FORMAL LOGIC: ITS SCOPE AND LIMITS

FORMAL LOGIC: ITS SCOPE AND LIMITS

Richard C. Jeffrey

McGraw-Hill Book Company

New York, St. Louis, San Francisco
Toronto, London, Sydney

To My Parents

PREFACE

This is a book for the beginner, designed to familiarize him with a complete system of quantificational logic in the course of a semester's study and to give him the wherewithal to see that the system *is* complete and that no system of quantificational logic is decidable. The principal novelty lies in the use of truth trees (one-sided semantic tableaux), which takes much of the drudgery out of the business of formalization and relates it in a natural way to the semantical interpretation. Completeness of the system is easy to prove; the detailed proof, in Chapters 5 and 8, can be read by the interested student on his own. There is no difficulty in seeing (as at the end of Chapter 7) that the tree method fails to provide a decision procedure for quantificational validity of inferences. The fact that *every* effective method fails in this respect is deduced from Church's thesis (construed as a thesis about Robinson arithmetic) in the last chapter, and a version of Gödel's incompleteness theorem is derived as a corollary. I think it important that this material be in the book, although it may well be omitted from the introductory course. Both philosophically and mathematically, *this* is what makes logic profoundly interesting and important; it would be a pity to emerge from one's only course in logic unaware of its existence.

Where techniques are to be acquired, I have included numerous worked examples in the text. Exercises at the end of each chapter provide material for further practice, or for getting a fresh perspective on matters treated in the text, or for seeing why the following chapter is there. The book is designed to be worked through selectively, with the guidance of an instructor. Thus, it would be pointless to work all the exercises; and certain chapters or parts of chapters can be omitted without loss of continuity. In particular, this is true of Chapters 5, 8, and 10 and the supplements at the end of Chapter 2. The first four chapters together with Chapters 6 and 7 amply cover the usual introductory course in deductive logic and can be gotten through handily in a semester, with time left over for Chapter 9 or for some discussion of the more theoretical matters treated in Chapters 5, 8, and 10.

Three small points should be mentioned. The first, and smallest, concerns quotation marks. I form the name of an expression by enclosing it in double quotes in the usual manner, so that punctuation signs immediately before the right-hand pair of quotation marks are not part of the expression so named but belong to the English sentence which contains the quoted material. Granted, this is not the simplest convention one could devise, but it is familiar and intelligible and, most important, corresponds to the way compositors' fingers work. I have adopted it to minimize cost and the number of typographical errors.

The second point concerns conditionals, which make their appearance in the course of a survey of all truth-functions in Chapter 3. There I argue as clearly as I can within a brief compass for the thesis that except in odd cases the truth conditions for the indicative English conditional are accurately given by the usual truth table. I have done this because I believe it and so that the instructor who does not will have a clearly stated position to attack.

The final point concerns the interpretation of quantifiers and predication. The notation of quantification theory makes its appearance in Chapter 6, alongside the apparatus of truth trees. Not until Chapter 7 is separate attention given to the interpretation of quantifiers, and only in Chapter 8 (which the instructor may well omit) is the notion of a valuation defined. All this is deliberate; I think that the method of truth trees is simple enough and suggestive enough to make *it* the best introduction to the basic semantical ideas. This is not quite a case of putting the formal cart before the semantical horse, for the tree formalism has the merits Alfred North Whitehead ascribed to a good notation; as Evert Beth's term "semantic tableaux" suggests, *this* formalism strongly suggests the right semantical interpretation. Explicit definitions of valuation and validity will seem pointless to the student outside the context in which they are really needed: the adequacy and completeness proofs in Chapter 8. Of course, the soundness of the rules can be roughly described and established prior to the strict definitions and proofs, and this is done in Chapters 6 and 7. But I have been at pains to minimize the *trappings* of rigor which, introduced prematurely, repel the thoughtful student as much as they attract the compulsive.

Beth's method of semantic tableaux (or Jaakko Hintikka's method of model sets) is now more than a decade old, although its roots go back further, say, to Jacques Herbrand. I learned of it late—from Saul Kripke (from whom I have borrowed the treatment of identity) and Raymond Smullyan (from whom I borrowed the idea of one-sidedness which reduces tableaux to trees)—and hastened to tell my students about it. So far, some three hundred of them have nearly unanimously found it easy to understand and fun to use—high time for its appearance in an introductory text!

Richard C. Jeffrey

CONTENTS

PART ONE
COMPOUND STATEMENTS

1
INTRODUCTION

"Every statement is either true or false; no statement is both." Much of logic is a series of literal-minded applications of this platitude.

The focus is on truth and falsity. We shall not be concerned with the purpose of making a statement (to inform, to mislead, to amuse ...) or even with how or whether the speaker knows that what he is saying is true. It *is* the job of pure logic to point out that if it is true to say

Tom stole it,

then it is equally true to say

Tom stole it or Dick stole it.

It is *not* the job of pure logic to point out that someone who makes the second statement, knowing that the first is also true, may be seriously misleading his hearers and slandering Dick. The truth (*a* truth) need not be the whole truth.

A near truth is a falsehood. Since there are albino crows in the world, it is false to say

All crows are black.

Since albino crows are rare, it is true to say

Nearly all crows are black.

Now if we wish to speak figuratively, we may say that the former statement is *nearly* true. No harm will have been done unless we make the mistake of thinking that a near truth is a kind of truth. It is not. A near truth is a kind of falsehood, and in logic, a miss is as good as a mile; we do not distinguish degrees of truth or of falsehood.

STATEMENTS AND SENTENCES

Strictly speaking, statements are not sentences. Rather, we *use* sentences to *make* statements, as when I utter the sentence "Father knew Lloyd George" in order to tell my wife (falsely, in fact) that M. M. Jeffrey knew the Prime Minister. But not every occasion on which a declarative sentence is spoken or written or tapped out in Morse code is an occasion on which a corresponding statement is being made; the sentence might have been uttered as part of a song, or written to practice calligraphy, or tapped out to see whether the circuit is working. Nor are sentences the only vehicles for making statements; in suitable circumstances a shrug or a nod or a silence will do the job.

It often happens that the same declarative sentence can be used to make one statement or another, depending on who utters it, when and where it is uttered, and to whom it is addressed. The sentence

1.1   *Of all the men of his time whom I have known, he was the wisest and justest and best*

is a case in point. Uttering it at the end of an account of the death of Socrates, Phaedo makes the same statement that anyone would make by saying

1.2   *Of all the men of Socrates' time whom Phaedo knew, Socrates was the wisest and justest and best.*

But when sentence **1.1** is uttered in another context (perhaps by Brutus, at Caesar's grave), a different statement is made. Sentence **1.1** is strongly *context-dependent,* for the statement made by uttering it depends very much on the context in which it is uttered. Other forms of context dependence are exhibited by the sentences "It is terribly hot" (when? where?) and "You are skating on thin ice" (which is interpreted literally or not, depending on the context). In contrast, sentence **1.2** is *context-free,* or nearly so; under a very wide range of circumstances, the same statement is made by uttering it, no matter who utters it, or where, or when, or how.

The ways in which sentence **1.2** fails to be completely context-free are ways in which every sentence fails: There are circumstances in which one makes no statement at all by uttering sentence **1.2,** as when it is uttered in an empty room or to practice elocution; and there are ways of uttering sentence **1.2** so as to make a statement, but a different statement from the one normally associated with that sentence. Thus, someone might utter sentence **1.2,** putting stress on the word "Phaedo" in such a way as to be saying in effect

> *Although Socrates was not the wisest and justest and best man of his time, he was the wisest and justest and best man of his time whom Phaedo knew.*

And similar effects can be produced by using the voice and face to utter a sentence ironically ("Brutus is an *honorable* man"), thus denying the statement normally associated with the sentence. But if we ignore context dependencies that are the common lot of all sentences, we may apply the term *context-free* to such sentences as **1.2** and "Brutus is an honorable man" and "2 + 2 = 4."

In logic it is harmless and useful to discuss context-free sentences in abstraction from their speakers. We shall speak of such sentences themselves as "making statements." Thus, we shall speak of the statement made by the sentence "Brutus is an honorable man," meaning, thereby, the statement that would be made by anyone who uttered that sentence in a normally assertive tone of voice under conditions that are right for statement making. We shall attribute truth-values to context-free sentences as well as to the statements associated with them. And we shall interpret the platitude at the beginning of this chapter as referring to such sentences as well as to the statements they make.

Difficulties about context dependence are at a minimum in scientific and mathematical discourse. If we were concerned only with sentences like "Whales are mammals" and "There are infinitely many prime numbers," we could plausibly have omitted all mention of statements and taken sentences to be the bearers of truth-values from the very beginning. But if we are to apply logic to everyday talk, we must first (at least in thought) replace context-dependent sentences like Phaedo's 1.1 by corresponding context-free sentences like 1.2.

In practice, we shall not often trouble to paraphrase sentences like 1.1 by sentences like 1.2. Instead, we shall use capital letters to represent the statements made by particular speakers on particular occasions so that such letters will function as context-free sentences in logical notation. As an example, consider the statements made by Herbert Hoover, Eleanor Roosevelt, and an unnamed bystander, by uttering the sentences

> *I voted for Eisenhower in 1952.* (Hoover)
> *I did not.* (Mrs. Roosevelt)
> *He did but she did not.* (Bystander)

We might then use the letter "A" as if it were a context-free sentence; anyone, any time, uttering "A" under conditions that are right for statement making, is imagined to be making the same statement that Hoover made on the occasion in question by uttering the context-dependent sentence "I voted for Eisenhower in 1952." Similarly, the sentence letter "B" might be used as a context-free substitute for Mrs. Roosevelt's utterance, and the bystander's statement can then be represented in logical notation by the sentence "$A \& B$," corresponding to the context-free English sentence "Hoover voted for Eisenhower in 1952 and Mrs. Roosevelt did not vote for Eisenhower in 1952."

If there is sometimes doubt about the exact sense of a statement or about whether some such statement as the bystander's is correctly representable in a particular way, say "$A \& B$," in terms of other statements, the fault may well lie with the speaker's use of language. Phrases like "wisest and justest and best man of his time" must be used with tact if a genuine statement is to be made having a definite truth-value. Occasionally, there are people to whom such a phrase may quite clearly apply; perhaps Socrates was one. And there are others to whom the phrase clearly does not apply. Between the two sorts of cases there is a fuzzy boundary where it is not at all clear how one would decide whether or not the phrase applies, and the judicious speaker will simply avoid using the phrase in such cases.

The problem is not that sentences like **1.2** have truth-values that we are unable to determine because the relevant data are lost in antiquity, for when we say that every statement is either true or false, we are not saying that we *know* which truth-value every statement has. But a problem does arise when we cannot even give clear *criteria* for determining truth-value. Consider the sentence "Socrates was bald when he drank the hemlock." This sentence makes a true statement if in fact Socrates had not one hair on his head when he drank the hemlock, and it makes a false statement if in fact he had a fine head of hair at that time. Under either of those conditions, the sentence does in fact make a statement, whether we know it or not. But if in fact Socrates had an amount and distribution of hair of the sort that lies within the vague boundary of application of the term "bald," the sentence has no truth-value, known or unknown, and in fact makes no statement, even though we may not *know* that it makes no statement.

Resolution of vagueness, ambiguity, and context dependence is a preliminary to formal logic, not a part of it. Thus, when we say that "*A*" follows logically from "*A* & *B*," we assume that the sentence letters "*A*" and "*B*" have definite truth-values, although we do not assume that these truth-values are known. Indeed, the claim that "*A*" follows from "*A* & *B*" is correct no matter what statements are made by the letters "*A*" and "*B*." Therefore we shall commonly discuss such questions in abstraction from particular interpretations of the letters. It is when we wish to apply logical analysis to ordinary talk that the sentence-statement distinction may become important. But in pure logic, sentence letters "*A*" and "*B*" and compound sentences like "*A* & *B*" can be treated simply as objects that have unknown truth-values associated with them. Thus, the claim that "*A*" follows from "*A* & *B*" will be interpreted as meaning that no matter what truth-values the letters "*A*" and "*B*" may have, the sentence "*A*" must be true if the sentence "*A* & *B*" is.

CONJUNCTION, DISJUNCTION, DENIAL

To show logical structure clearly, we use capital letters as sentences and special symbols as *connectives* for forming compound sentences out of simple ones. Thus, if "*R*" means that it is raining (at a certain place and time), if "*C*" means that it is cold (there, then), and if "*W*" means that it is windy (there, then), the expression

$(R \ \& \ C \ \& \ W)$

will be a sentence meaning that at the time and place in question,

> *It is raining* and *it is cold* and *it is windy.*

The expression

$$(R \lor C \lor W)$$

will be a sentence meaning that at the time and place in question,

> *It is raining* or *it is cold* or *it is windy.*

And the expressions

$$-R, \qquad -C, \qquad -W$$

will be sentences meaning that at the time and place in question,

> *It is* not *raining,*   *It is* not *cold,*   *It is* not *windy.*

Then the connectives

$$\&, \qquad \lor, \qquad -$$

do work that is done in English by the words

> *and,*   *or,*   *not.*

Some Jargon. The connective "&" (the *ampersand*) is called the sign of *conjunction*, and a sentence formed by writing other sentences in the blanks of any of the following expressions is said to *be a* conjunction:

$$(\quad \& \quad), \qquad (\quad \& \quad \& \quad), \qquad (\quad \& \quad \& \quad \& \quad), \qquad \dots$$

Such a sentence is said to be *the* conjunction *of* the sentences in the blanks, and the sentences in the blanks are called the *components* of the conjunction.

The connective "∨" (the *wedge*), called the sign of *disjunction*, is handled similarly. Sentences formed by writing sentences in the blanks of any of the following expressions are said to *be* disjunctions:

$$(\quad \vee \quad), \quad (\quad \vee \quad \vee \quad), \quad (\quad \vee \quad \vee \quad \vee \quad), \quad \ldots$$

Any such sentence is said to be *the* disjunction *of* the sentences in the blanks, which in turn are called the *components* of the disjunction.

Finally, the connective "−" (the *dash*) is called the sign of *denial*. A sentence formed by writing a dash before another sentence is said to *be* a denial, *the* denial *of* the sentence following the dash.

Interpreting the Connectives. By giving rough English translations, we have already indicated how the connectives are to be interpreted. But since each of the words "and," "or," and "not" has various uses in English, it will be well to be quite explicit about the interpretations of the corresponding connectives in our notation.

The use of "and" that corresponds to our use of the ampersand ("&") can be described as follows. Where "and" is written between adjacent sentences in a sequence of two or more, the result is a sentence which is true if all sentences in the original sequence are true and is false if even one is false. Our use of the symbol "&" can be described in the same way, except that we add parentheses on the outside:

> By writing ampersands between adjacent sentences in a sequence of two or more and enclosing the result in parentheses, a sentence is obtained which is true if all sentences in the sequence are true and is otherwise false.

Thus, the sentence "$(A \ \& \ B \ \& \ C)$" is true in the case where the sentences "A," "B," and "C" are all true and is false in each of the remaining seven cases concerning the joint truth and falsity of "A," "B," and "C":

	A	B	C	$(A \ \& \ B \ \& \ C)$
Case 1	t	t	t	t
Case 2	f	t	t	f
Case 3	t	f	t	f
Case 4	f	f	t	f
Case 5	t	t	f	f
Case 6	f	t	f	f
Case 7	t	f	f	f
Case 8	f	f	f	f

When only two sentence letters are involved, this *truth table* for "&" becomes shorter since we need only consider four cases:

	A	B	(A & B)
Case 1	t	t	t
Case 2	f	t	f
Case 3	t	f	f
Case 4	f	f	f

Similarly, the logical properties of the symbol "∨" (the wedge) correspond to those of the word "or" and can be summarized by truth tables. Reading the wedge as "or," we see clearly that "$(A ∨ B)$" is false when "A" and "B" separately are both false and is true when one letter is true and the other is false:

A	B	(A ∨ B)
t	t	
f	t	t
t	f	t
f	f	f

But what is the truth-value of "$(A ∨ B)$" in the first case, where "A" and "B" are both true?

If the wedge is simply a translation of the English "or," we are free to answer this question as we please, for English is ambiguous on this point. Sometimes, "or" is used in an *exclusive* sense, as when a child is told he may have candy *or* ice cream. Here, the qualification "but not both" is tacitly understood. But commonly, when "or" is written between declarative sentences, the resulting compound sentence is understood as being true if either *or both* of the sentences flanking the "or" are true. Latin provides two words for the two senses of "or": *aut* for the exclusive sense ("but not both") and *vel* for the inclusive sense ("or maybe both"). We use the symbol "∨" (reminiscent of *vel*) in the inclusive sense so that the blank in the foregoing truth table is to be filled with a "t." Then the rule for the wedge is as follows:

By writing wedges between adjacent sentences in a sequence of two or more and enclosing the result in parentheses, we obtain a sentence which is *false* if all sentences in the sequence are *false* and is otherwise true.

The logical properties of the dash (" − ") are simply stated:

The operation of prefixing a dash yields a sentence which is true (false) if the sentence following the dash is false (true).

Prefixing a dash turns truths into falsehoods and falsehoods into truths. Then the dash is the translation of the English phrase "it is not the case that" and has the following truth table:

A	$-A$
t	f
f	t

RULES OF FORMATION AND VALUATION

The parentheses in conjunctions and disjunctions are used to indicate grouping, much as in algebra, where the ambiguous expression

$$x + y \cdot z$$

is resolved into one of the two unambiguous expressions

$$x + (y \cdot z), \qquad (x + y) \cdot z$$

by inserting parentheses. To avoid ambiguities in our notation, we insist on flanking all conjunctions and disjunctions with parentheses. It is as if the rules for forming terms in algebra were as follows:

Each of the variables "x," "y," and "z," with or without subscripts, is a term. Furthermore, terms are obtained by applying any of the following operations:

1 Prefix a dash to a term.
2 Write pluses between adjacent terms in a sequence of two or more and enclose the result in parentheses.

3   Write dots between adjacent terms in a sequence of two or more and enclose the result in parentheses.

It is understood that nothing counts as a term unless it is a variable or can be obtained from variables by one or more applications of the operations **1, 2,** and **3.**

By these standards, the ambiguous expression "$x + y \cdot z$" is no term, although the following two unambiguous expressions do count as terms:

$$(x + (y \cdot z)), \qquad ((x + y) \cdot z)$$

Whatever parentheses are needed to eliminate ambiguity are provided by rules **2** and **3** for forming sums and products. When we apply rule **1** to form a negation, the result is unambiguous: the dash is always understood to apply to the complete term that immediately follows it, and there is always exactly one such term. Thus, the difference between the expressions

$$-(x + y), \qquad (-x + y)$$

is the difference between the negation of a sum and the sum of two terms (one of which happens to be the negation of a variable). There is no question of interpreting the dash in the second of these terms as applying to the expression "$x + y$," since that expression, lacking parentheses, is not a term by present standards. The difference between the two expressions we have been considering can be further emphasized by noticing that when values, say 1 and 2, are assigned to the variables "x" and "y," the two terms may take different values:

$$-(1 + 2) = -3, \qquad (-1 + 2) = 1$$

Of course, the outermost parentheses in terms like

$$(-x + y), \qquad (x + (y \cdot z)), \qquad ((x + y) \cdot z)$$

can be dropped without danger of ambiguity as can the outermost parentheses in the sentences

$$(-A \vee B), \qquad (A \vee (B \,\&\, C)), \qquad ((A \vee B) \,\&\, C)$$

when those terms or sentences stand alone. But when such expressions are to be compounded with others, it is often essential that the outermost parentheses be included. Thus, the negation of the sum of x and y must be formed by prefixing a dash to "$(x + y)$," not to "$x + y$."

Now our rules for forming sentences can be stated analogously.

RULES OF FORMATION

Each of the sentence letters "A," "B," ..., "Z," "A_1," ... counts as a sentence. Further sentences are produced by the following operations.

1 *Denial:* Prefix a dash to a sentence.
2 *Conjunction:* Write ampersands between adjacent sentences in a sequence of two or more sentences and enclose the result in parentheses.
3 *Disjunction:* Write wedges between adjacent sentences in a sequence of two or more sentences and enclose the result in parentheses.

Until Chapter 3, nothing counts as a sentence unless it is a sentence letter or can be obtained from sentence letters by one or more applications of operations **1, 2,** and **3.**

Our rules for determining the truth-values of compound sentences can be summarized in parallel fashion:

RULES OF VALUATION

1 A *denial* is true (false) if the sentence obtained by erasing the dash is false (true).
2 A *conjunction* is true if all its components are true but is false if even one component is false.
3 A *disjunction* is true if even one of its components is true but is false if all its components are false.

We give no rule for evaluating sentence letters; their truth-values are determined by facts about the world that lie outside the domain of logic. (Thus, if the letter "R" means that it is raining at a certain time and place, its truth-value is determined by facts about the weather at the time and place in question.) But, given the truth-values of all the letters that occur in a sentence, the truth-value of the entire sentence is determined by our rules of valuation. Indeed, the rules determine what the truth-value of a compound statement would be under every hypothesis about the truth-values of the ingredient sentence letters.

As an example, consider the sentence which (dropping outer parentheses) we write as

$$-R \vee W.$$

This corresponds to the English sentence

Either it is not raining, or it is windy.

Since there are two sentence letters, there are four possible cases and the truth table has four rows:

R	W	$-R$	$(-R \vee W)$
t	t	f	t
f	t	t	t
t	f	f	f
f	f	t	t

According to the rule of valuation for denial, the sentence " $-R$ " is opposite in truth-value from the sentence "R." This gives us the third column. And according to the rule for disjunction, the sentence "$(-R \vee W)$" is true if either of its components, "$-R$" or "W," is true and is false only if both components are false. Thus the fourth column is obtained from the third and the second. The process is like that of evaluating the expression "$(-x + y)$" under various hypotheses about the values of the variables. If we are interested only in the values 1 and 2 for the variables, the calculation goes like this:

x	y	$-x$	$(-x + y)$
1	1	-1	0
2	1	-2	-1
1	2	-1	1
2	2	-2	0

Formally, then, the logic of conjunction, disjunction, and denial is much like the arithmetic of multiplication, addition, and negation, with sentence letters playing the role of variables and truth-values playing the role of the numbers that variables may assume as values. But since there are only two truth-values, t and f, as against an infinity of numerical values, logic is notably simpler than arithmetic.

Meanings and Truth Conditions. If numerical values of terms correspond to truth-values of sentences, what corresponds in arithmetic to the *statements* that sentences make? The answer is clear enough if we think of some such concrete application of arithmetic as the following: Let x be the number of men in this room and let y be the number of adults in this room. Then $(-x + y)$ is the number of women in this room. Now the letters "x" and "y" have meanings as well as numerical values; their meanings indicate what facts must be determined in order to determine their values. Similarly in the sentence "$(-R \vee W)$," the meanings of "R" and "W" tell us what facts must be investigated in order to determine their truth-values, and these meanings may be identified with the statements that "R" and "W" make. Then we have the missing term of the proportion: the *meaning* of a term is to the *statement* made by a sentence as the *numerical value* of the term is to the *truth-value* of the sentence.

The rules of valuation make no mention of the meanings of sentences; they are couched entirely in terms of truth-values. Nevertheless, the rules of valuation determine the meanings of compound sentences in terms of the meanings of their ingredient sentence letters, for we know the meaning of a sentence (we know what statement the sentence makes) if we know what facts would make it true and what facts would make it false. Now if we have this information about the letters that occur in a sentence, the truth conditions supply the corresponding information about the whole sentence. Thus, referring to the truth table for "$(-R \vee W)$," we find that the entire sentence is true in cases 1, 2, and 4 and false in case 3. Then the facts that would make "$(-R \vee W)$" true are the facts that would make both "R" and "W" true (case 1: raining and windy) and also the facts that would make "R" false but "W" true (case 2: not raining but windy) and also the facts that would make both "R" and "W" false (case 4: not raining, not windy). In any of those cases, the sentence "$(-R \vee W)$" would be true, and in the remaining case (case 3: raining but not windy), that sentence would be false. Knowing the meanings (the *truth conditions*) of "R" and of "W," we can use the rules of valuation to discover the meaning of the compound sentence "$(-R \lor W)$" by reducing the question "What are the truth conditions for the compound sentence?" to the question "What are the truth conditions for the ingredient sentence letters?"

EXERCISES

1.1 Interpret the letters "F," "S," and "L" as meaning that *Flaubert was a Frenchman* (he was), that *all swans are white* (they are not), and that *Lloyd George knew my father* (he did not) and work out the truth-values of the following sentences:

a	$(S \& L) \lor F$	b	$S \& (L \lor F)$
c	$-(F \lor S \lor L)$	d	$-F \lor S \lor L$
e	$-(-F \lor -S \lor -L)$	f	$-(-F \& -S \& -L)$

1.2 Using the letters "R," "S," and "B" to mean *it is raining, it is snowing,* and *it is blowing,* translate the following sentences into logical notation. Interpret "either . . . or" as inclusive disjunction.
  a *It is raining, and either snowing or blowing.*
  b *Either it is raining and snowing, or it is blowing.*
  c *Either it is not both raining and snowing, or it is blowing.*
  d *It is raining but not snowing.*
  e *It is neither raining nor snowing.*
  f *It is doing both or neither.* (In reply to the questions "Is it raining? Snowing?")

1.3 Translate sentences **a** to **d** of Exercise 1.1 into unambiguous English.

1.4 Work out truth tables for the sentences in Exercise 1.1.

1.5 The sentences "$(R \& S)$" and "$(-R \& -S)$" cannot both be true; they are *logically exclusive* in the sense that any assignment of truth-values to the letters "R" and "S" that makes one of them true makes the other false. Is it therefore incorrect to write the sign "$\lor$" of *inclusive* disjunction between them, as you may have done in Exercise 1.2f? Explain. Hint: Symbolize exclusive disjunction by "$\circ$" and compare the truth tables for the sentences "$(R \& S) \lor (-R \& -S)$" and "$(R \& S) \circ (-R \& -S)$."

1.6 Suppose that all cases concerning the joint truth and falsity of the ingredient sentence letters are equally likely. Then the probability that a sentence is true is given by the ratio of the number of cases in which it comes out true to the total number of cases:

$$\frac{Number\ of\ t\ cases}{Total\ number\ of\ cases}$$

Thus, if all cases are equally likely, the probability is ¾ that the sentence "$-R \vee W$" is true. Now use "H_1" to mean that a certain coin lands head up on the first toss. Use "H_2" to mean that it lands head up on the second toss. The coin is tossed twice and cannot land on its edge. Work out the probabilities of the following sentences on the assumption that all four cases are equally likely:

a $\quad -(-H_1 \ \& \ -H_2)$ (They are not both tails.)
b $\quad -H_1 \vee -H_2$ (There is at least one tail.)
c $\quad (H_1 \ \& \ H_2) \vee (-H_1 \ \& \ -H_2)$ (The tosses have the same outcome.)
d $\quad$ The tosses have opposite outcomes.
e $\quad H_1 \vee H_2$
f $\quad H_1 \vee (-H_1 \ \& \ H_2)$

1.7 Cases need not be equally likely. In general,

The probability that a sentence is true is the sum of the probabilities of its t cases and is zero if the sentence has no t cases.

Find the probabilities that sentences **a** to **e** below are true on the assumption that the probabilities of the cases are as follows:

R	S	probability
t	t	.1
f	t	.2
t	f	.3
f	f	.4

a $\quad$ *It is raining or snowing.* $(R \vee S)$
b $\quad$ *It is raining or not snowing.*
c $\quad$ *It is not both raining and snowing.*
d $\quad -S \vee (R \ \& \ S)$
e $\quad -S \ \& \ (R \ \& \ S)$

2

LOGICAL EQUIVALENCE

"It is not the case that it will not rain" is a complicated way of saying that it will rain. In general, the sentences

$$A, \quad --A$$

make the same statement: they are *logically equivalent*. Similarly, the following sentences are logically equivalent:

$$-(A \ \& \ B), \quad -A \vee -B$$

Thus, "It will not both rain and snow" is another way of saying that either it will not rain or it will not snow. To see that this is so, work out the truth tables for the two sentences, and notice that they have the same truth conditions:

A	B	(A & B)	−(A & B)	−A	−B	−A ∨ −B
t	t	t	f	f	f	f
f	t	f	t	t	f	t
t	f	f	t	f	t	t
f	f	f	t	t	t	t

The columns of "t"s and "f"s under the two sentences are the same, and therefore the two sentences have the same meaning. Facts that would make one sentence true would make the other true as well, and facts that would make one of them false would falsify the other, too. Similarly, the proof that "A" and "$--A$" are logically equivalent can be given by truth tables:

A	$-A$	$--A$
t	f	t
f	t	f

Since the columns under "A" and "$--A$" are the same, these two sentences mean the same, make the same statement, and are logically equivalent.

Now for all sentences of the sort considered in these first five chapters, we define logical equivalence as follows:

Sentences are logically equivalent if and only if they have the same truth-values in all cases regarding the joint truth and falsity of the sentence letters that appear in them.

We have already used this definition to verify the logical equivalence of the following pair of sentences:

2.1 A, $--A$ *(Law of double denial)*

And we have used it to verify the logical equivalence of the first of the following two pairs:

2.2 $-(A \& B)$, $-A \lor -B$
                                                              (DeMorgan's laws)
2.3 $-(A \lor B)$, $-A \& -B$

To verify the logical equivalence of the second pair, **2.3**, work out the truth-values of the two sentences with a common listing of cases—say, with *tt, ft, tf,* and *ff* as successive values of *AB*—and notice that both sentences assume the same values, *f, f, f,* and *t* in the four cases. The logical equivalence of pair **2.3** is illustrated by the fact that the sentence "It will not either rain or snow" (or "It will neither rain nor snow") makes the same statement as the sentence "It will not rain and it will not snow."

LAWS OF EQUIVALENCE; SIMPLIFICATION

Strictly speaking, the logical equivalence of pair **2.1** is only an illustration of the law of double denial. The law itself says

Any sentence that begins with a pair "— —" of dashes (possibly followed by more dashes) is logically equivalent to the sentence obtained by erasing the first pair of dashes.

Example: " $- - -(A \lor -B)$ " is logically equivalent to " $-(A \lor -B)$."

Similarly, pairs **2.2** and **2.3** only illustrate DeMorgan's laws, which can be stated in general terms as follows:

The denial of a $\left\{ \begin{array}{l} conjunction \\ disjunction \end{array} \right\}$ is logically equivalent to

the $\left\{ \begin{array}{l} disjunction \\ conjunction \end{array} \right\}$ of the denials of the components.

Example: The denied conjunction

$$-(-A \ \& \ (A \lor -B) \ \& \ -B)$$

is logically equivalent to the disjunction

$$- -A \lor -(A \lor -B) \lor - -B$$

and the second component of this disjunction is logically equivalent to the conjunction " $(-A \ \& \ - -B)$." Substituting equivalents for equivalents, we find that the disjunction is logically equivalent to

$$- -A \lor (-A \ \& \ - -B) \lor - -B$$

and, erasing double dashes, we arrive at

$$A \lor (-A \ \& \ B) \lor B$$

as a sentence logically equivalent to the original denied conjunction.

Here we have applied DeMorgan's law twice, applied the law of double denial three times, and applied the further principle that

When a component of a sentence is replaced by something logically equivalent to it, the whole resulting sentence is logically equivalent to the whole original sentence.

This process of simplification can be carried much further, for as we can see by applying the truth table test, the original denied conjunction above is logically equivalent to "$A \lor B$." It is straightforward to verify this claim, but if we are to *discover* the simpler version by successively simplifying the clumsy one, we need more laws. DeMorgan's laws and the law of double denial got us from

$$-(-A \mathbin{\&} (A \lor -B) \mathbin{\&} -B)$$

to

$$A \lor (-A \mathbin{\&} B) \lor B.$$

Two more laws are needed to get us successively to

$$A \lor B \lor B$$

and

$$A \lor B.$$

The first of these laws is illustrated by the equivalent pairs

2.4 $A \lor (-A \mathbin{\&} B)$, $A \lor B$
2.5 $-A \lor (A \mathbin{\&} B)$, $-A \lor B$ *(Law of absorption)*

In general, the law of absorption allows us to simplify a disjunction which has a conjunction as one of its components, provided that

some component of the disjunction differs by only the presence or absence of a dash from some component of the conjunction.

In such a case the law allows us to drop the component of the conjunction. Thus, the sentence "$-A$" may be deleted from the disjunction "$A \lor (-A \mathbin{\&} B) \lor B$" to obtain a simpler equivalent disjunction, "$A \lor B \lor B$." Here the process of deleting " − A" is understood to include erasure of the accompanying ampersand and parentheses. As another example, notice that two applications of the law of absorption show the following sentences to be logically equivalent:

$$(A \& B \& -C \& D) \vee -B \vee C, \qquad (A \& D) \vee -B \vee C$$

Note, however, that the law of absorption does not license us to drop either the "A" or the " − A" from the sentence "(A & B) ∨ (− A & C)," for neither "A" nor " − A" is a full component of the disjunction.

Finally, the passage from "A ∨ B ∨ B" to "A ∨ B" is licensed by the principle:

A component of a disjunction may be dropped if it repeats another component; similarly, for conjunctions.

We may call this "the law of redundancy." The law allows us to delete an occurrence of "B" from "A ∨ B ∨ B" or from "A & B & B," but *not* from "(A & B) ∨ B" where neither occurrence of "B" is a component of the disjunction which simply repeats another whole component of the disjunction.

The law of absorption may need some further explanation. It asserts, for example, that

Either it is raining, or it is snowing but not raining

is merely a complicated way of saying

Either it is raining or it is snowing.

It is easy enough to verify that these sentences *are* logically equivalent by the truth table test:

	R	S	R ∨ (S & −R)	R ∨ S
Case 1	t	t	t	t
Case 2	f	t	t	t
Case 3	t	f	t	t
Case 4	f	f	f	f

Now lingering doubt about just *why* these sentences are logically equivalent can be dissolved by a closer examination of the *t* cases for the two sentences and their components. The *t* cases for a disjunction are obtained by pooling the *t* cases for the two components. The *t* cases for "$R \vee (S \ \& \ -R)$" are the *t* cases for "R" together with those for "$S \ \& \ -R$": 1 and 3 together with 2. And the *t* cases for "$R \vee S$" are the *t* cases for "R" together with those for "S": 1 and 3 together with 1 and 2. No matter how we list them, the result is the same: 1, 2, and 3. But the second, redundant list corresponds to the simpler of the two sentences.

Putting the same matter in terms of ordinary talk, the component "R" of each disjunction can come true in either of two ways: it could be raining and snowing, or raining but not snowing. Similarly, "S" can come true in either of two ways: it could be snowing and raining, or snowing but not raining. Then when all possibilities are considered, the sentence

> *Either it is raining or it is snowing*

means that

> *Either it is raining and snowing, or raining but not snowing, or snowing and raining, or snowing but not raining.*

Here the first and third components, "raining and snowing" and "snowing and raining," say the same thing. Deleting the third component, we have

> *Either it is raining and snowing, or raining but not snowing, or snowing but not raining.*

And now the first two components, which simply detail the two possible ways in which it could be raining, may be replaced by the simpler equivalent sentence "It is raining" to get

> *Either it is raining, or it is snowing but not raining.*

We have retraced, in English, the path from "$R \vee S$" to "$R \vee (S \ \& \ -R)$."

In discussing the law of absorption, we have noticed a principle that merits a name of its own: "the law of expansion." It was this principle that we used when we observed that the sentence "It is raining" can be expanded into a logically equivalent form "It is raining and snowing, or raining but not snowing." In general, any sentence, "A," can be expanded into a logically equivalent form "$(A \,\&\, B) \vee (A \,\&\, -B)$" in which two cases are distinguished as to the truth of "A," depending on whether the extraneous sentence "B" is true or false. Thus, the following are logically equivalent:

2.6 A, $(A \,\&\, B) \vee (A \,\&\, -B)$ (*Law of expansion*)

Two further principles are very simple but worthy of notice. The first, illustrated by the logical equivalence of the sentences

2.7 $A \vee B \vee C$, $(A \vee B) \vee C$, $A \vee (B \vee C)$

is the *associative law:*

> *A logically equivalent sentence is obtained when the grouping is changed in a conjunction or in a disjunction.*

Thus, the parentheses are unnecessary in the sentence

$(A \,\&\, B) \,\&\, (C \,\&\, D) \,\&\, E$,

although they *are* necessary in the sentence

$(A \,\&\, B) \vee (C \,\&\, D) \vee E$.

An equally obvious principle is the *commutative law:*

> *A logically equivalent sentence is obtained when the order of components is changed in a conjunction or in a disjunction.*

Then "$A \vee B$" and "$B \vee A$" make the same statement, and similarly, "$A \,\&\, B \,\&\, C$" is logically equivalent to "$B \,\&\, A \,\&\, C$."

Somewhat deeper are the *distributive laws,* analogous to the law

$$x \cdot (y + z) = (x \cdot y) + (x \cdot z)$$

of arithmetic. According to these laws, the sentences

2.8 $A \,\&\, (B \vee C),$ $(A \,\&\, B) \vee (A \,\&\, C)$

are logically equivalent, *and the sentences*

2.9 $A \vee (B \,\&\, C),$ $(A \vee B) \,\&\, (A \vee C)$

are logically equivalent. It is as if in arithmetic we were able to "add through" a product as we multiply through a sum; it is as if the equation

$$x + (y \cdot z) = (x + y) \cdot (x + z)$$

held for all numbers x, y, and z. According to **2.8**, the sentence

> *It is raining, and either snowing or blowing*

is logically equivalent to the sentence

> *It is raining and snowing, or it is raining and blowing.*

According to **2.9**, the sentence

> *It is raining, or it is snowing and blowing*

is logically equivalent to the sentence

> *It is raining or snowing, and it is raining or blowing.*

GROUPING

Notice the variety of devices that we use in English to indicate grouping. If "A," "B," and "C" mean that *it is raining, it is snowing,* and *it is blowing,* the sentence "$A \,\&\, (B \vee C)$" cannot be put into English simply as

> *It is raining and it is snowing or it is blowing,*

for nothing about this sentence shows that it is to be read as a conjunction, not as a disjunction. Since both sentences flanking the "or" have the same subject and verb ("it is"), we can make the grouping clear in this case by dropping a repetition:

It is raining and it is snowing or blowing.

This is clearly a conjunction of two sentences, the second of which has a compound predicate—"snowing or blowing." And we can resolve any remaining doubt by using a comma:

It is raining, and it is snowing or blowing.

It is still briefer, and no less clear, to turn this into a sentence with one verb and a doubly compound predicate:

It is raining, and snowing or blowing.

But when the ingredient sentences are grammatically unrelated, different devices must be used. To resolve the ambiguity in

All swans are white and Flaubert was a Frenchman or Lloyd George knew my father,

we use a comma and an "either" much as we might use a left parenthesis in logic:

All swans are white, and either Flaubert was a Frenchman or Lloyd George knew my father.

Notice that the "either" functions as a sign of grouping, not as an indication that the "or" is meant exclusively.

SEMANTICAL EQUIVALENCE

Two points remain to be made about logical equivalence. The first is illustrated by the pair of sentences

2.10 *Everyone loves everyone and everyone loves himself.*
         Everyone loves everyone.

If we use the sentence letter "E" to mean that everyone loves everyone and use "S" to mean that everyone loves himself, these go over into logical notation as

2.11 E & S, E

The truth table test does not classify the sentences in **2.11** as logically equivalent, for they have different truth-values in the *tf* case for *ES*:

E	S	E & S	E
t	t	t	t
f	t	f	f
$-t-$	$-f-$	$-f-$	$-t-$
f	f	f	f

Yet, given the interpretations of the sentence letters, it is clear that the sentences in **2.11** have the same truth conditions. The solution to the puzzle is that the meanings we have assigned to "E" and "S" are such that the troublesome *tf* case cannot arise, for if everyone loves everyone, then in particular, everyone loves himself. Of the four cases *tt*, *ft*, *tf*, and *ff* concerning the joint truth and falsity of "E" and "S," one is impossible. To indicate this, I have lined out the row of the truth table that corresponds to the impossible case. In all three *possible* cases, the two sentences in **2.11** have the same truth values: *t*, *f*, and *f*.

An even simpler example of the same phenomenon is provided by the pair of sentences

A, B

when "A" is interpreted as meaning that everyone loves everyone, and "B" is *also* interpreted as meaning that everyone loves everyone. Nothing in our notation demands that different letters be interpreted differently. Given that "A" and "B" are interpreted in the same way, two of the abstract possibilities concerning their joint truth and falsity are seen to be illusory, and in all *possible* cases, "A" and "B" have the same truth-value.

Moral: The truth table test is completely insensitive to the meanings of sentence letters. It classifies sentences as logically equivalent only if they have the same truth-values in all *abstractly* possible cases concerning the joint truth and falsity of the ingredient sentence letters and takes no account of the chance that one or more of the abstract possibilities may be semantical impossibilities—may be ruled out by the particular interpretations that have been assigned to the sentence letters. We might say that pairs like those in **2.11** and "*A*" and "*B*" above (where "*A*" and "*B*" are assigned the same interpretation) are *semantically equivalent*, but we shall not call them "logically equivalent." The term "logically equivalent" will be reserved for pairs of sentences which assume the same truth-values in all abstractly possible cases concerning the joint truth and falsity of their ingredient sentence letters.

Of course, since we are not looking for trouble when we symbolize, we would really not have chosen the same meaning for two different letters, as we did for "*A*" and "*B*" above. That would be self-defeating if our object is to show logical structure clearly. But there are cases, as in **2.10**, where the obvious transcription **2.11** into logical notation fails to show an essential aspect of the logical structure. In such cases we can do one of two things. One approach, indicated above, is to strike out as illusory one or more of the abstract possibilities concerning the joint truth and falsity of sentence letters. The other approach is to seek a more revealing symbolization, as we shall in later chapters.

TAUTOLOGIES AND CONTRADICTIONS

A final point about equivalence: we have seen in the case of the law of expansion that two sentences can be logically equivalent even though one contains a sentence letter that the other does not. The sentence letter "*B*" occurs vacuously in "(*A* & *B*) ∨ (*A* & −*B*)," contributing nothing to the sense of the whole. To say that

Either $2 + 2 = 4$ *and it is raining, or* $2 + 2 = 4$ *and it is not raining*

is to say something about numbers but nothing about the weather; we might just as well have said simply, that

$2 + 2 = 4.$

A more radical version of the same remark applies to the pair

2.12 $A \vee -A$, $B \vee -B$.   (*Law of tautology*)

These sentences are logically equivalent even though they have no sentence letters in common; each of them comes out true in every possible case concerning the joint truth and falsity of "*A*" and "*B*."

A B	$A \vee -A$	$B \vee -B$
t t	t	t
f t	t	t
t f	t	t
f f	t	t

The sentences "$A \vee -A$" and "$B \vee -B$" are *logical truths* or *tautologies* since they are true in every case concerning the truth and falsity of sentence letters. To know that either of them is true, we need not know which case is actual; to be told that one of them is true is to be told nothing we did not already know. In particular, the sentence

   It is raining or it is not

gives no news about the weather or about anything else, and the sentence

   $2 + 2 = 4$ or $2 + 2 \neq 4$

gives no more information about numbers than it does about the weather, for it gives no information at all. The first of these is only apparently about the weather, and the second is only apparently about numbers.

The case is similar for the logically equivalent pair

2.13 $A \& -A$, $B \& -B$ (*Law of contradiction*)

of *logical falsehoods* or *contradictions*. Since each of these comes out false in every case concerning the truth and falsity of sentence letters, they are logically equivalent. To know their truth-values, we need know nothing about the weather or numbers or anything else, nor need we even know what the letters "*A*" and "*B*" mean. The sentence

It is and is not raining

is only apparently about the weather, just as the sentence

$2 + 2 = 4$ and $2 + 2 \neq 4$

is only apparently about numbers. In fact, the two sentences have exactly the same meaning since they have exactly the same truth conditions: in all possible cases, both are false.

EXERCISES

2.1 Use truth tables to verify that the following three sentences are logically equivalent:

   2.14 $A \vee (A \mathbin{\&} B)$, $A \mathbin{\&} (A \vee B)$, A

2.2 Use the distributive and commutative laws to verify that the following two sentences are logically equivalent:

   2.15 $(A \vee B) \mathbin{\&} (C \vee D)$, $(A \mathbin{\&} C) \vee (B \mathbin{\&} C) \vee (A \mathbin{\&} D) \vee (B \mathbin{\&} D)$

Notice the analogy with the process of multiplying two sums in algebra:

$$\begin{array}{r} a + b \\ c + d \\ \hline ac + bc + ad + bd \end{array}$$

2.3 Translate each of the following into logical notation, simplify, and then translate back into English. Check your results by using truth tables and by paying attention to the meanings of the English sentences. In logical notation, use "M" for "Moriarty is guilty," use "C" for "Crumm is guilty," and use no additional sentence letters.

   a *Either Moriarty and Crumm are both guilty, or Crumm is innocent (= not guilty).*

   b *Either Crumm is guilty, or both he and Moriarty are.*

   c *Either Moriarty is guilty, or both he and Crumm are innocent.*

   d *Either Moriarty is guilty, or Crumm is innocent, or both are guilty.*

    e   *They are not both guilty, and at least one of them is innocent.*

    f   *Either they are both guilty, or Moriarty is but Crumm is not.*

    g   *They are both guilty or both innocent, and at least one of them is guilty.*

    h   *Either they are not both guilty or they are not both innocent.*

2.4 Translate, work out the truth tables, and try to think of simpler, logically equivalent versions.

    a   *Either Holmes is right, and the vile Moriarty is guilty, or he is wrong, and the scurrilous Crumm did the job; but those scoundrels are either both guilty or both innocent.* (Use just three sentence letters: do not translate the invective.)

    b   *Either Holmes is right, or Moriarty and Crumm are both guilty; but Crumm is innocent.*

    c   *Either Holmes is right, or Moriarty and Crumm are either both guilty or both innocent; and Crumm is guilty.*

2.5 Interpret "E" and "S" as in sentence pair **2.11**. Which of the following pairs are semantically equivalent?

    a E, $E \vee S$ b S, $E \vee S$ c S, $E \& S$

2.6 The following additional rules of simplification are often useful:

    2.16 a *If any component of a disjunction is a tautology, so is the whole disjunction.*

            b *If any component of a conjunction is a contradiction, so is the whole conjunction.*

            c *If a component of a disjunction is a contradiction, that component may be dropped.*

            d *If a component of a conjunction is a tautology, that component may be dropped.*

Use these rules together with the distributive law, the law of redundancy, and others, to simplify the three sentences in Exercise 2.4.

SUPPLEMENTS

Boolean Algebra. The facts about equivalence can be summarized in algebraic form by writing the sign "$=$" between sentences to indicate that they are logically equivalent, using the letters "x," "y," and "z" as variables for which arbitrary sentences may be substituted and the symbols "1" and

"0" to represent logical truth and logical falsehood, respectively. We now use " $+$ " as a sign of disjunction, in place of the wedge, and we indicate conjunction by a dot or simply by juxtaposition. Then the law of double denial can be written

2.17 $--x = x,$

and the four laws in **2.16** become

2.18   a $x + 1 = 1$ b $x \cdot 0 = 0$
           c $x + 0 = x$ d $x \cdot 1 = x$

Note that **2.18a** is *not* true for all x in ordinary algebra. The laws **2.12** and **2.13** of tautology and contradiction become

2.19   a $x + -x = 1$ b $x \cdot -x = 0$

Here again are two departures from ordinary algebra. Note that in our symbolism, " $x - y$ " is the conjunction of x with $-y$ and that we have no license to write " $x - y$ " in place of " $x + -y$." The notation " $x - y$ " is best avoided in favor of " $x \cdot -y$." The facts that the denial of a tautology is a contradiction and that the denial of a contradiction is a tautology are expressed

2.20   a $-1 = 0$ b $-0 = 1$

Again, we have two statements that would be false in their ordinary algebraic interpretation. Various other laws are expressed by equations as follows:

2.21 a $x + x = x$ b $xx = x$
2.22 a $x + y = y + x$ b $xy = yx$
2.23 a $-(x + y) = -x \cdot -y$ b $-(xy) = -x + -y$
2.24 a $x(y + z) = xy + xz$ b $x + yz = (x + y)(x + z)$
2.25 a $x + (y + z) = (x + y) + z$ b $x(yz) = (xy)z$

The last pair of equations say what we knew before: that parentheses are unnecessary in conjunctions and in disjunctions. We write " $x + y + z$ " for either side of **2.25a** and " xyz " for either side of **2.25b**. The five equations in **2.21**, **2.23**, and **2.24b** have no counterparts in ordinary algebra.

These nineteen equations are not independent; from various selections of them we can deduce the rest. One such selection consists of the ten equations in **2.18**, **2.19**, **2.22**, and **2.24**, and still smaller selections will suffice. But our concern here is with completeness, not economy. It turns out that two sentences are logically equivalent and would be shown so by the truth table test if and only if one can be obtained from the other by applying the foregoing equations. In particular, a sentence is a tautology if and only if it can be reduced to "1" by applying these equations, and a sentence is a contradiction if and only if it can be reduced to "0" by applying them.

EXERCISE

Use this method to show the equivalence of the paired sentences

a   2.4   b   2.5   c   2.6   d   2.14

and to simplify the following:

e   *Either Holmes has bungled, or Watson is on the job and Moriarty has been caught; but Watson is not on the job.*

f $(A \And B) \lor (A \And -B) \lor (-A \And B)$

g $(A \And B) \lor (A \And -B) \lor (-A \And B) \lor (-A \And -B)$

h $(A \lor B) \And (A \lor -B) \And -A$

i $-(A \And -(A \And -(A \And B)))$

Logical Networks. Electronic computing machines can be built of the following components, among others:

Inverter. A device with one input terminal and one output terminal and having the characteristic that when the input is at a high voltage level, the voltage at the output is low, and vice versa; when the input is low, the output is high.

"Or" gate. A device with two or more input terminals and one output terminal and having the characteristic that the output is high if even one input is high and the output is low if all inputs are low.

"And" gate. A device with two or more input terminals and one output terminal and having the characteristic that the output is high if all inputs are high and the output is low if even one input is low.

Now if the sentence letter "A" means that the voltage at the input to an inverter is high, the sentence "$-A$" will mean that the inverter's input (output) voltage is low (high). Then if "A" says that the input is high, "$-A$" says that the output is high, and we draw inverters as indicated in Figure 2.1. Similarly, we draw "and" and "or" gates as shown in Figures 2.2 and 2.3, for if "A," "B," "C," . . . mean that the respective inputs are high, the sentences "$A \& B \& C$" and "$A \lor B \lor C$" will be true if and only if the outputs of the "and" gate and of the "or" gate are high.

Figure 2.1 INVERTER   *Figure 2.2* "AND" GATE   *Figure 2.3* "OR" GATE

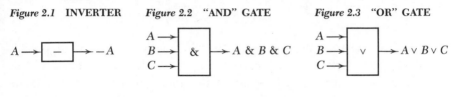

Figure 2.4

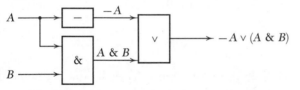

Networks of these devices can be formed by connecting outputs of some to inputs of others as illustrated in Figure 2.4. Again, sentences labeling terminals state the conditions under which those terminals are at high voltage levels. Then in Figure 2.4, the output of the entire network is at a high voltage level if the sentence "$-A \lor (A \& B)$" is true and is at a low voltage level if that sentence is false. Now as we can easily verify, the sentence "$-A \lor (A \& B)$" is logically equivalent to the simpler sentence "$-A \lor B$," so that the simpler sentence is a perfectly accurate description of the conditions under which the output of the network in Figure 2.4 is high. And by drawing a network that corresponds to this simpler sentence in the same way that Figure 2.4 corresponds to the more complicated one, we obtain the simpler network of Figure 2.5 which is equivalent to the

Figure 2.5

A ──→ [−] ───→
                    [∨] ├──→ $-A \lor B$
B ──────────────→

network of Figure 2.4: *equivalent* in the sense that under all possible conditions of voltage at the inputs, the new network will have the same output (high or low) as the old.

Figure 2.6

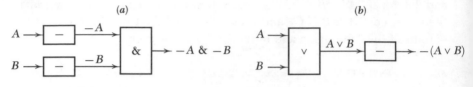

As a further example, notice that the two networks shown in Figure 2.6 are equivalent. Network b is simpler than network a if we measure the complexity of a network by counting the total number of boxes in it: inverters, "and" gates, and "or" gates. (Warning: Complexity, measured in this crude way, may fail to correspond to the actual cost or difficulty of building the electronic circuit.)

EXERCISE

Simplify each of the networks shown in Figure 2.7 by finding sentences that describe the conditions under which the outputs are high, simplifying those sentences, and finally drawing networks that correspond to the simplified sentences.

Meanings as Sets. To know the meaning of a statement is to know in what states of the world it would be true, and in what states it would be false. Now imagine that the various points in the rectangle of Figure 2.8a represent the various possible states of the world. The points inside the circle represent the states in which the sentence "A" would be true, and the rest of the points in the rectangle—the shaded region—represent the states in which "A" would be false. In general, the denial of a sentence is represented by whatever remains of the rectangle when the region representing that sentence is removed.

Since a disjunction is true if and only if at least one component is true, the region which represents a disjunction is the merger or *union* of the regions representing the components. Then the shaded region in Figure 2.8b represents "$A \vee B$," and the shaded region in Figure 2.8c represents "$A \vee B \vee C$."

Figure 2.7 NETWORKS TO BE SIMPLIFIED

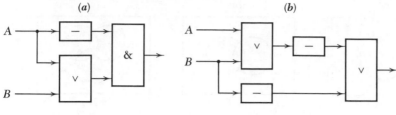

(a)

(b)

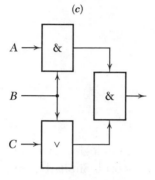

(c)

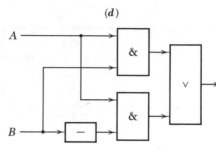

(d)

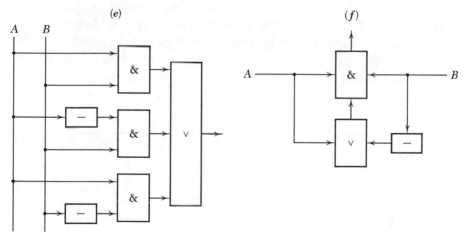

(e)

(f)

Since a conjunction is true if and only if all components are true, a conjunction is represented by the common part or *intersection* of all the regions which represent components (see Figure 2.8d and e).

Any tautology will be represented by the whole rectangle; thus, $A \vee -A$ is the union of the two regions into which the circle divides the

Figure 2.8

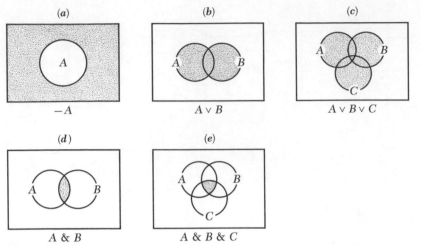

rectangle of Figure 2.8a. Figure 2.9 shows why all tautologies have the same meaning, being true in all possible states of the world. Similarly, any contradiction, such as "A & −A," will be represented by the empty "region," which has no points at all in it; thus, "A & −A" is represented by the (empty) intersection of the two shaded regions in Figure 2.8a.

Notice that the smallest nonempty regions into which one or two or three circles divide a rectangle correspond to the various possible cases

Figure 2.9

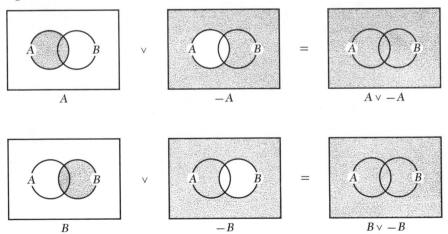

Figure 2.10

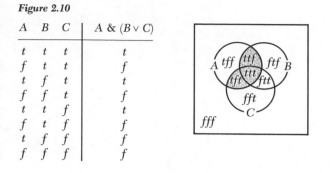

A	B	C	A & (B ∨ C)
t	t	t	t
f	t	t	f
t	f	t	t
f	f	t	f
t	t	f	t
f	t	f	f
t	f	f	f
f	f	f	f

concerning the joint truth and falsity of sentence letters and that the region which represents a sentence is obtained by shading the regions corresponding to that sentence's *t* cases (see Figure 2.10). Just as an unknown one of the cases concerning the joint truth and falsity of sentence letters is actual, so an unknown one of the points in a rectangle represents the actual state of the world. A sentence is true (false) if the point representing the actual state is in (out of) the region which represents that sentence. The logical truths—the tautologies—are the sentences which are true no matter which point in the rectangle represents the actual state. These are the sentences represented by the whole rectangle, to which *every* point belongs.

Now just as two sentences are logically equivalent if and only if they have exactly the same *t* cases, so two sentences are logically equivalent if and only if they are represented by the same region within the rectangle. This fact can be used to get an intuitive grasp on such facts as the logical equivalence of the sentences "*A*" and "*A* ∨ (*A* & *B*)." (Turn to Figure 2.8*d* and notice that the "*A* & *B*" region is inside the "*A*" region, so that in adding the former region to the latter we add nothing that was not already there.)

EXERCISE

Verify each of the equivalences in sentences **2.1** to **2.6**, **2.8**, **2.9**, **2.14**, and **2.16** by drawing separate circle diagrams for the sentences in each group and noticing that the shaded regions are identical. Finally, notice that where four or more sentence letters appear, as in **2.15**, the circles cannot be arranged so as to divide the rectangle into a number of compartments large enough to represent all rows of the truth table.

3

TRUTH-FUNCTIONS

How many different compound statements can be made using two sentence letters?

The question does not concern the number of different compound *sentences* that can be constructed but rather the number of distinct meanings that these sentences have. Thus, there is no end of different sentences that one can construct using only the two signs "A" and "−":

$$A, \quad -A, \quad --A, \quad ---A, \quad \ldots$$

But in this infinite list of distinct sentences, all the odd-numbered entries are logically equivalent, and all the even-numbered entries are logically equivalent; there are infinitely many sentences here, but only two statements.

To answer the question about *statements*, we recall that the meaning of a sentence is determined by its truth conditions, so that sentences mean the same if they come out true and false together, in all possible cases. Then if all four of the cases *tt*, *ft*, *tf*, and *ff* concerning *AB* are possible, there will be a different statement for every different way of filling in a column of four *t*'s and *f*'s in the following truth table:

A	B	
t	t	
f	t	
t	f	
f	f	

Thus, we obtain the disjunction of A and B if we assign values t, t, t, and f to the four cases; we obtain the conjunction if we assign the values t, f, f, and f; we obtain the denial of A if we assign f, t, f, and t; and we obtain B itself by assigning t, t, f, and f.

All told, there are sixteen different columns of four t's and f's; sixteen distinct statements that can be concocted out of two sentence letters, provided all four cases concerning their joint truth and falsity are possible.

A	B	1	2	3	4	5	6	7	8	9	10	11	12	13	14	15	16
t	t	t	t	t	t	t	t	t	t	f	f	f	f	f	f	f	f
f	t	t	t	t	t	f	f	f	f	t	t	t	t	f	f	f	f
t	f	t	t	f	f	t	t	f	f	t	t	f	f	t	t	f	f
f	f	t	f	t	f	t	f	t	f	t	f	t	f	t	f	t	f

Table   3.1

These can be surveyed as shown in Table 3.1. Column 1 represents the tautology, true in all cases and expressed equally well by any of the sentences

$$A \vee -A, \qquad B \vee -B, \qquad (A \mathbin{\&} B) \vee (-A \mathbin{\&} B) \vee (A \mathbin{\&} -B)$$
$$\vee (-A \mathbin{\&} -B), \qquad \ldots$$

Column 16 represents the contradiction, false in all possible cases and expressed by each of the sentences

$$A \mathbin{\&} -A, \qquad B \mathbin{\&} -B, \qquad (A \vee B) \mathbin{\&} (-A \vee B) \mathbin{\&} (A \vee -B)$$
$$\mathbin{\&} (-A \vee -B), \qquad \ldots$$

The statement made by "A" itself is represented by column 6. It is expressed by each of the sentences

$$A, \qquad (A \mathbin{\&} B) \vee (A \mathbin{\&} -B), \qquad (A \vee B) \mathbin{\&} (A \vee -B), \qquad \ldots$$

Similarly, the statement made by "B" is represented by column 4, and the denials of "A" and of "B" are represented by columns 11 and 13. Observe that the table is symmetrical about the dotted line between 8 and 9, in the sense that the columns symmetrically situated on opposite sides of the dotted line are denials of each other with t's in one column corresponding to f's in the other, and vice versa.

If "A" means that a certain coin lands head up the first time it is tossed and "B" means that it lands head up on the second toss, the simplest expressions in English and in logical notation for the sixteen statements are as indicated in Table 3.2.

$ftft$	A		
$fftt$	B		
$tttt$	1	$A \vee -A$	The first toss yields a head or a tail.
$fttt$	2	$A \vee B$	Head on the first or second toss.
$tftt$	3	$-A \vee B$	Head on toss 2 or tail on toss 1.
$fftt$	4	B	Head on the second toss.
$ttft$	5	$A \vee -B$	Head on toss 1 or tail on toss 2.
$ftft$	6	A	Head on the first toss.
$tfft$	7	$(A \,\&\, B) \vee (-A \,\&\, -B)$	Same outcomes on the two tosses.
$ffft$	8	$A \,\&\, B$	Heads on both tosses.
....			
$tttf$	9	$-A \vee -B$	Tail on at least one toss.
$fttf$	10	$(-A \,\&\, B) \vee (A \,\&\, -B)$	Opposite outcomes on the two tosses.
$tftf$	11	$-A$	Tail on the first toss.
$fftf$	12	$-A \,\&\, B$	Tail on toss 1 and head on toss 2.
$ttff$	13	$-B$	Tail on the second toss.
$ftff$	14	$A \,\&\, -B$	Head on toss 1 and tail on toss 2.
$tfff$	15	$-A \,\&\, -B$	Tails on both tosses.
$ffff$	16	$A \,\&\, -A$	The first toss yields a head and a tail.

Table 3.2

Similarly, there are exactly four distinct statements that can be made using just one sentence letter, provided both truth-values are semantically possible (see Table 3.3). Here, the first and last items again represent the tautology "$A \vee -A$" and the contradiction "$A \,\&\, -A$," the second column represents "A" itself, and the third represents the denial of "A."

A	1	2	3	4
t	t	t	f	f
f	t	f	t	f

Table   3.3

In general, with n sentence letters, each of which can be true or false independently of the others, there are $N = 2^n$ (the product of n twos) distinct cases concerning the joint truth and falsity of all n: every time we add a sentence letter, the number of cases doubles. And since a t or an f can be assigned to each of these n cases, independently of what has been assigned to the others, there will be 2^N distinct statements that we can make, using n sentence letters.

Number of sentence letters: 1, 2,   3,   4,....................

Number of cases: 2, 4,   8,   16,....................

Number of statements: 4, 16, 256, 65,536, ...

When a new sentence letter is added, the number of cases becomes the double of what it was before, and the number of statements becomes the square of what it was before. Then with only the four sentence letters "A," "B," "C," and "D," over sixty-five thousand distinct statements can be made; in particular, there are that many distinct statements that could be made about the outcomes of four tosses of a coin!

Of course, when the number of sentence letters increases by one and therefore the number of statements becomes the square of the previous number, the expanded collection of statements includes all the statements in the first collection, along with a large number of new statements. Thus, in going from one to two sentence letters, the tautology and the contradiction are repeated, as are the statements expressed by "A," "$-A$," "B," and "$-B$," all of which can be formulated using a single sentence letter. Then in Table 3.1, columns 1, 4, 6, 11, 13, and 16 represent statements that can be made with a single sentence letter, so that there are just ten *new* statements: statements that can be made with two sentence letters but not with one. (Similarly, among the 256 statements that can be made with three letters, only 218 are *new* in the sense that they can be made with three sentence letters but with no smaller number.)

NORMAL FORMS

Each of the ways we have been considering of forming new sentences out of old is called a *truth-function;* the truth-value of the result is determined by (is a function of) the truth-values of the ingredient sentences. So far, we have provided special symbols for only a very narrow selection of these truth-functions: the dash for the function which, applied to a single sentence, yields a sentence with the opposite truth-value; the ampersand for the function which, applied to two or more sentences, yields a sentence which is true if all ingredients are true and is otherwise false; and the wedge for the function which, applied to two or more sentences, yields a sentence which is false if all ingredients are false and is otherwise true. For the rest we have provided no special symbols, although we can, and in two cases, we shall.

Thus, we might adopt the special symbol

[, ,]

for the function which, applied to three sentences "*A*," "*B*," and "*C*," in that order, produces the sentence

[*A*, *B*, *C*]

which has the same truth-value as "*A*" or as "*C*," depending on whether "*B*" is true or false. The truth table for this connective must then be that of Table 3.4. But there is no real need to introduce a new symbol for this

A	B	C	[A, B, C]
t	t	t	t
f	t	t	f
t	f	t	t
f	f	t	t
t	t	f	t
f	t	f	f
t	f	f	f
f	f	f	f

Table   3.4

function since it can be expressed in terms of the three symbols we already have:

3.1 $(A \mathrel{\&} B) \vee (-B \mathrel{\&} C)$

It is straightforward to verify that sentence **3.1** is logically equivalent to the sentence "[A, B, C]" as defined by Table 3.4.

And as our survey (Table 3.2) of all sixteen truth-functions of two sentences has shown, each of those can be expressed in terms of the three symbols we already have. Indeed, it is easy to see that in general any truth-function of any finite number of sentences can be expressed in terms of the dash, the wedge, and the ampersand, for what a sentence says is that the actual case is one of its t cases, and in our notation we can easily describe each of the cases concerning the joint truth and falsity of sentence letters. Then the entire sentence can be expressed by (is logically equivalent to) the disjunction of the sentences that describe its t cases. Thus, any such case as

$$A \quad B \quad C$$
$$f \quad f \quad t$$

can be expressed as a conjunction of the sentence letters that are marked "t" with the denials of those that are marked "f":

$$(-A \mathrel{\&} -B \mathrel{\&} C)$$

When we apply our method to Table 3.4, we get the following sentence, which clearly is logically equivalent to "[A, B, C]."

3.2 $(A \mathrel{\&} B \mathrel{\&} C) \vee (A \mathrel{\&} -B \mathrel{\&} C) \vee (-A \mathrel{\&} -B \mathrel{\&} C) \vee (A \mathrel{\&} B \mathrel{\&} -C)$

The components of this disjunction correspond to the four t cases for the sentence "[A, B, C]":

ttt   tft   fft   ttf

This four-termed disjunction is markedly more complicated than sentence **3.1** which, as we have noted, is also logically equivalent to the sentence

"[A, B, C]." Our method need not yield the simplest expression for a given statement, but it does yield *an* expression for it, which can then be simplified by the methods of Chapter 2.

Two extreme situations ought to be noted. First, our method does not apply to contradictions, which have no *t* cases. But any contradiction is logically equivalent to the sentence "A & −A"; clearly, then, the contradictory statement can be expressed in terms of the dash, the ampersand, and the wedge (in fact, in terms of the first two alone). Second, if a sentence has only one *t* case, our method yields a "disjunction" with only one component: the sentence expressing that *t* case. Thus, applied to statement 12 in Table 3.1, our method yields the sentence "−A & B" which asserts that the one *t* case is actual.

Then by using parentheses, sentence letters, and the symbols "−," "&," and "∨," we can express any truth-functional compound of any collection of simple statements. The particular sentences that our method yields are called *disjunctive normal forms* of the corresponding statements. The disjunctive normal form of a statement is, in effect, its truth table, written out in a single line. Given any sentence, we can find a disjunctive normal form of the corresponding statement by simply working out the truth table and then applying our method.

Nor do we need all three of the symbols "−," "&," and "∨" to express all truth-functions. By DeMorgan's laws, we can do as much with the dash and either of the other two as we can with all three. Thus, the disjunctive normal form **3.2** of the sentence "[A, B, C]" can be expressed in terms of the dash and the wedge alone by applying DeMorgan's law to the components of the disjunction:

$$-(-A \lor -B \lor -C) \lor -(-A \lor B \lor -C) \lor -(A \lor B \lor -C)$$
$$\lor -(-A \lor -B \lor C)$$

And it can be equally well expressed in terms of the dash and the ampersand alone by applying DeMorgan's law to the whole disjunction **3.2**:

$$-(-(A \& B \& C) \& -(A \& -B \& C) \& -(-A \& -B \& C)$$
$$\& -(A \& B \& -C))$$

There are even individual truth-functions in terms of which we can express all truth-functional compounds of any sentences. One such is the

Sheffer stroke, |, which, applied to sentences "*A*" and "*B*," yields the sentence "$(A \mid B)$" which can be read

    not both A and B.

The sentence "$(A \mid B)$" is true if at least one of the ingredient sentences is false and is false if both ingredients are true. Then we have the following truth table:

A	B	$A \mid B$
t	t	f
f	t	t
t	f	t
f	f	t

Clearly, "$(A \mid B)$" is logically equivalent to "$-(A \ \& \ B)$." Then "$(A \mid A)$" is another way of saying "$-(A \ \& \ A)$" or, dropping the repetition, "$-A$"; thus, we can express denial in terms of the Sheffer stroke, writing

3.3   "$(A \mid A)$" for "$-A$."

Now since "$(A \ \& \ B)$" is the denial of "$(A \mid B)$," we have the means to eliminate ampersands in favor of strokes by writing

3.4   "$((A \mid B) \mid (A \mid B))$" for "$(A \ \& \ B)$."

Finally, since "$(A \lor B)$" is logically equivalent to "$-(-A \ \& \ -B)$" or to "$(-A \mid -B)$," we can write

3.5   "$((A \mid A) \mid (B \mid B))$" for "$(A \lor B)$."

    Now to express any statement in terms of the Sheffer stroke, first express it in terms of dashes, ampersands, and wedges (perhaps, by finding a disjunctive normal form for it), and then eliminate dashes, ampersands, and wedges in favor of strokes by applying substitutions of forms **3.3**, **3.4**, and **3.5**. In doing this we may have to insert extra parentheses to ensure that ampersands and wedges apply only to *pairs* of sentences, as in **3.4** and **3.5**.

Example. To apply the method to "$A \mathbin{\&} B \mathbin{\&} - C$," we must first rewrite it as, say,

$(A \mathbin{\&} B) \mathbin{\&} - C$.

Then we apply **3.4** and **3.3** to the components of the conjunction to get

$((A \mid B) \mid (A \mid B)) \mathbin{\&} (C \mid C)$.

Finally, we apply pattern **3.4** to this conjunction—replacing the "A"'s in **3.4** by "$((A \mid B) \mid (A \mid B))$" and replacing the "$B$"'s in **3.4** by "$(C \mid C)$"—to get the hideous result

$(((A \mid B) \mid (A \mid B)) \mid (C \mid C)) \mid (((A \mid B) \mid (A \mid B)) \mid (C \mid C))$

which is logically equivalent to the original sentence "$A \mathbin{\&} B \mathbin{\&} - C$."

CONDITIONALS

Obviously, the possibility of using the Sheffer stroke as our sole connective is only of theoretical interest. In practice, we do well to have various connectives, corresponding to various English locutions, with the aid of which we can write sentences that are easy to read and understand. This brings us to the question of whether there are not further truth-functions that merit special symbols. In fact, two such functions suggest themselves, corresponding to columns 7 and 3 in Table 3.1.

A	B	$(A \leftrightarrow B)$	$(A \to B)$
t	t	t	t
f	t	f	t
t	f	f	f
f	f	t	t

The first of these connectives is called the *biconditional.* Writing the double arrow between two sentences and enclosing the result in parentheses yields a sentence which is true (false) if the component sentences have identical (different) truth-values: "$(A \leftrightarrow B)$" means that "A" and "B" have the same truth-value—both true or both false. The closest English phrase is

if and only if.

We shall read "$(A \leftrightarrow B)$" as *A if and only if B.*

The second connective is called the *conditional.* Writing the arrow between two sentences and enclosing the result in parentheses yields a sentence which is true if the first component is false or if the second component is true. Then "$A \rightarrow B$" is equivalent to

$$-A \vee B$$

and to

$$-(A \mathrel{\&} -B).$$

In the second of these forms, the conditional statement is seen to deny that the first component is true while the second is false, and to that extent it is comparable with the conditional "if . . . then" construction in English; to say that

If it rains today, it will really pour

is at least in part to deny that it will rain today without really pouring.

But there is ground for doubt that the arrow conveys the full sense of the English conditional; many would claim that part of the meaning of the "if . . . then" construction in English is to assert some real connection between antecedent and consequent—between the "if" clause and the "then" clause. Thus, it is held that to assert "If it rains today, it will really pour" is not only to deny that it will rain today without really pouring, but is in addition to deny that it *could* rain today without really pouring. It is held that to assert "If A then B" is to claim that "$A \mathrel{\&} -B$" is not only false but impossible. Thus, the statement that

If Hitler had invaded England in 1940, he would have won the war.

is taken to assert a real connection between Hitler's invading England in 1940 and his winning the war, so that if the former had happened, the latter would surely have followed. But the statement that

Hitler invaded England in 1940 → Hitler won the war

is logically equivalent to

Either Hitler did not invade England in 1940 or he won the war.

Therefore, the arrow statement is true merely because in fact Hitler did not invade England in 1940; it is true whether or not invading would really have won him the war.

Similarly, if "*A*" means that I jump off the Empire State Building and "*B*" means that I float gently to the ground, "*A → B*" is true because "*A*" is false, but the English conditional

If I jump off the Empire State Building, then I float gently to the ground

may be taken to imply a causal connection between antecedent and consequent which in fact does not obtain, so that we might want to say that the English conditional is false although the arrow statement is true.

But there does seem to be a use of "if" in English that corresponds rather closely to our arrow, as when I say

If Hitler was a strategist, Napoleon was a plumber

in order to convey vividly that Hitler was no strategist. If "*B*" is false, "*A → B*" has the same truth-value as " *− A*," so that by asserting a conditional with an obviously false consequent we can in effect deny the antecedent. And we can do this whether or not there is any real connection between antecedent and consequent.

In defending "if . . . then" as a reading of the arrow, we must insist that antecedent and consequent be read as context-free declarative sentences. This means that

Hitler invaded England in 1940 → Hitler won the war

is not to be translated as a counterfactual conditional,

If Hitler had invaded England in 1940, then he would have won the war, but rather as the bland assertion

If Hitler invaded England in 1940, then Hitler won the war,

which we are more willing to accept as true merely because its antecedent is false. Similarly, the sentence

I jump off the Empire State Building → I float gently to the ground

is not to be rendered into English as

If I jump off the Empire State Building, then I float gently to the ground

if this English sentence is understood as a generalization about occasions when I might jump off the Empire State Building. Rather, we must suppose antecedent and consequent to refer to definite occasions, so that the whole is to be understood as saying something like this:

If I jumped off the Empire State Building on Washington's Birthday, 1966, then I floated gently to the ground on Washington's Birthday, 1966.

Here again, the whole conditional is trivially true because in fact I was nowhere near the Empire State Building on Washington's Birthday, 1966.

The situation for the arrow seems comparable with that for the wedge. Normally, I have no occasion to say "If A then B" when I know that "A" is false or that "B" is true. Knowing that "A" is false, I might say "If it had been the case that A, then it would have been the case that B," but this counterfactual conditional has a markedly different form and use from the simple indicative conditional that we are proposing as a translation of the arrow statement. Normally, the occasions on which I would say "If A then B" are those when I know the truth-value neither of "A" nor of "B" but for some reason am sure that if "A" is in fact true, so is "B": I am sure that "A & −B" is false. And typically, when I have such a belief, I have it because I know of some real connection between A and B; my confidence in the statement "If A then B" is based on my knowledge of the connection. But that statement itself (I would argue) *asserts* no such connection. It asserts only that −A ∨ B or that −(A & −B). As we said at the beginning of this book, the focus is on truth and falsity. We are not concerned with the purpose of making a statement or even with how or whether the speaker knows that what he is saying is true.

The case is similar for "or." I normally have no occasion to say "$A \lor B$" if I know the truth-value of either component. Rather it is when (somehow or other) I know that at least one of the two components is true but do not know which that I assert the disjunction. For this reason it is misleading, although true, to say

Tom did it or Dick did it

when the speaker knows that Tom did it and Dick did not. Similarly, it is misleading, although true, to say that $A \to B$ (that $-A \lor B$) when the speaker knows that "A" is false or when he knows that "B" is true.

Then we shall often use the arrow as a translation of the English "if . . . then"—bearing in mind the precise sense in which we are interpreting conditionals and distinguishing truth-value from grounds on which one knows the truth-value.

Translation. In translating between English and our notation, some confusion can arise because of the variety of ways in which we express conditionals in English. To begin with, notice that all of the following come to the same thing.

If *Hitler was a strategist,* then *Napoleon was a plumber.*
If *Hitler was a strategist, Napoleon was a plumber.*
Napoleon was a plumber if *Hitler was a strategist.*

Moral: The *"then"* can be omitted without changing the sense, and the *"if"* marks the antecedent (what comes before the arrow) even when in English the consequent is written first. Thus, each of the foregoing three sentences goes over into our notation as

$H \to N.$

A further variant can be obtained by analyzing the biconditional: "A if and only if B" means the same as

A if B, and A only if B

and as

> *If A then B, and if B then A.*

Now since "*A* if *B*" has been seen to have the same meaning as "If *B* then *A*," it appears that "*A* only if *B*" must be an English translation of "*A* → *B*," so that the English phrase

> *only if*

is a good translation of our arrow

> →.

We form conditionals in English by writing "only if" between sentences, to the same effect as if we had written the arrow between the same sentences in the same order. The word "if," *between* sentences, corresponds rather to the arrow written backward. "*A* if *B*" goes over into our notation as "*B* → *A*."

There is a strong tendency, which we should resist, to assume that someone who says "*A* if *B*" really means "*A* if and only if *B*." Perhaps he does, but if so, he has expressed himself inaccurately. The statements "*A* → *B*" and "*A* ↔ *B*" are quite different, as their truth tables show: since they have different truth-values in the case where "*A*" is false but "*B*" is true, the one is by no means equivalent to the other unless, for some reason, the *ft* case for "*AB*" cannot arise. (Thus, the sentences "If Socrates was bald, then he was quite hairless" and "Socrates was bald if and only if he was quite hairless" are semantically equivalent, although they are not logically equivalent.)

Now for a final version of the conditional. The sentence

> *H* → *N*

can also be translated into English as follows:

> *Hitler was not a strategist unless Napoleon was a plumber.*

In other words, the sentences

$$H \to N, \qquad -H \vee N, \qquad -H \text{ unless } N$$

are all equivalent. Comparing the second with the third, we see that our wedge, the inclusive

   or

has the same sense as

   unless.

Furthermore, the wedge, and also "unless," must come to the same thing as

   if not

(written *between* sentences), for "A if not B" means the same as " $-B \to A$," which in turn means the same as "$B \vee A$" or, since the order doesn't matter, "$A \vee B$." And by the same reasoning,

   unless not

comes to the same thing as

   if

for, translating "unless" by the wedge, "A unless not B" becomes "$A \vee -B$" and then "$B \to A$" which is equivalent to "A if B."

NON-TRUTH-FUNCTIONAL CONNECTIVES

We are *not* claiming that all ways of combining sentences to get new sentences are truth-functional and can be represented in terms of *not, and,* and *or.* We often assert compound statements whose truth-values are not determined by (are not functions of) the truth-values of their components. Thus, the phrase

   Jeffrey believes that,

written before a declarative sentence, yields a declarative sentence that may be true or false, but whose truth or falsity is not determined solely by the truth-value of what follows the phrase. Since some of my beliefs are true and others of them are false, "Jeffrey believes that A" can be true when "A" is true or when "A" is false. And since there are truths and there are falsehoods that I *fail* to believe, the sentence "Jeffrey believes that A" can be *false* when "A" is true or when "A" is false.

Another example is the connective

It is more probable that . . . than that—

which may yield a true or a false sentence when declarative sentences are written in the blanks, irrespective of the truth or falsity of those component sentences. To see that this connective is not truth-functional, consider the process of drawing a card from a well-shuffled deck. Suppose that in fact the ace of spades is destined to be drawn. Now it is true that (A) an ace is drawn and that (B) a black card is drawn, so that both components are true in each of the following sentences:

It is more probable that A than that B.
It is more probable that B than that A.

Yet the first sentence is false, while the second is true; clearly, it is not the truth-values of the components that determine the truth-value of the whole here. If we symbolize

It is more probable that A than that B

by

$A \gg B,$

then $\gg$ is a genuine connective which, written between sentences, yields a new sentence. But it is no truth-function, and none of the sixteen columns in Table 3.1 represents the statement $A \gg B$. Similarly, we might represent "Jeffrey believes that" by "*"; but although "*A" is then genuinely a compound sentence, it is not compounded truth-functionally out of "A" and is represented nowhere in Table 3.3.

EXERCISES

3.1 Let "A" mean that everyone loves everyone, and let "B" mean that everyone loves himself. How many different statements are made by the infinitely many different sentences that can be built out of "A" and "B" by truth-functional connectives? (Assume that two sentences make the same statement if and only if they are equivalent logically or semantically.)

3.2 Interpret "A" as making the contradictory statement that Socrates was an Athenian and Socrates was not an Athenian. How many different statements are made by the infinitely many different sentences that can be built out of "A" by truth-functional connectives?

3.3 Let "A" mean that Moriarty is guilty and let "B" mean that Crumm is guilty. (Then "$-A$" means that Moriarty is innocent, and "$-B$" means that Crumm is innocent.) Write clear, idiomatic English sentences corresponding to the sixteen truth-functional compounds of "A" and "B" in the manner of Table 3.2.

3.4 Explain exactly why it is that (a) all tautologies have the same meaning, regardless of what sentence letters appear in them, and why it is that, similarly, (b) there is only one self-contradictory statement, although that statement can be expressed by various sentences involving various sentence letters.

3.5 Reread Exercise 1.7 and then explain the following facts.

    a Logically equivalent sentences must have the same probability.

    b If a conditional is a tautology, then the probability of its consequent is at least as great as that of its antecedent.

3.6 Verify that the following pairs of sentences are logically equivalent:

    a $[A, B, C]$, $(B \rightarrow A) \mathbin{\&} (-B \rightarrow C)$

    b $[A, B, -A]$, $A \leftrightarrow B$

    c $[f, A, t]$, $-A$

    d $[A, A, B]$, $A \vee B$

3.7 Explain how it is that every truth-functional compound of sentence letters can be expressed using those letters together with the signs "t," "f," and "$[\; , \; , \;]$."

3.8 *Another Normal Form.* Every sentence can be interpreted as saying of its f cases that none is actual. Thus, looking at Table 3.4, we see that the f cases for "$[A, B, C]$" are cases 2, 6, 7, and 8, and that these can be described as follows:

2:     $(-A \& B \& C)$ 6: $(-A \& B \& -C)$
7:     $(A \& -B \& -C)$ 8: $(-A \& -B \& -C)$

To say that none of these is actual is to say this:

$$-(-A \& B \& C) \& -(-A \& B \& -C) \& -(A \& -B \& -C)$$
$$\& -(-A \& -B \& -C)$$

Then the statement $[A, B, C]$ can be expressed as *a conjunction of denials of its f cases* as can any statement that has f cases. Apply the same technique to the statements:

    a $A \leftrightarrow B$ **b** $A \rightarrow B$ **c** $A \vee B$ **d** $A \,|\, B$

3.9 The Sheffer stroke is not the only single connective that is adequate for all purposes of truth-functional composition. Another is the connective $\downarrow$ where "$A \downarrow B$" means *neither A nor B*.

    a   Write the truth table for $\downarrow$.

    b   Express $-A$ and either $A \vee B$ or $A \& B$ in terms of $\downarrow$ and sentence letters and parentheses alone, thereby showing that $\downarrow$ is adequate for all purposes of truth-functional composition.

3.10 Show that each of the pairs

    a $\rightarrow$, $-$ **b** $\rightarrow$, f

is adequate for all purposes of truth-functional composition.

3.11 Mathematical proofs of theorems of biconditional form "$A \leftrightarrow B$" are usually broken up into a proof of "$A \rightarrow B$" and a proof of "$B \rightarrow A$," and the latter two proofs together are spoken of as showing that A *is a necessary and sufficient condition for B.*

    a   Which proof shows necessity (that for B to be true, it is necessary that A be true)?

    b   Which proof shows sufficiency (that for B to be true, it is sufficient that A be true)?

3.12 Verify that the following pairs are logically equivalent:

    a $-(A \rightarrow B)$, $A \& -B$
    b $-A \rightarrow B$, $-B \rightarrow A$
    c $A \rightarrow B$, $-B \rightarrow -A$
    d $A \leftrightarrow B$, $(A \rightarrow B) \& (-A \rightarrow -B)$

3.13 Verify that the following pairs are *not* logically equivalent:

a $A \rightarrow B$, $A \leftrightarrow B$
b $A \rightarrow B$, $B \rightarrow A$
c $A \rightarrow (B \rightarrow C)$, $(A \rightarrow B) \rightarrow C$
d $A \rightarrow B$, $-A \rightarrow -B$

3.14 Which of the following sentences are logically equivalent to which others?

a A b $-A$ c $A \rightarrow A$ d $-A \rightarrow A$
e $A \rightarrow -A$ f $-(A \rightarrow A)$ g t h f

3.15 Interpret the sentence letters as follows. A: You pay me. B: I do the job. C: The job is not too hard. Translate into logical notation:
a *If you pay me, then I shall do the job unless it is too hard.*
b *I shall do the job if you pay me, unless it is too hard.*
c *Unless it is too hard, I shall do the job if you pay me.*
d *If it is not too hard, I shall do the job if you pay me.*
e *If you pay me, then if the job is not too hard, I shall do it.*

3.16 A: I did the job. B: I was paid. Translate:
a *I was paid, if I did the job.*
b *I was paid, unless I did not do the job.*
c *If I did the job, I was paid.*
d *If I was not paid, I did not do the job.*
e *Unless I was paid, I did not do the job.*

3.17 *Inference.* To say that a collection of sentences (the *premises*) implies a sentence (the *conclusion*) is to say that

> In none of the cases concerning the joint truth and falsity of the sentence letters are *all* premises true while the conclusion is false.

Example. The premises "$A \vee B$" and "$-A$" imply the conclusion "B."

		premises		conclusion
A	B	$A \vee B$	$-A$	B
t	t	t	f	t
f	t	t	t	t
t	f	t	f	f
f	f	f	t	f

Reason: In the only case (case 2) in which both premises are true, the conclusion is true as well. On the other hand, the premises "$A \to B$" and "B" do *not* imply the conclusion "A" because there is a case (case 2, again) in which both premises are true but the conclusion is false:

		premises		conclusion
A	B	$A \to B$	B	A
t	t	t	t	t
f	t	t	t	f
t	f	f	f	t
f	f	t	f	f

Now test the following inferences for validity; in other words, see whether the premises (the sentences above the bar) really do imply the conclusion (below the bar):

a $A \lor B$ b $A \to B$ c $A \to B$

     $\dfrac{A}{B}$ $\dfrac{A \to -B}{-A}$ $\dfrac{A \lor B}{B}$

d $A \to B$ e $A \leftrightarrow B$

     $\dfrac{-B}{-A}$ $\dfrac{-(A \,\&\, B)}{-A \,\&\, -B}$

3.18   Test each of the following inferences for validity:

a   *Crumm is not guilty.*   b   *Moriarty is guilty.*
    Moriarty is guilty if Crumm is.   *Moriarty is not guilty.*
    Moriarty is not guilty.   *Holmes is on the job.*

c   *If Moriarty has escaped, then either Holmes has bungled or Watson is on the job.*
    Holmes has not bungled unless Moriarty has escaped.
    Watson is not on the job.
    Moriarty has escaped if and only if Holmes has bungled.

d   *If Holmes has bungled or Watson is windy, Moriarty will escape.*
    Moriarty will escape unless Holmes bungles.

e   *Moriarty will escape unless Holmes acts.*
     We shall rely on Watson only if Holmes does not act.
     _____
     If Holmes does not act, Moriarty will escape unless we rely on Watson.

f   *Moriarty will escape only if Holmes bungles.*
     Holmes will not bungle if Watson is to be believed.
     _____
     If Watson is to be believed, Moriarty will not escape.

g   *We shall fish if it rains, and we shall swim if it does not.*
     _____
     We shall fish or swim.

h   *We shall fish if it rains, and we shall swim if it does not.*
     We shall fish unless we do not swim.
     _____
     We shall swim unless we do not fish.

i   *We shall swim even if it rains.*
     _____
     We shall swim.

j   *There is coffee on the stove if you want some.*
     _____
     There is coffee on the stove.

Note: **i** and **j** illustrate deviant uses of "if."

3.19   It is plausible to view the indicative English conditional as at least half truth-functional, for when the antecedent is true, the whole conditional has the same truth-value as its consequent. Then if the conditional "If A then B" is *fully* truth-functional, its truth table must be given by one of a certain four columns in Table 3.1; but three of those columns define statements which clearly are not conditionals. Identify the three columns, and identify the corresponding statements both in English and in logical notation. You will then have shown by a process of elimination that if the English conditional is truth-functional, its truth table must be the one we have given for the arrow.

3.20   Explain why the conditional must have the truth table we have given for it if it is truth-functional and the following *deduction theorem* holds:

A conditional is a logical truth if and only if its antecedent logically implies its consequent.

TRUTH TREES

To say that some premises imply a conclusion is to deny that a case can be found in which all premises are true but the conclusion is false. Such a case is called a *counterexample*. Then to say that the premises

$$A \rightarrow -B$$
$$-C \rightarrow A$$

imply the conclusion

$$B \rightarrow C$$

is to say that none of the eight cases concerning the joint truth or falsity of the letters "A," "B," and "C" is a counterexample: none of them makes both premises true while making the conclusion false.

The most straightforward way to verify such a claim is to compute the truth-values of both premises and of the conclusion in each of the eight cases and then check to see that the premises are never both true when the conclusion is false. But since the number of cases doubles every time a new sentence letter is introduced, the straightforward way can be impossibly laborious. (If there are ten letters, 1,024 cases have to be examined!)

AN EXAMPLE

Even in the foregoing inference where only three sentence letters appear and where there are only eight cases, there is much effort wasted in a straightforward examination of all cases to see that none is a counterexample. By using a little subtlety, we can greatly reduce the labor; what is wanted is a way of eliminating whole groups of cases at once. A systematic technique of this sort is given by the method of *truth trees* that will now be explained. As an example, we use the inference already mentioned:

$$A \to -B$$
$$\underline{-C \to A}$$
$$B \to C$$

The truth tree for this inference is as follows:

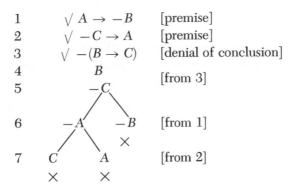

1	$\sqrt{\ }\ A \to -B$	[premise]
2	$\sqrt{\ }\ -C \to A$	[premise]
3	$\sqrt{\ }\ -(B \to C)$	[denial of conclusion]
4	B	[from 3]
5	$-C$	
6	$-A$ $-B$	[from 1]
7	C A	[from 2]

First Step. The first step in the construction of this tree was to *list the premises and the denial of the conclusion.* The counterexamples are the cases in which all three of these sentences are true. We want to see if there are any such cases. This accounts for lines 1, 2, and 3.

Second Step. It makes no great difference which of lines 1, 2, and 3 we examine first. Let us begin with line 3. Any counterexample must make this line true. Therefore, it must make "$B \to C$" false, and this will happen if and only if "B" is true and "C" is false. We indicate this by writing "B" and "$-C$" as lines 4 and 5 of the tree. At this point we also check ($\sqrt{\ }$) line 3

B	C	$B \to C$
t	t	t
f	t	t
t	f	f
f	f	t

to show that we have taken account of all possible ways in which it can be true. The procedure can be summarized by the following *rule of inference* in which the circle and triangle stand for arbitrary sentences.

$$\sqrt{\ -(\bigcirc \to \triangle)}$$
$$\bigcirc$$
$$-\triangle$$

Third Step. Let us take line 1 next. Any counterexample must also make this line true. Here the relevant rule of inference is this:

In words: The cases in which a conditional is true are the cases in which its antecedent is false together with the cases in which its consequent is true. (Some cases fall into both categories, but that is all right.)

	$\bigcirc$	$\triangle$	$\bigcirc \to \triangle$
Consequent true	t	t	t
	f	t	t
Antecedent false	t	f	f
	f	f	t

Then the fork in the rule for conditionals has the sense of "or": a conditional $\bigcirc \to \triangle$ is true if and only if either its antecedent $\bigcirc$ is false or its consequent $\triangle$ is true (or both). Then we check the first line of the tree and introduce a fork at the bottom (after line 5) with the left prong labeled "$-A$" (denial of the antecedent) and the right prong labeled "$-B$" (the consequent). This accounts for all possible ways in which line 1 might be true.

Fourth Step. In the right-hand path down through the tree we now have the following sentences:

$$A \to -B, \qquad -C \to A, \qquad -(B \to C), \qquad B, \qquad -C, \qquad -B$$

But two of these sentences contradict each other: "*B*" and "*— B.*" The path is accordingly said to be *closed,* and we indicate this fact by marking it with a cross ($\times$) under its last entry, "*—B.*" A closed path is one that contains a sentence together with its denial. It is impossible for all sentences in a closed path to be true.

Fifth Step. Only line 2 remains to be dealt with. Any counterexample must make this line true as well as lines 1 and 3. Since line 2 is a conditional, "*— C* $\to$ *A,*" we treat it as line 1 was treated in the third step. Now, the circle represents "*— C*" and the triangle represents "*A.*" Applying the rule, we *place a fork at the bottom of every open path that contains the checked sentence,* labeling the left-hand prong "*— — C*" ($- \bigcirc$) and labeling the right-hand prong "*A*" ($\triangle$):

But since the two denials undo each other, we *omit both dashes.* ("*— — C*" is logically equivalent to "*C.*") This gives us line 7.

Final Step. Ignoring the path that we have already marked "$\times$," there are two paths from top to bottom of the tree. Each of these is closed: the left-hand path contains both "*C*" and "*— C,*" while the other contains both "*A*" and "*— A.*" Accordingly, we mark each path with a cross.

Every path is now closed. The tree itself is then said to be closed, and *the inference has been found to be valid.*

Why? Because the two rules of inference were so designed that when we check a sentence, we display all possible ways in which that sentence can be true. The different paths through the tree then represent different possible ways in which the sentences with which we started might all be true, and every such possibility is represented by some path. If a path is closed, then the "possibilities" that it represents do not really exist. If all paths are closed, it is impossible for all the sentences with which we started the tree to be true: *there are no counterexamples.*

In contrast, notice what happens when we test an *invalid* inference such as the following, in which the conclusion is not really implied by the premises:

$A \rightarrow B$
$-A$
—————
B

Here we have a tree in which one path is open:

1	$\sqrt{} \ A \rightarrow B$	[premise]
2	$-A$	[premise]
3	$-B$	[denial of conclusion]
4	$-A \qquad B$	[from 1]
	$\times$	

The open path represents a counterexample: a case in which both premises are true while the conclusion is false. To see what case this is, note what sentence letters appear, with or without dashes, in the open path:

$-A, \qquad -B$

The counterexample is the case in which "A" and "B" are both false: case 4, in the standard listing. There, indeed, "$A \rightarrow B$" and "$-A$" (premises) are both true, and "B" (conclusion) is false:

		premises		conclusion
A	B	$A \rightarrow B$	$-A$	B
f	f	t	t	f

The procedure we have followed in constructing these truth trees is purely mechanical. It can be put into the form of a *flow chart* as in Figure 4.1.

Now try the method on the following inferences. Solutions are given below. You will get one tree or another (but the same *answer*—valid or invalid) depending on the order in which you choose to check sentences.

Figure 4.1

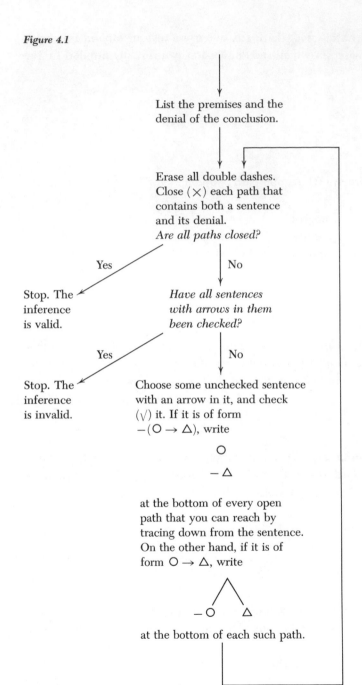

The trees shown in the solutions are the ones you will get if you first check the denial of the conclusion and then check the premises in order, from top to bottom.

EXAMPLES

a A
   $\dfrac{A \to B}{B}$

b B
   $\dfrac{A \to B}{A}$

c $\dfrac{-A}{A \to B}$

d $A \to B$
   $B \to C$
   $\overline{A \to C}$

e $\dfrac{-A \to B}{B \to A}$

f $\dfrac{A \to B}{-B \to -A}$

SOLUTIONS

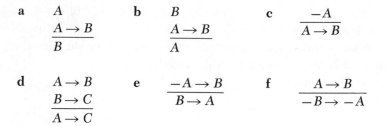

a

      A
   $\sqrt{} \ A \to B$
        $-B$

   $-A \qquad B$
   $\times \qquad \times$

   valid

b

      B
   $\sqrt{} \ A \to B$
        $-A$

   $-A \qquad B$

   invalid

c

      $-A$
   $\sqrt{} \ -(A \to B)$
        A
        $-B$
        $\times$

   valid

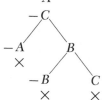

d

   $\sqrt{} \ A \to B$
   $\sqrt{} \ B \to C$
   $\sqrt{} \ -(A \to C)$
        A
        $-C$

   $-A \qquad\qquad B$
   $\times$
        $-B \qquad C$
        $\times \qquad \times$

   valid

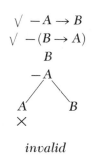

e $\sqrt{} \ -A \to B$
   $\sqrt{} \ -(B \to A)$
        B
        $-A$

   $A \qquad B$
   $\times$

   invalid

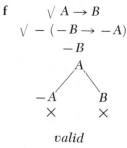

f $\sqrt{} \ A \to B$
   $\sqrt{} \ -(-B \to -A)$
        $-B$
        A

   $-A \qquad B$
   $\times \qquad \times$

   valid

Notice that if even one path is open after all formulas containing arrows have been checked, the inference is invalid, for *each* open path represents a class of counterexamples. Thus, in example **e,** the right-hand path represents a class of counterexamples consisting of all cases in which "*A*" is false and "*B*" is true. (If you are considering only the four cases concerning the joint truth and falsity of "*A*" and "*B*," there is only one such case.)

As a matter of strategy, it is well to check denials of conditionals before checking conditionals: $-(O \rightarrow \triangle)$ before $(O \rightarrow \triangle)$. This prevents the tree from branching out unnecessarily. But the method works no matter in what order you apply the rules of inference.

For further practice, try these:

EXAMPLES

g $\dfrac{(A \rightarrow B) \rightarrow C}{-C \rightarrow A}$ h $\dfrac{(A \rightarrow B) \rightarrow A}{A}$

i $\dfrac{(A \rightarrow B) \rightarrow B}{A}$ j $A \rightarrow B$
  $B \rightarrow C$
  $\dfrac{C \rightarrow D}{A \rightarrow D}$

k   *Moriarty will escape unless Holmes acts.*
  We shall rely on Watson only if Holmes does
  not act.
  _____
  If Holmes does not act, Moriarty will escape
  unless we rely on Watson.

SOLUTIONS

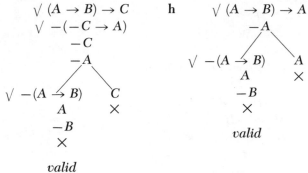

g
$$\sqrt{} \;\; (A \to B) \to C$$
$$\sqrt{} \;\; -(-C \to A)$$
$$-C$$
$$-A$$

$\sqrt{}\; -(A \to B) \qquad C$
$\qquad A \qquad\qquad \times$
$\qquad -B$
$\qquad \times$

valid

h
$$\sqrt{} \;\; (A \to B) \to A$$
$$-A$$

$\sqrt{}\; -(A \to B) \qquad A$
$\qquad A \qquad\qquad \times$
$\qquad -B$
$\qquad \times$

valid

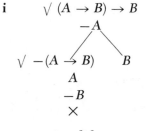

i
$$\sqrt{} \;\; (A \to B) \to B$$
$$-A$$

$\sqrt{}\; -(A \to B) \qquad B$
$\qquad A$
$\qquad -B$
$\qquad \times$

invalid

j
$$\sqrt{} \;\; A \to B$$
$$\sqrt{} \;\; B \to C$$
$$\sqrt{} \;\; C \to D$$
$$\sqrt{} \;\; -(A \to D)$$
$$A$$
$$-D$$

$-A \qquad B$
$\times$
$\qquad -B \qquad C$
$\qquad \times$
$\qquad\qquad -C \qquad D$
$\qquad\qquad \times \qquad \times$

valid

k   In an obvious notation, the argument is:

$$-H \to M$$
$$W \to -H$$
$$\overline{-H \to (-W \to M)}$$

The tree test shows this to be valid:

$$\sqrt{} -H \to M$$
$$W \to -H$$
$$\sqrt{} -(-H \to (-W \to M))$$
$$-H$$
$$\sqrt{} -(-W \to M)$$
$$-W$$
$$-M$$

$$
\begin{array}{cc}
H & M \\
\times & \times
\end{array}
$$

Note: We did not need the second premise.

RULES OF INFERENCE

So far, our method applies only to inferences in which the only connectives to appear are "$-$" and "$\to$"; but we can easily extend it so as to apply to sentences in which any truth-functional connectives at all may appear. For each connective, we merely have to provide two rules of inference, as follows:

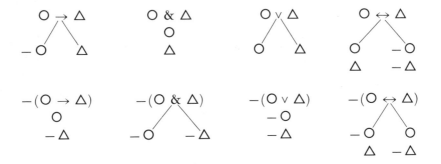

Any one of these rules can be applied to any unchecked sentence which has the form indicated in the first line of the rule. Thus, the lower rule for & can be applied to the sentence

$$-((A \rightarrow B) \, \& \, (-A \, \& \, B))$$

because it has the form *denial of a conjunction:* $-(\bigcirc \, \& \, \triangle)$ with "$(A \rightarrow B)$" in place of "$\bigcirc$" and "$(-A \, \& \, B)$" in place of "$\triangle$." None of the other rules apply to this sentence, for the sentence *is* the denial of a conjunction and *is not* of any other form. It is true that *parts* of the sentence have other forms: the part "$(A \rightarrow B)$" is a conditional and the part "$(-A \, \& \, B)$" is a conjunc-

Figure 4.2

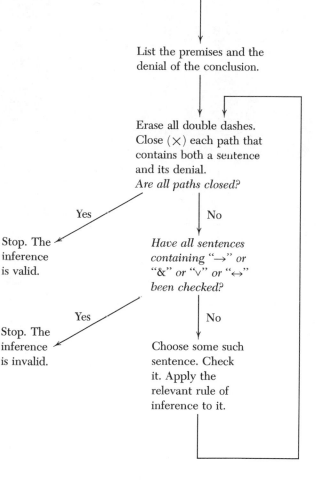

tion. But *the rules of inference are not to be applied to parts of sentences; they are to be applied only to whole sentences.*

The program for applying the rules of inference is the same as it was when we had only the two rules for → (see Figure 4.2). The instruction "Apply the relevant rule of inference" at the lower right of Figure 4.2 means: *Write the material shown below the first line of the rule at the bottom of every open path that passes through the checked formula.* To any sentence which contains connectives other than the dash, one and only one rule of inference will be relevant (will apply).

Now try these examples. Solutions follow.

EXAMPLES

l $\dfrac{A \leftrightarrow B}{A \to B}$ m $\dfrac{A \to B}{A \leftrightarrow B}$ n $\dfrac{A \,\&\, B}{A \lor B}$

SOLUTIONS

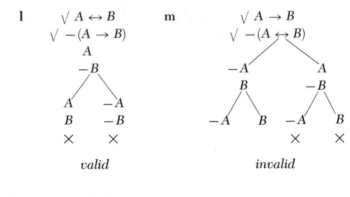

l $\sqrt{}\ A \leftrightarrow B$

    $\sqrt{}\ -(A \to B)$

       A

      $-B$

    A $-A$

    B $-B$

    $\times$ $\times$

      valid

m $\sqrt{}\ A \to B$

    $\sqrt{}\ -(A \leftrightarrow B)$

   $-A$ A

    B $-B$

 $-A$ B $-A$ B

     $\times$ $\times$

     invalid

n $\sqrt{}\ A \,\&\, B$

   $\sqrt{}\ -(A \lor B)$

    $-A$

    $-B$

     A

     B

    $\times$

   valid

COMMENTS ON THE RULES

The rules may be applied in any order, but usually it is best to begin with rules that involve no branching: the lower rules for → and ∨ and the upper rule for &, if there are any sentences to which these rules apply.

For simplicity, the rules for & and ∨ have been given only for conjunctions and disjunctions that have two components, but the rules are similar when three or more terms are involved. Thus, for three components, the rules are these:

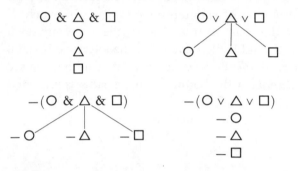

There are no such three-component rules for → or for ↔ because expressions like "A → B → C" and "A ↔ B ↔ C" do not count as sentences.

The two rules for each connective are justified by consulting the truth table for that connective. Thus, the upper rule for & is justified by the fact that the one and only way in which a conjunction O & △ can be true is for both conjuncts, O and △, to be true. The lower rule for & is justified by the fact that the ways in which a conjunction can be false are precisely described as the ways in which the first conjunct can be false together with the ways in which the second conjunct can be false. This description is a bit redundant since one way of falsifying a conjunction is to falsify both conjuncts at once, but this redundancy is harmless, for exclusiveness is not implied when we draw a fork in a tree. In fact, the redundancy makes for simplicity, as we can see by noticing that an irredundant version of the lower rule for & would look like this:

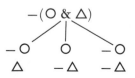

Use of this rule in place of the one we have adopted would lead to no mistakes in classifying inferences as valid or not, but the trees it would lead to would be unnecessarily large.

Rules for the other connectives are justified similarly.

The truth-value of a sentence is determined by the truth-values of its subsentences. Truth trees grow as their sentences are checked (indicating that subsequently they can be ignored), and the ways in which they can be true are indicated by adding material at the bottoms of open paths as indicated in the rules of inference. When all sentences containing the connectives "→," "&," "∨," and "↔" have been checked, each open path through the tree represents a class of counterexamples: cases in which all the sentences at the top of the tree are true. Then if there are any open paths, the inference is invalid. And if there are none, the inference is valid, for as each sentence is checked, *all* the ways in which it could be true are accounted for by adding material at the bottoms of open paths as indicated by the rules of inference.

Now use the method to test the following inferences:

EXAMPLES

o $A \leftrightarrow B$ **p** $A \vee B$ **q** A **r** $\dfrac{A}{A \vee B}$

    $\dfrac{A \vee B}{A \,\&\, B}$ $\dfrac{-A}{B}$ $\dfrac{B}{A \,\&\, B}$

s $(A \,\&\, B) \rightarrow C$
     $\dfrac{-A \rightarrow D}{B \rightarrow (C \vee D)}$

t   *We shall fish if it rains and swim if it does not.*
     We shall fish or swim.

u   *If Holmes has bungled or Watson is windy, Moriarty will escape.*
     Moriarty will escape unless Holmes bungles.

SOLUTIONS

o

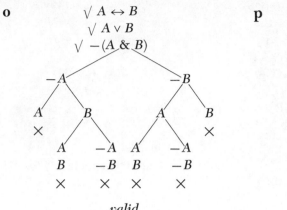

√ A ↔ B
√ A ∨ B
√ −(A & B)

valid

p

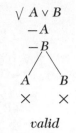

√ A ∨ B
−A
−B

valid

q

A
B
√ −(A & B)

valid

r

A
√ −(A ∨ B)
−A
−B
×

valid

s

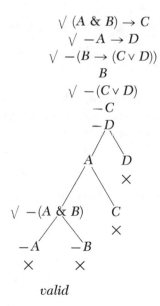

√ (A & B) → C
√ −A → D
√ −(B → (C ∨ D))
B
√ −(C ∨ D)
−C
−D

valid

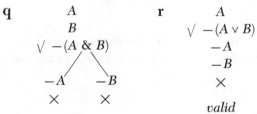

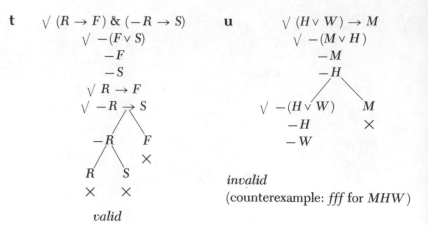

t $\checkmark$ $(R \to F)$ & $(-R \to S)$ u $\checkmark$ $(H \lor W) \to M$
        $\checkmark$ $-(F \lor S)$ $\checkmark$ $-(M \lor H)$
             $-F$ $-M$
             $-S$ $-H$
        $\checkmark$ $R \to F$
        $\checkmark$ $-R \to S$ $\checkmark$ $-(H \lor W)$ M
                                                           $-H$ $\times$
          $-R$ F $-W$

        R S $\times$ *invalid*
        $\times$ $\times$ (counterexample: *fff* for *MHW*)

          valid

EXERCISES

4.1   Rework Exercises 3.17 and 3.18 by the tree method.

4.2   Give the simplest rules of inference you can for the connectives

    a | **b**   ↓   **c**   [, ,]

Now use these rules to test the validity of the following inferences:

d $\dfrac{A \downarrow B}{A \mid B}$ **e** $\dfrac{A \mid B}{A \downarrow B}$ **f** $\dfrac{[A, B, C]}{A \downarrow C}$ **g** $\dfrac{[A, (A \downarrow B), C]}{A \mid C}$

                                                        B

4.3   The tree method can be used as follows to see whether a sentence is a tautology. Start the tree with the denial of the sentence, and proceed as if you were testing an inference for validity. If the tree closes, the sentence is a tautology; if the tree does not close, the sentence is not a tautology.

    Example. "$A \to A$" is a tautology because its tree closes, as shown here.

$\checkmark$ $-(A \to A)$
    A
   $-A$
   $\times$

    a   Explain why this technique works.
Use the technique to tell which of the following are tautologies:

    b $A \rightarrow (B \rightarrow A)$
    c $A \rightarrow (-A \rightarrow A)$
    d $(A \rightarrow -A) \rightarrow A$
    e $(A \rightarrow (B \rightarrow C)) \rightarrow ((A \rightarrow B) \rightarrow (A \rightarrow C))$
    f $-(A \leftrightarrow B) \leftrightarrow (-A \leftrightarrow B)$

4.4 How can the tree method be used to test sentences for logical equivalence? Describe a method and use it on the pairs in Exercise 3.13.
4.5 A set of sentences is *consistent* if and only if there is a case in which they are all true. Such a case is called a *model* for the set of sentences. Thus, a set of sentences is *inconsistent* if it has no model: if there is no case in which all sentences of the set are true.

    a   Describe how the tree method can be used to test sets of sentences
        for consistency.
Apply your method to determine which of the following sets are consistent.

    b $A,$ $-A$
    c $A \rightarrow B,$ $-A \rightarrow B$
    d $B \rightarrow A,$ $B \rightarrow -A$
    e   *Both Crumm and Moriarty are guilty if either is.*
        If neither is guilty, then Holmes has not bungled.
        Unless Holmes has bungled, exactly one of them is guilty.

4.6 The method of Exercise 4.3 provides the following alternative way of testing inferences for validity. To see whether some premises imply a conclusion, form a conditional of which the antecedent is the conjunction of the premises (or *the* premise, if there is only one) and of which the consequent is the given conclusion. Test this conditional to see whether it is a tautology; if so, the inference is valid, and if not, the inference is invalid. Try this method on one or two inferences, and then explain why it works.

5

ADEQUACY OF THE METHOD. TREES AND PROOFS

Chapter 4 was at once a description and a sketchy justification of a certain method for testing validity of inferences. We now fill in the details of the justification, showing that the tree method really does the job for which it was designed. We show that

> An inference is valid (invalid) if the corresponding tree does (does not) eventually close.

As described by the graph of Figure 4.2, the tree method is all but mechanical. What latitude there is consists in choosing an order of application for the rules of inference in the lower right-hand corner of the graph, but this latitude is inessential and could easily be eliminated by arbitrarily stipulating an order of application for the rules. The fact that order is inessential will be demonstrated when we prove the adequacy of the tree method, for in that proof we make no special assumption about the order in which the rules of inference are applied.

PRELIMINARIES

It is obvious, but worth mentioning, that the process of constructing a tree as in Chapter 4 must eventually end. (The corresponding process for the more elaborate trees that will be encountered in later chapters can go on forever.) The process of Chapter 4 must terminate after some finite number of steps simply because (1) the tree begins with a finite number of sentences, each of which has finite length, and (2) the tree grows by a process of choosing an unchecked sentence in an open path, checking it, and adding at the bottom some finite number of sentences, each of which is shorter than the sentence checked. Eventually the point must be reached at which all unchecked sentences in open paths have length 1 or 2, and the process ends.

Preliminary to the proof of adequacy, we recall some features of the tree method and illustrate them with the aid of the tree shown in Figure 5.1 for the following inference:

$$A \to (-B \lor C)$$
$$\underline{B \to (A \,\&\, -C)}$$
$$C \to B$$

Each open path through a finished tree describes a valuation which is in fact a counterexample to the inference being tested: an assignment of truth-values to sentence letters which makes all initial sentences (1, 2, and 3 in Figure 5.1) assume the value t. The fact that the valuation is indeed a counterexample has become familiar through many examples and will be proved below. Here, the key concept is

the valuation described by an open path through a finished tree,

which we define as

the assignment of truth-values to sentence letters in which letters that appear as full lines of the path have the value t and letters whose denials appear as full lines of the path have the value f.

Path 1 through Figure 5.1 describes the valuation fft of the letters ABC, while paths 2 and 3 both describe a single valuation: ft for the letters BC.

A counterexample need not assign truth-values to all the sentence

Figure 5.1

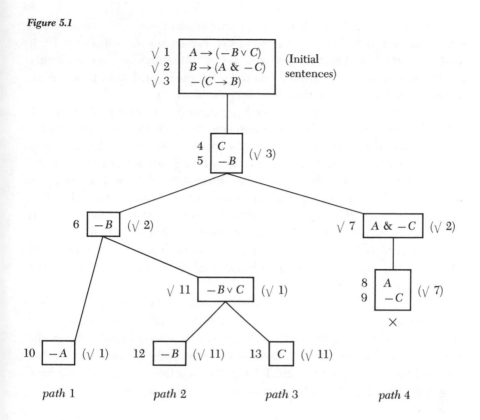

letters that appear in an inference, and distinct paths may describe one and the same counterexample. These facts are illustrated by paths 2 and 3 of Figure 5.1. Notice, too, that the counterexample described by path 1 is an *extension* of the one described by paths 2 and 3:

A	B	C	
·	f	t	(paths 2 and 3)
f	f	t	(path 1)

Here, the key concept can be defined as follows:

> An *extension* of a counterexample is obtained by assigning truth-values to additional sentence letters whose truth-values are not specified by the given counterexample.

Not only is the valuation *fft* of *ABC* an extension of the counterexample in which the letters *BC* receive the values *ft*, but so are the valuations *tft* of *ABC* and *tftff* of *ABCDE*. These last two valuations are not explicitly described by any path through the tree of Figure 5.1, but both are compatible with the valuation described by paths 2 and 3.

Any valuation obtained by extending a counterexample to an inference is itself a counterexample to that inference. Thus, the assignment *ft* to *BC* is a counterexample to the inference of Figure 5.1: when "*B*" has the value *f* and "*C*" has the value *t*, the rules of valuation given in Chapter 1 (or the truth tables that define the connectives) force all three initial sentences to assume the value *t*. For the initial sentences to assume the value *t*, it is sufficient that "*B*" and "*C*" assume the values *ft*, regardless of what (if any) values are assigned to other sentence letters. Then since the valuation *ft* of *BC* is a counterexample, so are the valuations *tft* and *fft* of *ABC* and the valuation *tftff* of *ABCDE* and all other extensions of the given counterexample.

We have seen that the tree method will always supply a "yes" or "no" answer to the question "Is this inference valid?" To say that the method is adequate is to say that the answer is always correct. Since the answer is "no" if and only if there is an open path through the finished tree and since an inference is invalid if and only if there is a counterexample to it, our claim that the method is adequate amounts to this:

5.1   *There is an open path through a finished tree if and only if some valuation of sentence letters forces all initial sentences to assume the value t.*

We shall prove the "only if" clause by proving something a bit stronger:

5.2   *Each open path in a finished tree describes a valuation in which all full sentences in the path are true.*

Since the initial sentences are full sentences in every path, **5.2** implies the "only if" clause of **5.1**. (Remember that "only if" is English for "→.") We shall then prove the "if" clause of **5.1** by proving something a bit stronger than *it*:

5.3   *Given a valuation that makes all initial sentences true, we can find a path through the finished tree in which every full sentence is true in the given valuation.*

The path mentioned in **5.3** must be open, for if some full sentence in it were the denial of another, there could be no valuation that makes all full sentences in the path true.

The proof of adequacy will turn on the fact that each rule of inference is correct in two senses: upward and downward. To see what is meant, recall that each rule of inference has a single *premise* and one or more *lists of conclusions*. Thus, each of the following three rules has a single premise: the checked sentence.

The rule at the left has three lists of conclusions, each of which is only one sentence long. The rule in the middle has only one list of conclusions, which is three sentences long. And the rule at the right has two lists of conclusions, each of which is two sentences long.

We shall say that a list of sentences is true if all sentences in the list are true and that a list is false if even one sentence in it is false.

Now to say that a rule of inference is correct in the *downward* sense is to say that if the premise is true in a valuation, so is at least one list of conclusions.

A rule of inference is downward correct if and only if every valuation that makes the premise true makes at least one list of conclusions true.

And to say that a rule of inference is correct in the *upward* sense is to say that the premise is true in every valuation that makes even one list of conclusions true.

A rule of inference is upward correct if and only if every valuation that makes at least one list of conclusions true makes the premise true.

To show that a particular rule of inference is correct in both senses, we must compare it with the corresponding rule of valuation: with the corresponding truth table. Thus, the rule given above for the biconditional is downward correct because both cases (1 and 4) in which the premise is

true are cases in which one or the other (left or right) list of conclusions
is true:

	$\bigcirc$	$\triangle$	$-\bigcirc$	$-\triangle$	$\bigcirc \leftrightarrow \triangle$
Case 1	t	t	f	f	t
Case 2	f	t	t	f	f
Case 3	t	f	f	t	f
Case 4	f	f	t	t	t

And the rule is upward correct because the cases (1 and 4, again) in which
at least one list of conclusions is true are cases in which the premise is also
true. Entirely similar reasoning is involved in showing the correctness of
each of the other rules of inference: a rule is correct in both senses if and
only if the t cases for the premise coincide with the cases in which at least
one list of conclusions is true.

> A rule of inference is *both* upward and downward correct if and only
> if the valuations that make the premise true are precisely the valuations
> that make at least one list of conclusions true.

> We can now proceed to the proof of statement **5.1** via **5.2** and **5.3**.

PROOF OF 5.2

It is the upward correctness of our rules that ensures the truth of
claim **5.2** that

> the valuation described by an open path in a finished tree forces the
> value t on every sentence that appears as a full line in that path.

The valuation described by an open path through a finished tree, say
path 2 in Figure 5.1, is the one in which a sentence letter has the value t
or f depending on whether it or its denial makes an appearance as a full
line in that path. Then every full sentence of length 1 or 2 that appears in
the path is certainly true in this valuation. (Thus, sentences 4, 5, 6, and 12
are true in the valuation described by path 2 of Figure 5.1.) Since the path
is open and the tree is finished, any longer sentence that occurs as a full
line of the path must have been checked and must have a list of con-

clusions in the path, each of which is shorter than the checked premise. Among the checked sentences there must be one or more which have only sentence letters and denials of sentence letters as conclusions in the path. (In path 2 of Figure 5.1 these are the checked sentences 2, 3, and 11.) The upward correctness of our rules of inference assures us that each such checked sentence must be true in the valuation described by the path, for it has a list of conclusions in the path which is known to be true in that valuation. And we continue reasoning in this way until all checked sentences in the path are accounted for; among the sentences already known to be true in the valuation described by the path must be a list of conclusions of some sentence whose truth in the valuation has not yet been established. (See sentence 1 in path 2 of Figure 5.1.) But since the rules of inference are upward correct, the truth of that sentence in the valuation follows from the previously established truth of its conclusions. (The truth of sentence 11 ensures the truth of sentence 1 in the valuation described by path 2 of Figure 5.1.)

This argument can be converted into a rigorous proof of **5.2** by *mathematical induction,* according to which we prove that a statement is true of all natural numbers 0, 1, 2, . . . by proving (*basis*) that it is true of the number 0 and (*induction step*) that it is true of the successor of any natural number that it is true of. We shall prove **5.2** by *induction on the number of checked sentences* in the path that is under consideration. In other words, we prove that the following statement is true for all values 0, 1, 2, . . . of "*n*" by proving (*basis*) that it is true when we write "0" for "*n*" and (*induction step*) that if the statement is true as it stands, it remains true when we write "*n* + 1" for "*n*" in it.

5.4   *The valuation described by an open path* with *n* checks *in a finished tree forces the value t on every sentence that appears as a full line in that path.*

Basis. If an open path in a finished tree contains no checked sentences at all, then that path must be the whole tree, all sentences in it must be initial, and they must be either sentence letters or denials of sentence letters. In this case, **5.4** is true by definition of "the valuation described by an open path."

Induction Step. Consider a finished tree in which some open path has *n* + 1 checked sentences where *n* is a natural number. We shall describe another finished tree in which a certain open path has n checked sentences. According to **5.4** this latter path describes a valuation in which all full sentences in the path have the value t. We shall then prove that the very same valuation is described by the original path, with $n + 1$ checked sentences, and that all sentences in the original path are true in that valuation. We shall thus have proved that if **5.4** is true, it remains true when "n" is replaced by "$n + 1$" in it; we shall have proved the induction step.

To begin, focus attention on some one open path through the original tree. By hypothesis, this path contains at least one checked sentence ($n + 1$ checked sentences where n is at least 0). Consider the first sentence that was checked in the construction of this path. It must be an initial sentence and must, in fact, be the first initial sentence that was checked in the construction of the tree.

Now consider the *diminished path,* obtained from the chosen path by deleting the first sentence that was checked in the construction of the tree. There are exactly n checked sentences in the diminished path. Notice that among the sentences in the diminished path are all the members of one of the lists of conclusions that were added to the tree upon checking the sentence we have deleted.

For concreteness, consider two examples: path 2 through the tree of Figure 5.1, and the rightmost path through the tree of Figure 5.2. In the first example, the deleted sentence is the initial sentence 3; in the second, the deleted sentence is the initial sentence 1.

Observe that the diminished path must be a path through a certain finished tree, which we shall call the *diminished tree.* In Figure 5.1, the diminished tree is obtained by simply deleting sentence 3, the first sentence to be checked, from the original tree. In Figure 5.2, the diminished tree is obtained by deleting sentence 1, the first to be checked, and also sentences 3, 5, and 6. In general, when the first sentence to be checked is one to which a nonbranching rule of inference applies, the diminished tree is obtained by simply deleting the first sentence to be checked. But when the

Figure 5.2

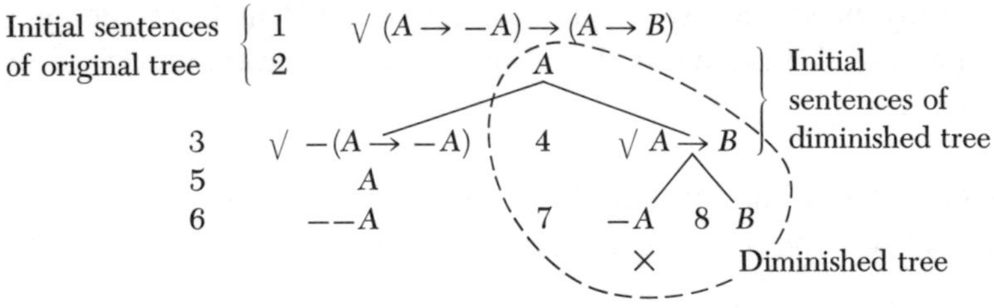

first sentence to be checked is one to which a branching rule of inference applies (one with two or more lists of conclusions), the diminished tree is obtained by deleting not only the first sentence to be checked but also the extraneous lists of conclusions which were added to the tree upon checking that sentence but which do not lie on the chosen path and by deleting as well the remainders of all paths that descend from the deleted lists of conclusions.

The initial sentences for the diminished tree include all the initial sentences for the original tree except for the first sentence to be checked, as well as all sentences in the list of conclusions that were added to the chosen path when the first sentence was checked. It should be clear that the diminished tree is a genuine finished tree, obtainable by our rules of inference from the initial sentences of the diminished tree.

Now we can complete the induction step. Given any open path through a finished tree where the given path has $n + 1$ checks, the diminished path has n checks and is an open path in a finished tree, namely, the diminished tree. Then according to statement **5.4**, the diminished path describes a valuation in which all full sentences in that path assume the value t. Among the sentences in the diminished path are all members of one of the lists of conclusions which had the deleted sentence as their premise. Then *by upward correctness of the rules of inference,* the deleted sentence must be true in the valuation described by the diminished path. Thus every full sentence in the original path must be true in that valuation, for we got the diminished path from the original path by simply deleting a sentence known to be true in the valuation that the diminished path describes. And this is the same valuation as the one described by the original path, which differs from the diminished path only in lacking a *checked* sentence; hence, a sentence which is not simply a sentence letter or the denial of a sentence letter. Then if **5.4** is true, so is the statement obtained by writing "$n + 1$" for "n" in **5.4**. The induction step has been established, and **5.2** is proved.

PROOF OF 5.3

It is the downward correctness of our rules that ensures the truth of claim **5.3** that

if a valuation makes all initial sentences true, it makes all the full sentences in some whole path true.

We prove **5.3** by mathematical induction on the number of checks in the finished tree. For this purpose we reformulate **5.3** as the claim that the following statement is true for every value 0, 1, 2, ... of "*n*."

5.5   *If a valuation makes all initial sentences true in a finished tree that has no more than n checks, it makes all the full sentences in some whole path true.*

Basis. If there are no checks in the finished tree, the initial sentences constitute the whole tree, and there is nothing to prove.

Induction Step. Assume that **5.5** is true, consider a finished tree with $n + 1$ checks, and imagine we are given a valuation that makes all initial sentences in this tree true. Among the initial sentences is the first sentence that was checked in constructing the tree. *By downward correctness of the rules of inference*, at least one of the lists of conclusions that was added to the tree upon checking this sentence is true in the given valuation. Choose one such list, and consider the corresponding diminished tree. The given valuation makes all initial sentences of the diminished tree true, and since the diminished tree contains at most n checks, **5.5** assures us that all full sentences in some path through it are true in the given valuation. By adding the deleted sentence to this path, we obtain a path through the original tree in which all full sentences are true in the given valuation. This completes the induction step and the proof of **5.5**.

DIRECT AND INDIRECT PROOFS

Having proved its adequacy, let us now compare the tree method with more familiar methods of proof.

A *direct proof* of a conclusion from one premise or more can be represented as a single list of sentences, the last of which is the conclusion, and each of which is either a premise or a consequence, by one or another *rule of proof*, of sentences higher in the list. Rules of proof differ from what we have been calling "rules of inference" in that each rule of proof has just one conclusion and may have more than one premise. Here are three examples, with their names:

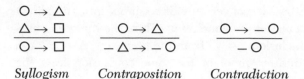

| Syllogism | Contraposition | Contradiction |

Each of these rules is *sound* in a sense related to our notion of downward correctness: if all premises are true, the conclusion must be true.

As an illustration of the notion of a direct proof, consider the following inference:

$$A \to B$$
$$\underline{A \to -B}$$
$$-A$$

This inference can be shown valid by the following five-line direct proof, in which the notation at the right of each line gives its provenance.

1	$A \to B$	[premise]
2	$A \to -B$	[premise]
3	$-B \to -A$	[from 1 by contraposition]
4	$A \to -A$	[from 2 and 3 by syllogism]
5	$-A$	[from 4 by contradiction]

But proofs need not be direct.

An *indirect proof* of a conclusion from one or more premises is a list of sentences, one of which is the denial of another, and each of which is either (1) a premise or (2) the denial of the conclusion or (3) a consequence, by one or another rule of proof, of sentences higher in the list.

The rationale of indirect proof is that where a sentence and its denial are both deducible from a set of assumptions, those assumptions cannot all be true. In an indirect proof, the assumptions are the premises and the denial of the conclusion of an inference, so that the deduction of contradictory consequences from the assumptions shows that the premises cannot all be true while the conclusion is false.

It is simple (and pointless) to convert any direct proof into an indirect proof by appending the denial of the conclusion. Thus, the foregoing five-line direct proof of the conclusion "$-A$" from the premises "$A \rightarrow B$" and "$A \rightarrow -B$" becomes an indirect proof of the same conclusion from the same premises when we append a sixth line:

6        $--A$ [denial of the conclusion]

But often, indirect proofs are simpler than direct proofs and easier to discover. Thus, suppose we have the following two rules of inference:

$$\frac{--\bigcirc}{\bigcirc} \qquad \frac{\begin{array}{c}\bigcirc \\ \bigcirc \rightarrow \triangle\end{array}}{\triangle}$$

Double negation   *Detachment*

These are simpler and less numerous than the three rules used in the foregoing proofs, and they readily suggest a simpler indirect proof of "$-A$" from the same premises as before:

1        $A \rightarrow B$ [premise]
2        $A \rightarrow -B$ [premise]
3        $--A$ [denial of the conclusion]
4   A [from 3 by double negation]
5   B [from 4 and 1 by detachment]
6        $-B$ [from 4 and 2 by detachment]

Our method of truth trees is akin to the method of indirect proof; the various paths down through a tree represent the various ways in which the premises and denial of the conclusion might all be true, and closed paths represent ways that are impossible. Then if all paths are closed, it is impossible for the conclusion to be false while all premises are true, and the inference is seen to be valid. The most striking difference between trees and indirect proofs is that a proof is a single list of sentences, but a tree that has more than one path is, in effect, a bundle of lists.

COUPLED TREES

The tree method can be modified in order to yield analogues of direct proofs: arrays of sentences that bear much the same relation to direct proofs that trees bear to indirect proofs. The idea can be illustrated in the case of the inference we have been considering:

$$A \to B$$
$$\underline{A \to -B}$$
$$-A$$

In a direct proof, we start with the premises and try to get to the conclusion via sound rules of inference. In the corresponding modification of the tree method, we start a tree with the premises, omitting the conclusion:

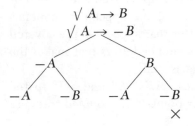

The three open paths represent all possible ways in which the premises can both be true, and each path contains the conclusion "$-A$." Then every possible way in which the premises can both be true is a way in which the conclusion would be true. We indicate the fact that all open paths lead to "$-A$" as follows:

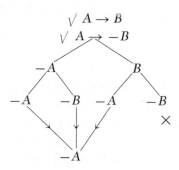

   In general, our modified tree method involves working from the
premises down and from the conclusion up, as illustrated below for the
inference from "$A \to B$" to "$-B \to -A$":

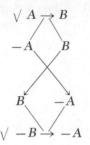

Here we have two trees: a normal tree going down from the premises and
an upside-down tree going up from the conclusion. The arrows linking the
two trees indicate that each open path in the upper tree *covers* one or
another path in the lower tree in the sense that the upper path contains
every sentence letter or denied sentence letter that appears in the covered
lower path. Therefore, every valuation of sentence letters that makes the
premises true must make the conclusion true as well.

   The valid inference from the premises "A," "B," and "C" to the
conclusion "$A \leftrightarrow B$" illustrates two further points. The coupled trees are
as follows:

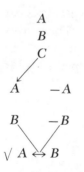

Here we see that for an inference to be valid, it is enough that each open
path in the upper tree cover some path in the lower tree; it is *not* necessary, for validity, that each open path in the lower tree be covered. Notice,
too, that the single path in the upper tree covers the left-hand path in the
lower tree even though there is a letter in the upper path that does not

appear in the covered lower path; all we require for covering is that the covering path contain all the sentence letters and denials of sentence letters that appear in the covered path.

A final point is illustrated by the valid inference:

$$\frac{A}{B \vee (A \mathbin{\&} -B)}$$

Here the single open path in the upper tree fails to cover either path in the lower tree:

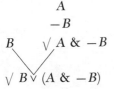

To remedy this defect we observe that "A" can come true in two ways: with or without the truth of "B." Then we add a fork

under "A" in the upper tree to obtained coupled trees in which each open path in the upper tree covers a path in the lower:

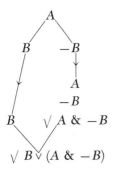

The device of introducing additional forks may even have to be applied more than once in order to get every open path in the upper tree to cover a path in the lower. Thus, since "$B \lor C \lor (-B \& -C)$" is a tautology, the following inference is a valid one:

$$\frac{A}{B \lor C \lor (-B \& -C)}$$

But to demonstrate the validity of this inference by the coupled tree method, we must introduce two additional forks, as indicated by the three successive coupled trees below:

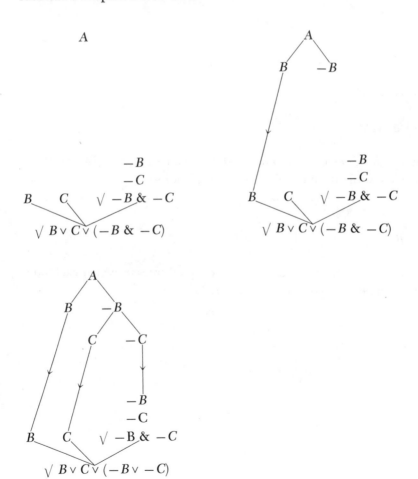

Summary. To test an inference for validity by the *coupled tree* method, construct two trees: one, down from the premises, and the other, up from the conclusion (*not* the denial of the conclusion). The inference is valid if each open path in the upper tree *covers* some path in the lower tree in the sense that *every sentence letter and denial of a sentence letter that appears in the covered path appears also in the covering path.* If some open path in the upper tree covers no path in the lower, it may be possible to remedy the defect by adding a fork at the bottom of the upper path in question, labeled with some sentence letter and its denial, and this device may be repeated if necessary, using another sentence letter. But if the introduction of additional forks (perhaps for *every* sentence letter that appears in the conclusion) fails to make each open path in the upper tree cover a path in the lower, the inference is invalid.

EXAMPLES

a $$\dfrac{A}{A \vee (-B \mathbin{\&} A)}$$ b $$\dfrac{A \vee B}{A \vee (-A \mathbin{\&} B)}$$ c $$\dfrac{A \to B}{B}$$

SOLUTIONS

a and b are valid; c is invalid.

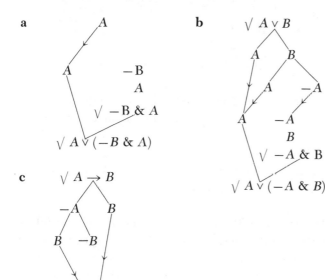

In **b** it was necessary to introduce an additional fork in the third line of the upper tree, in order to get an upper tree in which each open path covers a path in the lower tree. In **c** an extra fork was introduced in line 3 of the upper tree, but this left us with an open path (the middle one) in the upper tree that covered no path in the lower tree, and indeed, the inference is invalid.

EXERCISES

5.1 We have proved that the tree method is adequate as a test of validity of inferences. Make the additional remarks that are necessary in order to prove that the method is also adequate as a test of (1) logical truth of sentences and (2) consistency of sets of sentences.

5.2 Explain why the coupled tree method is adequate as a test of validity of inferences.

5.3 Test the following inferences for validity by the coupled tree method:

a $\dfrac{A \to (B \to C)}{B \to (A \to C)}$ b $\dfrac{A \to B}{A \to (A \,\&\, B)}$ c $\dfrac{A}{A \to B}$

d $\dfrac{B}{A \to B}$ e $\dfrac{\begin{array}{c} B \to A \\ -B \to A \end{array}}{(A \to A) \to A}$

5.4 How would you use the coupled tree method to test logical truth of individual sentences? Explain your method and test it on the following sentences:

a $A \to A$ b $B \vee C \vee (-B \,\&\, -C)$ c $A \to (B \to A)$
d $A \vee A$ e $[A \to (B \to C)] \to [(A \to B) \to (A \to C)]$

5.5 When the coupled tree test shows an inference to be invalid, a counterexample can be read off the finished coupled trees. Explain how.

5.6 A single rule of proof—the rule of detachment—suffices for direct proofs in which no connectives other than the dash and the arrow appear if we make use of *axioms* as follows. An axiom is any sentence of form **a** or **b** or **c**:

a $\quad \bigcirc \to (\triangle \to \bigcirc)$
b $\quad (\bigcirc \to (\triangle \to \square)) \to ((\bigcirc \to \triangle) \to (\bigcirc \to \square))$
c $\quad (-\triangle \to -\bigcirc) \to (\bigcirc \to \triangle)$

A proof of a conclusion from 0 or more premises is a list of sentences, the last of which is the conclusion, and each of which is either a premise or an axiom or a consequence by the rule of detachment of two sentences higher in the list.

A *theorem* is a sentence that can be proved without premises. Example: The following is a proof of the sentence "$A \to A$" using no premises:

1 $\quad (A \to ((A \to A) \to A)) \to ((A \to (A \to A)) \to (A \to A)) \qquad$ b
2 $\quad A \to ((A \to A) \to A) \qquad$ a
3 $\quad (A \to (A \to A)) \to (A \to A) \qquad$ 1, 2
4 $\quad A \to (A \to A) \qquad$ a
5 $\quad A \to A \qquad$ 3, 4

The notations at the right give the provenance of each line. Thus, line 3 follows from lines 1 and 2 by detachment, and line 4 is an axiom of form **a**. Now find proofs for the following:

a $\quad \dfrac{B}{A \to B} \qquad$ b $\quad \dfrac{B}{\dfrac{-A \to -B}{A}} \qquad$ c $\quad \dfrac{--A}{-A \to ---A}$

d $\quad \dfrac{--A}{A} \qquad$ e $\quad \dfrac{A}{--A} \qquad$ f $\quad \dfrac{A \to B}{-B \to -A}$

5.7 We know what it is for a set of sentences (the premises) to imply an individual sentence (the conclusion). It is natural to extend this terminology as follows:

One set of sentences implies another *set of sentences* if and only if each individual sentence in the second set is implied by the first set.

Prove that implication is *transitive* in the sense that

if one set of sentences implies another set which in turn implies a third set, then the first implies the third.

5.8   Prove that implication has the *compactness* property:

If a conclusion is implied by an infinite set of premises, it is implied by some finite subset of those premises.

5.9   Prove the *deduction theorem:*

A set of premises implies the conditional $(O \rightarrow \triangle)$ if and only if the set consisting of those premises together with the antecedent O implies the consequent $\triangle$.

PART TWO
QUANTIFICATION

6

INFERENCE RULES FOR QUANTIFIERS

In Part One we analyzed sentences into atoms which were themselves sentences. Example:

> *If Watson can trap Moriarty, Holmes can.*
> *Holmes cannot.*
> _____
> *Watson cannot.*

Here, premises and conclusion were viewed as molecules constructed out of atomic sentences by truth-functional connectives. The logical forms of the premises and conclusion were displayed by using sentence letters to represent the atoms of the analysis and by using parentheses, dashes, and arrows to show how the atoms are connected to form molecules:

$$W \rightarrow H$$
$$-H$$
$$\overline{-W}$$

Formal validity of an inference was validity in virtue of the molecular forms of its premises and conclusion; there was no need to investigate the structures of the atomic sentences. To see that the foregoing inference is valid, it was enough to see that the second premise is the denial of the consequent of the first and that the conclusion is the denial of the antecedent of the first premise.

But much of our reasoning defies analysis in such terms.

AN EXAMPLE

> Holmes, if anyone, can trap Moriarty.
> Holmes cannot.
> _____
> No one can.

To show that this inference is valid, we carry the analysis on below the atomic level; we analyze sentences into parts which are not themselves sentences or truth-functional connectives.

To begin, we restate the premises and the conclusion so as to make their logical structures evident:

> For all x, if x can trap Moriarty then Holmes can trap Moriarty.
> It is not the case that Holmes can trap Moriarty.
> _____
> It is not the case that there is an x such that x can trap Moriarty.

We already have symbols for the phrases "if . . . then" and "it is not the case that" which appear above. Then in a mixture of English and the language of logic, the argument is as follows:

> For all x (x can trap Moriarty → Holmes can trap Moriarty)
> — Holmes can trap Moriarty
> _____
> — There is an x such that x can trap Moriarty

Now we introduce the symbol

$$(x)$$

for the phrase "for all x"; we introduce the symbol

$$(\exists x)$$

for the phrase "there is an x such that"; we introduce symbols

a, b

as names for Holmes and Moriarty; and we introduce the symbol

T

for the relational phrase "can trap" so that "xTy" means that x can trap y. The inference can now be written in the language of logic:

$$(x)(xTb \rightarrow aTb)$$
$$-aTb$$
$$\overline{}$$
$$-(\exists x)xTb$$

Showing that this inference is valid amounts to showing that the premises and the denial of the conclusion cannot all be true, regardless of how the names "a" and "b" are understood, regardless of how the relational symbol "T" is understood, and regardless of what things are allowed as values of the variable "x" (provided that a and b themselves are allowable values of x). Now let us see how the method of truth trees can be extended so as to show the validity of this inference.

We begin by listing the premises and the denial of the conclusion, suppressing double dashes:

STAGE 1

1	$(x)(xTb \rightarrow aTb)$
2	$-aTb$
3	$(\exists x)xTb$

None of the rules of inference of Part One are directly applicable. Still, there is an obvious move we might make to augment the methods of Part One: Since sentence 1 says that something is true of *all* x, that thing must be true in particular of the two x's for which we have names:

STAGE 2

| 4 | $aTb \rightarrow aTb$ |
| 5 | $bTb \rightarrow aTb$ |

We now have a five-sentence tree in which the new sentences were obtained by dropping the "(x)" from sentence 1 and then replacing "x" by "a" to get sentence 4 and by "b" to get sentence 5.

The rules of inference of Part One can be applied to sentences 4 and 5 to extend the tree as follows:

STAGE 3

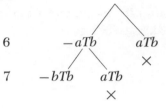

6        $-aTb$ aTb
7        $-bTb$ aTb

There is still one open path—but there is still a sentence, 3, that we have not used. This sentence says that *something* bears the relation T to b. But in the sole open path, we have sentences which deny that a bears T to b and that b bears T to itself. Then if there is something that bears T to b, it must be a third thing, say c:

STAGE 4
8   cTb

Now we have a new name, "c," and therefore sentence 1 has some more work to do. Sentence 1 says that "$xTb \rightarrow aTb$" is true of *every* x. Then it is true of every x for which we have a name, c as well as a and b:

STAGE 5
9        $cTb \rightarrow aTb$

When the rules of inference of Part One are applied to sentence 9, the tree closes:

STAGE 6

10        $-cTb$ aTb
               ×   ×

Then the inference is valid. Overall, the tree is as shown in Table 6.1. Note that checking a sentence is equivalent to erasing it: once a sentence has been checked, it can be ignored. Do you see why sentences beginning with "$(\exists x)$" are checked but sentences beginning with "(x)" are not? (Reread the explanation preceding stage 5 if you do not see.)

$$
\begin{array}{cl}
1 & (x)(xTb \rightarrow aTb) \\
2 & -aTb \\
3 & \surd\ (\exists x)xTb \\
4 & \surd\ aTb \rightarrow aTb \\
5 & \surd\ bTb \rightarrow aTb \\
\end{array}
$$

```
 6                      -aTb      aTb
                        /  \       ✕
 7        -bTb      aTb
 8        cTb        ✕
 9     √ cTb → aTb
          /  \
10   -cTb      aTb
      ✕         ✕
```

Table   6.1

EXAMPLES

For further exercise, try the method on the following two inferences:

If Watson can trap Moriarty, anyone can.
Holmes cannot.

Watson cannot.

Everyone is mortal.

No one is immortal.

Using "a," "b," and "c" as names of Holmes, Moriarty, and Watson and interpreting "Mx" as *x is mortal*, we can symbolize the two arguments as follows:

$$cTb \rightarrow (x)xTb \qquad \underline{(x)Mx}$$
$$\underline{-aTb} \qquad\qquad -(\exists x)-Mx$$
$$-cTb$$

SOLUTIONS

The trees for the two arguments are these:

1	$\sqrt{\ } cTb \rightarrow (x)xTb$		1	$(x)Mx$
2	$-aTb$		2	$\sqrt{\ } (\exists x)-Mx$
3	cTb		3	$-Ma$
			4	Ma
4	$-cTb \qquad (x)xTb$			$\times$
	$\times$			
5	aTb			
	$\times$			

Since the trees are closed, the arguments are valid. Before going further, you should try to explain why each sentence is in each of these trees, and then read the following two paragraphs to see whether your explanations are correct.

In the tree at the left, lines 1 and 2 are the premises and line 3 is the denial of the conclusion: "$--cTb$" without the superfluous double dash. Line 4 comes from line 1 by the methods of Part One, by applying the rule for $\bigcirc \rightarrow \triangle$ with "cTb" in the role of the circle and "$(x)xTb$" in the role of the triangle. The left-hand formula in line 4 is the denial of line 3, so that the left-hand path is closed. The right-hand formula in line 4 asserts that "xTb" is true for every x. Accordingly, we make the assertion for the three x's that we have names for: We assert it for "a" in line 5 and would then go on to assert it for "b" and for "c" (getting "bTb" as a sixth line and "cTb" as a seventh) if it were not for the fact that the right-hand path is now closed: line 2 is the denial of line 5.

In the tree at the right, line 1 is the premise and line 2 is the denial of the conclusion: "$--(\exists x)-Mx$" without the superfluous double dash. Line 2 says that there is an x for which "$-Mx$" is true. Accordingly, we introduce "a" as a name of that object and say, in line 3, that it is an x for which "$-Mx$" is true. We then check line 2 since no further use can be made of it. Line 1 says that "Mx" is true for all x. Therefore, in line 4 we say that "Mx" is true of the x that we have a name for. Since line 3 is the denial of line 4, the tree is closed.

Using these examples as patterns, we have the means to test the validity of the following inferences. Try them, and then check your results against the solutions given below:

EXAMPLES

a   *Holmes, if anyone, can trap Moriarty.*
        Moriarty can trap himself.
        Holmes can trap Moriarty.

(Hint about translation: The second premise means that Moriarty can trap Moriarty.)

b   *Alma does not love Bert.* $-aLb$
        Not everyone loves Bert. $-(x)xLb$

c   *Everyone loves Alma.*
        Alma loves herself.

d   *Alma loves everyone who loves her.*
        Alma does not love Bert.
        Bert does not love Alma.

(Hint: The first premise means that for all x, if x loves Alma then Alma loves x.)

e $(x)(Mx \rightarrow H)$
        $((\exists x)Mx \rightarrow H)$

SOLUTIONS

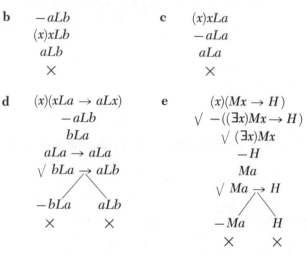

a 1 $(x)(xTb \rightarrow aTb)$ Line 4 says about a what line 1 says
  2   bTb about everything, and line 5 says about
  3          $-aTb$ b what line 1 says about everything.
  4     $aTb \rightarrow aTb$ The decision to check line 5 before
  5   $\surd\ bTb \nrightarrow aTb$ line 4 saved us the trouble of checking
                                    line 4 at all.

  6   $-bTb$ aTb
        $\times$ $\times$

b $-aLb$ c $(x)xLa$
     $(x)xLb$ $-aLa$
     aLb aLa
     $\times$ $\times$

d $(x)(xLa \rightarrow aLx)$ e $(x)(Mx \rightarrow H)$
      $-aLb$ $\surd\ -((\exists x)Mx \rightarrow H)$
       bLa $\surd\ (\exists x)Mx$
    $aLa \rightarrow aLa$ $-H$
    $\surd\ bLa \nrightarrow aLb$ Ma
                                 $\surd\ Ma \nrightarrow H$
   $-bLa$ aLb
     $\times$ $\times$ $-Ma$ H
                                   $\times$ $\times$

Notice that the conclusion of **e** is a conditional with antecedent "$(\exists x)Mx$"
and consequent "H," which can be written without ambiguity as "$(\exists x)Mx \rightarrow$
H." But the outer parentheses must be restored when we deny the conclusion
in the second line of the tree: the denial is "$-((\exists x)Mx \rightarrow H)$," not
"$-(\exists x)Mx \rightarrow H$." The latter sentence is not the denial of a conditional but
is itself a conditional of which the antecedent happens to be the denial of
the sentence "$(\exists x)Mx$."

Moral. The symbols "(x)" and "$(\exists x)$" behave like the sign "$-$" of
denial in that each of these three signs is taken to govern as little of the
sentence as possible. In particular, these signs govern only the antecedents
of the following conditionals:

$(x)Mx \rightarrow H,$ $(\exists x)Mx \rightarrow H,$ $-W \rightarrow H$

To indicate that the entire conditional is to be governed, we must introduce parentheses which make the other interpretation impossible:

$$(x)(Mx \rightarrow H), \qquad (\exists x)(Mx \rightarrow H), \qquad -(W \rightarrow H)$$

Handle conjunctions, disjunctions, and biconditionals similarly. The sentences

$$(x)Mx \vee H, \qquad (\exists x)Mx \vee H, \qquad -W \vee H$$

are short for

$$((x)Mx \vee H), \qquad ((\exists x)Mx \vee H), \qquad (-W \vee H),$$

not for

$$(x)(Mx \vee H), \qquad (\exists x)(Mx \vee H), \qquad -(W \vee H).$$

THE COMPLETE METHOD

The symbols "(x)" and "$(\exists x)$" are called *quantifiers:* "(x)" is a *universal* quantifier and "$(\exists x)$" is an *existential* quantifier. We have seen how to deal with universally quantified sentences, of form

$$(x) \ldots x \ldots,$$

when they appear in trees, and with existentially quantified sentences, of form

$$(\exists x) \ldots x \ldots.$$

But what about denials of such sentences?

Such denials are easily handled, simply by rewriting

"$-(x)$" as "$(\exists x)-$"

and rewriting

"$-(\exists x)$" as "$(x)-.$"

In other words:

> Move the dash to the other side of the quantifier, and change universal "(x)" to existential "$(\exists x)$" and vice versa.

It is easy to see why this procedure is justified: "$-(x)Px$" and "$(\exists x)-Px$" have the same meaning because to deny that everything has the property P is to assert that something lacks P, and "$-(\exists x)Px$" and "$(x)-Px$" have the same meaning because to deny that there is something that has P is to assert that everything lacks P. It follows that

"$-(x)-$" has the same meaning as "$(\exists x)$"

and

"$-(\exists x)-$" has the same meaning as "(x)."

Our rules of inference are now complete; they allow us to test the formal validity of any inference whose premises and conclusion are expressed in our notation. The old and new rules are collected in Table 6.2. Warning: These rules are to be applied only to complete sentences which are not occurring as parts of longer sentences. Thus, the rule for $(\exists x)$ may be applied to the sentence "$(\exists x)(Mx \rightarrow H)$" but *not* to either of the sentences "$(\exists x)Mx \rightarrow H$" or "$H \rightarrow (\exists x)Mx$." To these last two sentences, the rule for $\bigcirc \rightarrow \triangle$ applies.

In the rules for the quantifiers, "$(x) \ldots x \ldots$" and "$(\exists x) \ldots x \ldots$" represent sentences which, written with all their parentheses, begin with the sequence "(x)" of three signs or with the sequence "$(\exists x)$" of four signs. Thus, "$(x)(Mx \rightarrow H)$" is of form $(x) \ldots x \ldots$, but "$(x)Mx \rightarrow H$" is not; written with all its parentheses, this latter sentence is seen to be a conditional, "$((x)Mx \rightarrow H)$," which does not *begin* with the sequence "(x)" of three signs.

The sentences

$$(x)(xLa \rightarrow aLx), \qquad (\exists x)(xTb \ \& \ -aTb)$$

are of forms $(x) \ldots x \ldots$ and $(\exists x) \ldots x \ldots$ respectively. If the name n is "b," then the corresponding sentences of form $\ldots n \ldots$ are

$$bLa \rightarrow aLb, \qquad\qquad bTb \ \& \ -aTb.$$

Denial	Erase "− −" wherever it appears in unchecked sentences in open paths. Check sentences of forms "−(x)...x..." and "−(∃x)...x..." in open paths and rewrite them as "(∃x) − ...x..." and "(x) − ...x..." at the bottoms of those paths.
Connectives	$\sqrt{}\ \bigcirc \to \triangle$ $\sqrt{}\ \bigcirc \vee \triangle$ $\sqrt{}\ \bigcirc\ \&\ \triangle$ $\sqrt{}\ \bigcirc \leftrightarrow \triangle$ $-\bigcirc\quad\triangle$ $\bigcirc\quad\triangle$ $\bigcirc$ ... $\triangle$ $\bigcirc\quad -\bigcirc$ ... $\triangle\quad -\triangle$ $\sqrt{}\ -(\bigcirc \to \triangle)$ $\sqrt{}\ -(\bigcirc \vee \triangle)$ $\sqrt{}\ -(\bigcirc\ \&\ \triangle)$ $\sqrt{}\ -(\bigcirc \leftrightarrow \triangle)$ $\bigcirc$ $-\bigcirc$ $-\bigcirc\quad -\triangle$ $-\bigcirc\quad\bigcirc$ $-\triangle$ $-\triangle$ ... $\triangle\quad -\triangle$
Universal Quantifier	Given an open path in which a sentence of form (x)...x... occurs: for *each* name n that appears anywhere in the path, write the sentence ...n... at the bottom of the path unless that sentence already occurs in the path. (If no name appears in the path, choose some name n and write ...n... at the bottom of the path.) When you are done, *do not* check the sentence (x)...x....
Existential Quantifier	Given an unchecked sentence of form (∃x)...x... that occurs in an open path: inspect the path to see whether it contains a sentence of form ...n... where n is some name or other. If not, choose a name n that is not used anywhere in the path, and write the sentence ...n... at the bottom of the path. When this has been done for every open path on which the given sentence of form (∃x)...x... occurs, check that sentence.

Table 6.2 Rules of Inference

In this chapter, the sentence ...n... is obtained from (x)...x... or (∃x)...x... by dropping the initial quantifier and rewriting all remaining x's as n's.

A flow graph for applying the rules of Table 6.2 is given in Figure 6.1. The order of procedure shown there is not the only possible one, but it is fairly efficient (usually) and does ensure that if the tree *can* close, it eventually *will*. The inference is invalid if we ever get to stage 7 *or if the procedure never terminates.* (For the inferences encountered in this chapter, the procedure always terminates.)

Figure 6.1

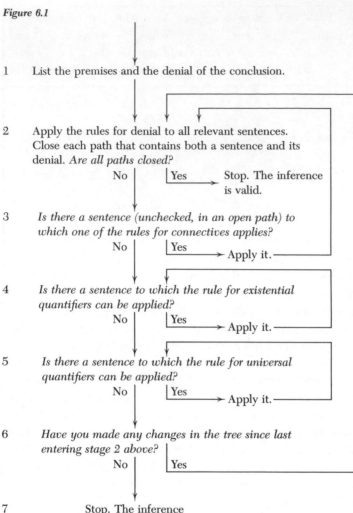

1   List the premises and the denial of the conclusion.

2   Apply the rules for denial to all relevant sentences.
     Close each path that contains both a sentence and its
     denial. *Are all paths closed?*
                    No   │Yes   Stop. The inference
                                              is valid.

3   *Is there a sentence (unchecked, in an open path) to
     which one of the rules for connectives applies?*
                    No   │Yes
                                        ⟶ Apply it.

4   *Is there a sentence to which the rule for existential
     quantifiers can be applied?*
                    No   │Yes
                                        ⟶ Apply it.

5   *Is there a sentence to which the rule for universal
     quantifiers can be applied?*
                    No   │Yes
                                        ⟶ Apply it.

6   *Have you made any changes in the tree since last
     entering stage 2 above?*
                    No   │Yes

7   Stop. The inference
               is invalid.

APPLYING THE RULES

To illustrate the use of the rule for −, we apply the tree method
to show that the sentence

$(\exists x)Px \vee (x) - Px$

is a logical truth, deducible from any premises we please or from no premises at all. Then the argument we wish to test is

$$\overline{(\exists x)Px \lor (x)-Px}$$

This argument has a conclusion but has no premises. The tree is this:

1	$\sqrt{\ } \ -[(\exists x)Px \lor (x)-Px]$	[denial of conclusion]
2	$\sqrt{\ } \ -(\exists x)Px$	[from 1 by rule
3	$-(x)-Px$	for $-(\bigcirc \lor \triangle)$]
4	$(x)-Px$	[from 2 by rule for $-$]
	$\times$	

This tree is closed because 3 is the denial of 4.

The simplest sort of use of the rule for (x) is illustrated by the argument

$$\frac{(x)Px}{Pa}$$

for which the tree is as follows:

1	$(x)Px$	[premise]
2	$-Pa$	[denial of conclusion]
3	Pa	[from 1 by rule for (x)]
	$\times$	

To see how the rule for (x) applies when no name appears in the path in question, consider the inference

$$\frac{(x)Px}{(\exists x)Px}$$

according to which *something* or other must have the property P if *everything* has it. Intuitively, this inference is valid because we always assume that *variables have values*, so that at least one thing (named "a" perhaps) counts as an allowable value of the variable "x." The tree begins as follows:

```
1        (x)Px          [premise]
2     √ −(∃x)Px         [denial of conclusion]
3        (x)−Px         [2 by −]
```

This one-path tree is still open; line 3 is *not* the denial of line 2. (To deny a sentence, put a dash *out front*.) Now since no name appears in this path, the rule for (x) as applied to line 1 directs us to choose a name, say "*a*," and write "*Pa*" at the bottom of the path:

```
4     Pa     [1 by (x)]
```

Now there *is* a name, "*a*," that appears in the path. Taking this into account, we apply the rule for (x) to line 3 and get a sentence that closes the tree:

```
5     −Pa     [3 by (x)]
         ×
```

Finally, to illustrate the use of the rule for $(∃x)$, consider the argument

$$\frac{(∃x)Mx → H}{(x)(Mx → H)}$$

which is the converse of the argument in example **e** on page 109. The tree is as follows:

```
1              (∃x)Mx → H           [premise]
2           √ −(x)(Mx → H)          [denial of conclusion]
3           √ (∃x)−(Mx → H)         [2 by −]
4             √ −(Ma → H)           [3 by (∃x)]
5                  Ma               [4 by
6                  −H                 −(○ → △)]
                  /  \
7     √ −(∃x)Mx     H       [1 by ○ → △]
                    ×
8        (x)−Mx             [7 by −]

9         −Ma               [8 by (x)]
            ×
```

LOGICAL STRUCTURE

In conclusion, let us return to the inference which we studied at length at the beginning of this chapter:

> *Holmes, if anyone, can trap Moriarty.*
> *Holmes cannot.*
> _____
> *No one can.*

We symbolized this as follows:

$(x)(xTb \rightarrow aTb)$
$-aTb$
_____
$-(\exists x)xTb$

But this symbolization displays more of the logical structure of the premises and conclusion than needs to be shown in order to establish the inference as valid. Thus, instead of using the relational symbol "T" for "can trap," we could have used a predicate symbol, say "M," for "can trap Moriarty," for in the three sentences with which we are concerned, "T" is followed by "b" (for Moriarty) wherever it occurs. Reading "Mx" as "x can trap Moriarty," the symbolization becomes

$(x)(Mx \rightarrow Ma)$
$-Ma$
_____
$-(\exists x)Mx$

This inference is logically valid, for the tree closes:

$(x)(Mx \rightarrow Ma)$
$\quad -Ma$
$\quad \sqrt{} \ (\exists x)Mx$
$\qquad Mb$
$\quad Ma \rightarrow Ma$
$\sqrt{} \ Mb \rightarrow Ma$

$-Mb \qquad Ma$
$\times \qquad\quad \times$

But even this symbolization shows more of the structure of the premises and conclusion than is needed to see that the inference is valid. Instead of writing "Holmes can trap Moriarty" as "aTb" or as "Ma," we can represent it still less revealingly by a single sentence letter "H." The inference then becomes

$$(x)(Mx \rightarrow H)$$
$$\underline{-H}$$
$$-(\exists x)Mx$$

In this form, too, the inference passes the tree test:

$(x)(Mx \rightarrow H)$
$\quad -H$
$\sqrt{} \ (\exists x)Mx$
$\quad Ma$
$\sqrt{} \ Ma \nrightarrow H$

$-Ma \qquad H$
$\times \qquad \times$

This form shows only as much of the logical structure of the premises and conclusion as is needed to demonstrate the validity of the inference.

Finally, observe that we could have begun on a very different tack, construing "Holmes, if anyone, can trap Moriarty" not as

For all x, if x can trap Moriarty then Holmes can trap Moriarty

but in the logically equivalent form:

If there is an x such that x can trap Moriarty, then Holmes can trap Moriarty.

Using "T" for "can trap" would have led to the symbolization

$$(\exists x)xTb \rightarrow aTb$$
$$\underline{-aTb}$$
$$-(\exists x)xTb$$

In this form, the inference can be seen to be valid by the methods of Part One:

$\sqrt{}\ (\exists x)xTb \rightarrow aTb$
$\quad -aTb$
$\quad (\exists x)xTb$

$-(\exists x)xTb \qquad aTb$
$\quad \times \qquad\quad \times$

Here we used only the rule for $\bigcirc \rightarrow \triangle$. We could just as well have rewritten the original inference in English as

> *If there is someone who can trap Moriarty then Holmes can trap Moriarty.*
> *It is not the case that Holmes can trap Moriarty.*
> ___
> *It is not the case that there is someone who can trap Moriarty.*

Then writing "S" for "There is someone who can trap Moriarty" and writing "H" for "Holmes can trap Moriarty," the inference goes over into the notation of Part One as follows:

$S \rightarrow H$
$-H$
___
$-S$

This is readily seen to be valid by the methods of Part One.

Then by judiciously rewriting the inference in English before symbolizing it, we might have shown *this* inference to be valid without using the new notation and rules of Part Two; but more commonly, inferences that seem to involve quantifiers really do involve them, and no amount of rephrasing will turn them into inferences that can be symbolized and tested by the methods of Part One.

EXERCISES

6.1 Use the tree method to show that the following arguments are valid:

a
$$\frac{Pa}{(\exists x)Px}$$

b
$$\frac{aLb}{(\exists x)aLx}$$

c
$$\frac{(x)xLx}{aLa}$$

d
$$\frac{(\exists x)Px}{(x)(Px \rightarrow Qx)} \\ \overline{(\exists x)Qx}$$

6.2   Use the tree method to show that the two sentences are logically equivalent in each of the following pairs. (This involves two trees per pair since you must show that each member of the pair is deducible from the other.)

a $(x)Px,$ $-(\exists x)-Px$ **b** $(\exists x)Px,$ $-(x)-Px$
c $(\exists x)(Px \vee Qx),$ $(\exists x)Px \vee (\exists x)Qx$
d $(x)(Px \,\&\, Qx),$ $(x)Px \,\&\, (x)Qx$

6.3   Use the tree method to show that each of the following sentences is a logical truth:

a $Pa \rightarrow (\exists x)Px$ **b** $(x)xLx \rightarrow aLa$
c $[H \rightarrow (x)Mx] \leftrightarrow (x)(H \rightarrow Mx)$
d $(x)(Ax \leftrightarrow Bx) \rightarrow [(\exists x)Ax \leftrightarrow (\exists x)Bx]$

SOLUTIONS

6.1 a Pa **b** aLb **c** $(x)xLx$
$\sqrt{}\;\; -(\exists x)Px$ $\sqrt{}\;\; -(\exists x)aLx$ $-aLa$
$(x)-Px$ $(x)-aLx$ aLa
$-Pa$ $-aLa$ $\times$
$\times$ $-aLb$
$\times$

d $\sqrt{}\;\; (\exists x)Px$
$(x)(Px \rightarrow Qx)$
$\sqrt{}\;\; -(\exists x)Qx$
$(x)-Qx$
Pa
$-Qa$
$\sqrt{}\;\; Pa \nrightarrow Qa$
$-Pa$ Qa
$\times$ $\times$

6.2 **a** $(x)Px$ $\sqrt{}\ -(\exists x)-Px$
              $\sqrt{}\ (\exists x)-Px$ $-(x)Px$
                  $-Pa$ $(x)Px$
                  Pa $\times$
                  $\times$

b $\sqrt{}\ (\exists x)Px$ $\sqrt{}\ -(x)-Px$
         $(x)-Px$ $-(\exists x)Px$
          Pa $(\exists x)Px$
         $-Pa$ $\times$
          $\times$

[In **a** and **b** above, line 3 of the right-hand tree comes from line 1 by *two* applications of the $-$ rule.]

c $\sqrt{}\ (\exists x)(Px \lor Qx)$
         $\sqrt{}\ -[(\exists x)Px \lor (\exists x)Qx]$
            $\sqrt{}\ -(\exists x)Px$
            $\sqrt{}\ -(\exists x)Qx$
            $(x)-Px$
            $(x)-Qx$
            $\sqrt{}\ Pa \lor Qa$
              $-Pa$
              $-Qa$

         Pa Qa
         $\times$ $\times$

         $\sqrt{}\ (\exists x)Px \lor (\exists x)Qx$
         $\sqrt{}\ -(\exists x)(Px \lor Qx)$
         $(x)-(Px \lor Qx)$

   $\sqrt{}\ (\exists x)Px$ $\sqrt{}\ (\exists x)Qx$ [It would have been equally correct
      Pa $Qb \longleftarrow$ to have written "*a*" instead of "*b*"
   $\sqrt{}\ -(Pa \lor Qa)$ $\sqrt{}\ -(Pb \lor Qb)$ here (and below) since the name "*a*"
      $-Pa$ $-Pb$ is new *to this path*, as required by
      $-Qa$ $-Qb$ the rule for $(\exists x)$.]
      $\times$ $\times$

d $(x)(Px \, \& \, Qx)$
                     $\sqrt{} \;\; -[(x)Px \, \& \, (x)Qx]$

        $\sqrt{} \;\; -(x)Px$ $\sqrt{} \;\; -(x)Qx$
       $\sqrt{} \;\; (\exists x)-Px$ $\sqrt{} \;\; (\exists x)-Qx$
          $-Pa$ $-Qa$
       $\sqrt{} \;\; Pa \, \& \, Qa$ $\sqrt{} \;\; Pa \, \& \, Qa$
           Pa Pa
           Qa Qa
            $\times$ $\times$

   $\sqrt{} \;\; (x)Px \, \& \, (x)Qx \longleftarrow$ —[This is checked
   $\sqrt{} \;\; -(x)(Px \, \& \, Qx)$ because it is a
   $\sqrt{} \;\; (\exists x)-(Px \, \& \, Qx)$ *conjunction.*
      $\sqrt{} \;\; -(Pa \, \& \, Qa)$ It is only
         $(x)Px \longleftarrow$ here and
         $(x)Qx \longleftarrow$ here that the
           Pa rule for (x)
           Qa can be applied.]

      $-Pa$ $-Qa$
       $\times$ $\times$

6.3 a $\sqrt{} \;\; -[Pa \rightarrow (\exists x)Px]$ **b** $\sqrt{} \;\; -[(x)xLx \rightarrow aLa]$
               Pa $(x)xLx$
            $\sqrt{} \;\; -(\exists x)Px$ $-aLa$
               $(x)-Px$ aLa
                $-Pa$ $\times$
                 $\times$

c

$$\sqrt{\ } -\{[H \rightarrow (x)Mx] \leftrightarrow (x)(H \rightarrow Mx)\}$$

$\sqrt{\ } H \rightarrow (x)Mx$	$\sqrt{\ } -[H \rightarrow (x)Mx]$
$\sqrt{\ } -(x)(H \rightarrow Mx)$	$(x)(H \rightarrow Mx)$
$\sqrt{\ } (\exists x)-(H \rightarrow Mx)$	H
$\sqrt{\ } -(H \rightarrow Ma)$	$\sqrt{\ } -(x)Mx$
H	$\sqrt{\ } (\exists x)-Mx$
$-Ma$	$-Ma$
	$\sqrt{\ } H \rightarrow Ma$

$-H$	$(x)Mx$
$\times$	Ma
	$\times$

$-H$	Ma
$\times$	$\times$

[A biconditional is logically true if and only if each side implies the other. Then the fact that this tree is closed shows that "$H \rightarrow (x)Mx$" is logically equivalent to "$(x)(H \rightarrow Mx)$." Of course, this equivalence can equally well be demonstrated by the method of Exercise 6.2.]

d

$$\sqrt{\ } -\{(x)(Ax \leftrightarrow Bx) \rightarrow [(\exists x)Ax \leftrightarrow (\exists x)Bx]\}$$
$$(x)(Ax \leftrightarrow Bx)$$
$$\sqrt{\ } -[(\exists x)Ax \leftrightarrow (\exists x)Bx]$$

$\sqrt{\ } (\exists x)Ax$	$\sqrt{\ } -(\exists x)Ax$
$\sqrt{\ } -(\exists x)Bx$	$\sqrt{\ } (\exists x)Bx$
$(x)-Bx$	$(x)-Ax$
Aa	Ba
$-Ba$	$-Aa$
$\sqrt{\ } Aa \leftrightarrow Ba$	$\sqrt{\ } Aa \leftrightarrow Ba$

Aa	$-Aa$	Aa	$-Aa$
Ba	$-Ba$	Ba	$-Ba$
$\times$	$\times$	$\times$	$\times$

[A conditional is logically true if and only if its antecedent implies its consequent. Then the fact that this tree is closed shows that the inference from "$(x)(Ax \leftrightarrow Bx)$" to "$(\exists x)Ax \leftrightarrow (\exists x)Bx$" is a valid one.]

FURTHER EXERCISES

Test the following inferences for validity by the tree method. Write "*a*" for Alma, "*b*" for Bert, and "*xLy*" for *x* loves *y*.

6.4   *Alma does not love herself.*
    Not everyone loves Alma.

6.5   *Everyone loves himself.*
    Bert does not love himself.

6.6   *Everyone whom Alma loves, loves Alma, i.e., $(x)(aLx \rightarrow xLa)$*
    If Alma loves everyone, everyone loves Alma.

6.7   *All who love Alma are loved by her.*
    There is someone whom Alma does not love.
    Someone does not love Alma.

6.8   *Alma does not love all her lovers, i.e., $-(x)(xLa \rightarrow aLx)$*
    Alma has a lover whom she does not love, i.e., $(\exists x)(xLa \ \& \ -aLx)$

6.9   *Alma loves herself.*
    Alma's love is sometimes reciprocated.

6.10   *Unless Alma loves herself, she loves no one.*
    Alma loves Bert if she loves herself.

6.11   *Unless Alma loves herself, she loves no one.*
    Alma loves Bert only if she loves herself.

6.12   Use the tree method to determine whether these are logical truths.
   a   *If Alma's love is never reciprocated, she does not love herself.*
   b   *Alma loves herself if she loves everyone.*
   c   *Alma loves herself, if anyone.*
   d   *Alma, if anyone, loves Alma.*

7

MULTIPLE QUANTIFICATION. TRANSLATION

We shall have occasion to use letters other than "x" as variables, and for each of these, say "y," we have a rule for (y) and a rule for $(\exists y)$. These will be identical with the rules given above for (x) and $(\exists x)$ except that "y" appears in place of "x" throughout the statement of each rule.

As an example, consider the argument

> *Everybody is related to everybody.*
> *Everybody is related to himself.*

If we take the values of the variables "x" and "y" to be people and if we use "R" for the phrase "is related to," the argument goes over into the language of logic as follows:

$$\frac{(x)(y)xRy}{(x)xRx}$$

The premise says something about all persons x and y, namely, that x is related to y. It is to be interpreted as if it had been written "$(x)[(y)(xRy)]$," just as "$--H$" is interpreted as if it had been written "$-[-(H)]$," but in neither case are the signs of grouping needed, for no other interpretation makes sense. The tree method shows this argument to be valid:

1	$(x)(y)xRy$	[premise]
2	$\sqrt{\ } \ -(x)xRx$	[$-$conclusion]
3	$\sqrt{\ } \ (\exists x)-xRx$	[2 by $-$]
4	$-aRa$	[3 by $(\exists x)$]
5	$(y)aRy$	[1 by (x)]
6	aRa	[5 by (y)]
	$\times$	

To get line 5 from line 1 by the rule for (x), we observed that line 1 is of form $(x)\ldots x\ldots$ where $\ldots x\ldots$ is "$(y)xRy$." Then $\ldots a\ldots$ is line 5, viz., the result of writing "a" for "x" in $\ldots x\ldots$.

As a further example, consider the argument

$$\frac{(\exists x)(y)xLy}{(y)(\exists x)xLy}$$

If the values of the variables are people and "L" means *loves*, this is a valid argument from the premise

> *There is someone who loves everyone*

to the conclusion

> *Everyone is loved (by someone or other).*

The conclusion could be true without the premise being true: If everyone loved himself and only himself, then indeed everyone would be loved, but no one person would love everybody. But the opposite situation is not possible: If some one person does love everybody, then indeed, everyone is loved. Then the argument has no counterexamples, and is valid. We now use the tree method to show that the argument is valid.

1	$\sqrt{\ } \ (\exists x)(y)xLy$	[premise]
2	$\sqrt{\ } \ -(y)(\exists x)xLy$	[$-$conclusion]
3	$\sqrt{\ } \ (\exists y)-(\exists x)xLy$	[2 by $-$]

4	$(y)aLy$	[1 by $(\exists x)$]
5	$\sqrt{}\ -(\exists x)xLb$	[3 by $(\exists y)$]
6	$(x)-xLb$	[5 by $-$]
7	$-aLb$	[6 by (x)]
8	aLb	[4 by (y)]
	×	

It is essential that the rules for quantifiers be applied only when the quantifier governs the *whole* sentence in which it occurs. Thus, the rule for (y) cannot be applied to line 1 above, and neither can the rule for (y) nor the rule for $(\exists x)$ be applied to line 2.

INTERPRETATION OF QUANTIFIERS

Now that quantifiers are being used within the scopes of other quantifiers, it will be well to have a close look at their interpretation. For definiteness, suppose that "Ma" means *a is male*, that "aLb" means *a loves b*, and that the allowable values of the variables are the people a, b, c, . . . , some of whom are women.

Quantifiers as Connectives. The false sentence "$(x)Mx$" means that everybody is male. It means that each of the sentences "Ma," "Mb," "Mc," . . . is true and can thus be interpreted as the conjunction of all those sentences:

$(x)Mx$ Ma & Mb & Mc & . . .   *Everyone is male.*

Similarly, the sentence "$(\exists x)Mx$" means that someone is male. It means that at least one of the sentences "Ma," "Mb," "Mc," . . . is true and can thus be interpreted as their disjunction:

$(\exists x)Mx$ $Ma \vee Mb \vee Mc \vee$ . . .   *Someone is male.*

The statement that everyone loves himself comes out as the conjunction of the sentences "aLa," "bLb," "cLc," . . . which say about each of a, b, c, . . . that he loves himself:

$(x)xLx$ aLa & bLb & cLc & . . .   *Everyone loves himself.*

The statement that someone loves himself comes out as the corresponding disjunction:

$(\exists x)xLx$ $aLa \lor bLb \lor cLc \lor \ldots$ *Someone loves himself.*

In general, a universally quantified sentence, which makes a statement about everybody, comes out as the conjunction of the sentences which make that same statement about a, about b, about c, and so on; and the corresponding existentially quantified sentence comes out as the disjunction of those same sentences.

The difference in meaning between the sentences

$(x)(\exists y)xLy,$ $(\exists y)(x)xLy$

can be brought out clearly in these terms. The former sentence is universally quantified, saying that

$(\exists y)xLy$ *x loves someone*

is true for *every* value a, b, c, $\ldots$ of "x." The latter sentence is existentially quantified, saying that

$(x)xLy$ *Everyone loves y*

is true for *some* value a, b, c, $\ldots$ of "y." (Note that the variables "x" and "y" have the same objects as their possible values.) Then the two sentences are interpreted as a conjunction and as a disjunction, respectively:

$(x)(\exists y)xLy,$ $(\exists y)aLy \,\&\, (\exists y)bLy \,\&\, (\exists y)cLy \,\&\, \ldots$
$(\exists y)(x)xLy,$ $(x)xLa \lor (x)xLb \lor (x)xLc \lor \ldots$

The first says that

a loves someone & b loves someone & c loves someone & . . . ,

and the second says

Everyone loves a $\lor$ *everyone loves b* $\lor$ *everyone loves c* $\lor \ldots$.

Thus, the first says

Everyone loves,

and the second says

Everyone loves the same person.

Similarly, the difference in meaning between the sentences

$$(y)(\exists x)xLy, \qquad (\exists x)(y)xLy$$

is the difference between the conjunction

Someone loves a & someone loves b & someone loves c & . . .

and the disjunction

a loves everyone ∨ b loves everyone ∨ c loves everyone ∨ . . . .

The first of these says

Everyone is loved,

and the second says

Everyone is loved by the same person.

Logic into English. The information that is conveyed in logical notation by the order of quantifiers is conveyed in English by a variety of devices. The most reliable way to translate logical notation into English is to begin with the ponderous readings

For every x,   There is an x such that

of the quantifiers "(x)" and "$(\exists x)$" and then work in stages toward idiomatic English. Thus, the sentence

$$(x)(\exists y)xLy$$

might first be rendered in near English as

For every x there is a y such that x loves y.

Since the variables are understood to range over people, we might recast this more explicitly as follows:

For every person x there is a person y such that x loves y.

To turn this into English we must eliminate the variables and find another way of doing their job of cross-indexing. A clumsy but reliable expedient is simply to drop the first occurrence of each variable and replace later occurrences by references to *the former* and *the latter:*

For every person there is a person such that the former loves the latter.

This is English of a sort. It only remains to improve the style, by methods that belong not to logic but to the art of English composition. The clearest expressions of this statement in English seem to be

Everyone loves,   *Everyone is a lover,*

which achieve their clarity by burying one of the quantifiers. Both quantifiers appear on the surface in the version

Everyone loves someone,

but this might be misinterpreted as meaning that everyone loves the same person: all love one.

LINKAGE

Each of the sentences

$(x)(\exists y)xLy,$ $(y)(\exists x)yLx$

goes over into the same clumsy English sentence:

For every person there is a person such that the former loves the latter.

The only purpose of the variables in the former pair of sentences is to show which member of the pair, *lover* or *beloved,* is governed by which quantifier. This job of cross-indexing is done in clumsy English by the locutions *the former* and *the latter* and is done in logical notation in a way that can be clarified by actually drawing links between quantifiers and the variables they govern. The two sentences above are logically equivalent because they show the same pattern of links:

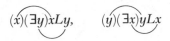

$$(x)(\exists y)xLy, \qquad (y)(\exists x)yLx$$

All cross-indexing is shown by the links alone:

$$(\ )(\exists \ ) \ L \ )$$

Indeed, we could express the claim that everyone is a lover without using variables at all by adopting the link notation just shown. But for typographical reasons it is convenient to identify the links without actually showing them. We do this by marking the two ends of each link by two occurrences of the same variable, taking care to do this in a way that makes it possible to reconstruct the original pattern of links. Thus, in our example, we might use the letter "z" to mark the ends of the upper link, and we might use "x" for the lower:

$$\overset{z}{(\ )(\exists \ ) \ L \ )}\underset{x}{}$$

Writing these letters in place of the ends of the links, we have an expression from which the pattern of links can be recovered:

$$(z)(\exists x)zLx$$

The order in which quantifiers are written at the beginning of a sentence can be significant, as can the position (subject or object of "L") governed by each quantifier. But all relevant information about order and position can be shown in the link notation without using variables. The decision about which variables to use in the standard notation is a completely trivial one;

all that matters is that the desired pattern of links be shown unambiguously by the variables.

Of course, a single quantifier may govern two or more positions within a sentence. "Alma loves everyone who loves her" may be translated as

$$(x)(xLa \rightarrow aLx),$$

where the universal quantifier is linked to the subject of the first "L" and the object of the second:

$$(\,\,\widehat{)(\,\, La} \rightarrow aL\,\,)$$

For a more involved example, consider the sentence "Someone loves everyone who loves her," which we translate as

$$(\exists y)(x)(xLy \rightarrow yLx).$$

Here we have the following pattern of links:

$$(\exists \,)(\,\,)(\,\, L \,\,\rightarrow\, L\,\,)$$

The distinct statement that someone is loved by everyone she loves has the same order of quantifiers but exhibits a different linkage pattern:

$$(\exists y)(x)(yLx \rightarrow xLy), \qquad (\exists \,)(\,\,)(\,\, L \,\,\rightarrow\, L\,\,)$$

Each of these last two linkage patterns is of the sort that requires us to associate different variables with the two quantifiers if the original pattern is to be recoverable from the standard logical notation. But the logical truth

$$(x)[(y)Py \rightarrow Px]$$

illustrates the contrary situation, in which the same linkage pattern would have been indicated even if we had used a single variable for both quantifiers:

$(x)[(x)Px \rightarrow Px]$

To recover the linkage pattern from this sentence, we work from the inside out. Since the "x" after the "P" in the antecedent is linked to the inner quantifier, it is not free to be linked to the outer quantifier, and the pattern must be the following:

$(\ ^\backprime)[(\ ^\backprime)P^\backprime \rightarrow P^\backprime\ ]$

It is instructive to work out the tree which shows "$(x)[(x)Px \rightarrow Px]$" to be a logical truth:

1	$\sqrt{\ } -(x)[(x)Px \rightarrow Px]$	[− conclusion]
2	$\sqrt{\ } (\exists x) - [(x)Px \rightarrow Px]$	[1 by −]
3	$\sqrt{\ } -[(x)Px \rightarrow Pa]$	[2 by $(\exists x)$]
4	$(x)Px$	[3 by
5	$-Pa$	$-(\bigcirc \rightarrow \triangle)$]
6	Pa	[4 by (x)]
	$\times$	

Notice how the step from line 2 to line 3 is accomplished. When the existential quantifier is checked, a new name is written in each position which is linked to *that* quantifier. The whole tree could have been constructed in the link notation without using variables at all:

1	$-(\ ^\backprime)[(\ ^\backprime)P^\backprime \rightarrow P^\backprime\ ]$	[− conclusion]
2	$(\exists\ ^\backprime) - [(\ ^\backprime)P^\backprime \rightarrow P^\backprime\ ]$	[1 by −]
3	$-[(\ ^\backprime)P^\backprime \rightarrow Pa]$	[2 by $(\exists \cdot)$]
4	$(\ ^\backprime)P^\backprime$	[3 by
5	$-Pa$	$-(\bigcirc \rightarrow \triangle)$]
6	Pa	[4 by $(\cdot)$]
	$\times$	

Moral. When, in applying the rules of inference for the quantifiers, we check a sentence of one of the forms

$$(x) \ldots x \ldots, \qquad (\exists x) \ldots x \ldots$$

and write

$$\ldots a \ldots$$

at the bottom of the path, the sentence $\ldots a \ldots$ is obtained by erasing the leftmost quantifier in the checked sentence and writing "a" for every occurrence of "x" which was linked to *that* quantifier.

Variables in separate sentences have nothing to do with each other. Thus, the valid inference

> *Everything is material.*
> *Something is material.*

can be transcribed indifferently as any of the following:

$(x)Mx$	$(x)Mx$	$(y)My$	$(y)My$	$(\frown)M\frown$
$(\exists x)Mx$	$(\exists y)My$	$(\exists x)Mx$	$(\exists y)My$	$(\exists \frown)M\frown$

The fact that in the first and fourth of these the same variables are used in premise and conclusion is entirely without significance. The truth trees are essentially the same, whether the same or different variables are used in premise and conclusion:

$(x)Mx$	$(x)Mx$	$(y)My$	$(y)My$	$(\frown)M\frown$
$\surd -(\exists x)Mx$	$\surd -(\exists y)My$	$\surd -(\exists x)Mx$	$\surd -(\exists y)My$	$\surd -(\exists \frown)M\frown$
$(x)-Mx$	$(y)-My$	$(x)-Mx$	$(y)-My$	$(\frown)-M\frown$
Ma	Ma	Ma	Ma	Ma
$-Ma$	$-Ma$	$-Ma$	$-Ma$	$-Ma$
$\times$	$\times$	$\times$	$\times$	$\times$

Of course, the case is different for *names* "a" and "b" and the like, which must have the same meanings wherever they appear in sentences of an inference.

TRANSLATION

The business of translating English sentences into logical notation is largely a matter of rephrasing the sentences within a very limited fragment of English, augmented by variables. Examples are provided by the four forms of *categorical statements* in traditional logic. These were thought of as subject-predicate statements, classified as *affirmative* or *negative* depending on whether the subject was affirmed or denied of the predicate and classified as *universal* or *particular* depending on whether all or some of the things described by the subject were under discussion. The scheme is presented in Table 7.1 where the traditional nomenclature "A," "E," "I," and "O" is used to identify the four forms.

	Affirmative	*Negative*
Universal	A: All S are *P*.	E: No S are *P*.
Particular	I: Some S are *P*.	O: Some S are not *P*.

Table   7.1

Categorical Statements. The first thing to be noted is that both in English and in logical notation, each of these forms can be expressed in a variety of equivalent ways. Thus, reading "*S*," the subject term, as "swans" and reading "*P*," the predicate term, as "pretty," the A form can be expressed in English in at least the following six ways:

All swans are pretty.
Any swan is pretty.
Each swan is pretty.
Every swan is pretty.
Swans are all pretty.
Swans are pretty.

To express this A statement in logical notation, we must abandon the traditional idea that we are dealing with a sentence in subject-predicate form for which the *universe of discourse* (the class of things under discussion) consists of the swans: the things described by the subject. Instead, we view the statement as an assertion about *everything:* nonswans as well as swans.

We construe the statement as having the form

The following is true of everything: if it is a swan then it is pretty.

To translate this into logical notation, read the preamble as "(x)" and replace the two occurrences of the pronoun "it" by occurrences of the variable "x." Then we have

A: $(x)(Sx \rightarrow Px)$

as a translation of "all S are P," with "Sx" meaning that x is an S and "Px" meaning that x is a P.

The claim is not that "$(x)(Sx \rightarrow Px)$" can always be relied upon to say the same thing or to assume the same truth-value, as "All S are P." Rather, the claim is that the statement-making jobs normally done by English sentences of the latter form are done quite adequately by corresponding statements of the former form in logical notation and that

the cases in which the two sentences have different meanings are cases in which the English sentence can plausibly be said to fail in its statement-making function.

In particular, consider the sentence

All griffins are purple,

which is of the A form with "griffins" for "S" and "purple" for "P." Since there are no griffins, the question "Are they all purple?" seems to have no answer, and so this A sentence seems to have no truth-value and seems to make no statement. But the corresponding sentence "$(x)(Sx \rightarrow Px)$" in logical notation makes a statement and has a truth-value whether or not there are any griffins. Since in fact there are none, the antecedent of the conditional "$Sx \rightarrow Px$" is false for each x, and therefore the whole conditional is true for each x. Then the transcription of this A sentence into logical notation is true, although the corresponding English sentence seems to have neither truth-value.

Furthermore, the E sentence

No griffins are purple

which answers "no" to the seemingly unanswerable question "Are all griffins purple?" also goes over into a truth in logical notation, for we read it as

The following is false of everything: it is a griffin and it is purple.

Then "No S are P" goes over into logical notation in any of the following logically equivalent ways:

E: $(x) - (Sx \mathbin{\&} Px)$, $-(\exists x)(Sx \mathbin{\&} Px)$, $(x)(Sx \rightarrow -Px)$

In case there are no S's, each of these is true.

Clearly, every sentence of form

$(x)(x$ *is a griffin* $\rightarrow \ldots x \ldots)$

is true simply because the antecedent of the inner conditional is false for every value of "x." Since our transcription of "All griffins are purple" and our third transcription of "No griffins are purple" have this form, both are true. If this is an oddity, it is a more manageable one than the corresponding oddity in English where it seems that sentences of form "All griffins are . . ." have, not the truth-value t, but no truth-value at all. Here is a point at which logic can profitably diverge from English.

No such difficulties are encountered in the traditional analysis of the particular statement forms I and O: "Some S are P" and "Some S are not P." Each of these asserts the nonemptiness of some class of things: the things that are both S and P in the I form and the things that are S but not P in the O form. Then these are handily translated into our notation as follows:

I: $(\exists x)(Sx \mathbin{\&} Px)$
O: $(\exists x)(Sx \mathbin{\&} -Px)$

Tense. Tense distinctions are one of the things that can make different utterances of the same English sentence have different truth-values. Choice of the right tense is a matter of comparing the time of utterance of a sentence with the time of occurrence of the event it is about. To say

It is raining in Boston

is to say that

> *It is raining in Boston as this statement is being made.*

Therefore the sentence, uttered at two different times, may be the vehicle for making statements with two different truth-values. But happily, choice of the right tense is often a matter of style, not substance. This will generally be the case when the time of the event under discussion is explicitly indicated in the sentence or when it has no relevance to the matters being considered, as in the inference

> *Ramsey was born on February 22.*
> *Washington was born on February 22.*
> ---
> *Ramsey and Washington have (had?) the same birthday.*

In translating logic into English, "*Pa*" is to be read "*a* is *P*" or "*a* was *P*" or "*a* will be *P*," as appropriate; if it is not clear which tense is appropriate, the present tense will do. In translating English into logic, we must explicitly express any *relevant* information that is conveyed by the tenses of the verbs, and we must take care that the result is a context-free sentence. But commonly, in the inferences we consider, the tenses of the verbs convey no information relevant to validity and can be ignored in translation. The inference about birthdays can be represented straightforwardly as follows, where the universe of discourse consists of the 366 dates that can be birthdays, where "*a*" is used as a name of February 22, where "*Rx*" means that *x* is Ramsey's birthday, and where "*Wx*" means that *x* is Washington's birthday.

> Ra
> Wa
> ---
> $(\exists x)(Rx \mathbin{\&} Wx)$

Choosing a Universe of Discourse. In discussing the sentence "All griffins are purple" we noted that in our usage the universe of discourse comprises the nongriffins as well as the griffins and is therefore a nonempty class. But how broad a class is it? Does the universe of discourse include decks of cards? Shadows of butterflys? The number three? Beethoven's Ninth Symphony? Chicago? Tuesday morning? There is no one answer. In discussing Alma's love life it is appropriate to choose a universe of discourse consisting of people, but in analyzing the inference about birthdays above, we found it convenient to take days of the year as values of the variables.

In English there are standard clues that partly indicate what the universe of discourse is supposed to be. These clues are provided by various special pronouns which indicate that we are discussing, say, people, places, or times. The statements

    Everyone loves Alma
    Everybody loves Alma
    Someone loves Alma
    Somebody loves Alma

are clearly intended to have some class of people (perhaps all people presently alive) as its universe of discourse. The first two might go over into logic as "$(x)xLa$" and the second two as "$(\exists x)xLa$," and in both cases it is clear that the variable "x" takes people as values. A further clue is given by the tense of the verb: Use of the present tense suggests that the universe of discourse is a class of people presently alive. Similarly, use of "somewhere" as an existential quantifier indicates that the universe of discourse is some class of places, although much remains to be clarified by the context: All places on this planet? In the galaxy? But logical notation provides no such grammatical clues; the universe of discourse is not indicated by the notation and must be specified separately, just as the meanings of names like "a" and predicate symbols like "S" must be specified separately.

Restricted Quantifiers. It is tempting to symbolize sentences like

7.1   *Everyone was born somewhere*

by using two different variables having two different universes of discourse. Thus, if "xBy" means that x is y's birthplace, the temptation is to use a class of places as the universe of discourse for "x" and to use a class of people as the universe of discourse for "y" and to write **7.1** as

7.2 $(y)(\exists x)xBy.$

But in our system of logic, all variables in an inference must have the same universe of discourse; otherwise, the tree method cannot be relied upon to classify correctly inferences as valid or not. Of course, we could modify the tree method to allow for *restricted quantifiers*. If "*Pa*" means that *a* is a person and "*Sa*" means that *a* is a place, we might indicate the restrictions on the quantifiers in **7.2** by means of subscripts:

7.3 $(y)_P(\exists x)_S xBy$

And we might then introduce special rules of inference for such restricted quantifiers. But it is ultimately simpler to use the standard notation, in which all variables have the same universe of discourse. Sentence **7.1** would then be translated as

7.4 $(y)[\,Py \rightarrow (\exists x)(Sx \,\&\, xBy)]$

and the variables "*x*" and "*y*" would be understood to have a common universe of discourse, consisting of people and places.

But we can use the notation of **7.3** as a halfway house between the English of **7.1** and the standard logical notation of **7.4** by giving rules for removing restrictions on quantifiers:

> Rewrite $(x)_P \ldots x \ldots$ as $(x)(Px \rightarrow \ldots x \ldots)$ and
> rewrite $(\exists x)_P \ldots x \ldots$ as $(\exists x)(Px \,\&\, \ldots x \ldots)$.

Although these rules are stated for the particular variable "*x*" and the particular predicate symbol "*P*," rules of the same form apply to other variables and other predicate symbols. The rationale is the one that underlay our translations of the A and I forms of categorical sentences: To say that all *P*'s are *Q*'s is to say that everything is a *Q* if a *P*, and to say that some *P*'s are *Q*'s is to say that something is both a *P* and a *Q*:

> All *P*'s are *Q*'s $(x)_P Qx$ $(x)(Px \rightarrow Qx)$
> Some *P*'s are *Q*'s $(\exists x)_P Qx$ $(\exists x)(Px \,\&\, Qx)$

To see how **7.4** comes from **7.3** according to our rules, notice that **7.3** has the form

7.5 $(y)_P \ldots y \ldots$

where $\ldots y \ldots$ is "$(\exists x)_S xBy$." Our rule instructs us to rewrite **7.5** as

7.6 $(y)(Py \rightarrow \ldots y \ldots)$

or, here, as

7.7 $(y)(Py \rightarrow (\exists x)_S\, xBy).$

Our rule also instructs us to rewrite

$(\exists x)_S \ldots x \ldots$

as

$(\exists x)(Sx \,\&\, \ldots x \ldots).$

Here, $\ldots x \ldots$ is "xBy," so that in **7.7** we are to replace

$(\exists x)_S\, xBy$

by

$(\exists x)(Sx \,\&\, xBy).$

This transforms **7.7** into the standard notation of **7.4.**

An Example. Skill in any sort of problem solving is in large part a matter of knowing how to divide difficulties so as to solve parts of the problem and then combining the parts into a complete solution. Our rules for eliminating restrictions on quantifiers are codifications of one way of dividing difficulties in translating English into standard logical notation. For a further example of the process, let us translate

7.8   *Horses' tails are animals' tails*

into standard logical notation, using "T" for "is a tail of" and using "Ha" and "Aa" for "a is a horse" and "a is an animal." The universe of discourse is to include all animals and all tails. We need no explicit rules to see that **7.8** has the form

7.9 $(x)(x$ *is a horse's tail* $\rightarrow x$ *is an animal's tail* $).$

In rewriting **7.8** as a mixture of English and logical notation **7.9**, we are effectively dividing difficulties, for we have reduced the problem of translating **7.8** into logical notation to the two easier problems of translating

7.10   *x is a horse's tail,*   *x is an animal's tail*

into logical notation. Now to say that x is a horse's tail is to say that there is a horse that x is the tail of, and to say that x is an animal's tail is to say that there is an animal that x is the tail of. Using restricted quantifiers, we see the two clauses in **7.10** become

7.11 $(\exists y)_H xTy,$ $(\exists y)_A xTy$

Our rules then direct us to rewrite **7.11** as

7.12 $(\exists y)(Hy \ \& \ xTy),$ $(\exists y)(Ay \ \& \ xTy)$

Substituting these for antecedent and consequent of the inner conditional in **7.9**, we finally have this as a translation of **7.8** into standard logical notation:

7.13 $(x)[(\exists y)(Hy \ \& \ xTy) \rightarrow (\exists y)(Ay \ \& \ xTy)]$

INFINITE TREES

In conclusion, let us note a general structural feature of the tree method. If an inference is valid, the tree method will show it to be valid in some finite number of steps: the tree for the inference will eventually close. But for an invalid inference the case may be different: the tree will fail to close either because (1) there comes a point at which none of the rules of inference is applicable, while at least one path is open or because (2) *the tree continues to grow forever.* In terms of Figure 6.1, this corresponds to the difference between (1) eventually reaching stage 7 and thus halting when there is an open path through the tree and (2) answering "yes" to question 6 every time it is asked and thus never halting.

To illustrate the possibility that the tree will grow forever, we apply the tree method to the "inference"

$$\overline{(\exists x)(y) - xLy}$$

in order to see whether the sentence under the bar is a logical truth.

1	$(x)(\exists y)xLy$	[— conclusion, by three uses of —]
2	$\checkmark\ (\exists y)aLy$	[1 by (x)]
3	aLb	[2 by $(\exists y)$, using a *new* name "b"]
4	$\checkmark\ (\exists y)bLy$	[1 by (x)]
5	bLc	[4 by $(\exists y)$, using a *new* name "c"]
6	$\checkmark\ (\exists y)cLy$	[1 by (x)]
7	cLd	[6 by $(\exists y)$, using a *new* name "d"]

$$\vdots$$

Clearly, this process will continue forever, generating an infinite path which never closes in which all the following sentences eventually appear:

$$aLb, \qquad bLc, \qquad cLd, \qquad dLe, \qquad \ldots$$

These sentences tell an infinitely long story about characters named "a," "b," "c," ..., each of whom loves his successor. For all its length, this story is incomplete, for there are infinitely many questions about the loves of these characters that it leaves unanswered. Thus, no hint is given about whether any of these loves are reciprocated, for the statements

$$bLa, \qquad cLb, \qquad dLc, \qquad eLd, \qquad \ldots$$

are neither affirmed nor denied in the story. But the story is consistent and *could* be completed in infinitely many different ways. And, incomplete as it is, the story serves to describe a situation in which line 1 of the foregoing tree is true; it describes a counterexample to the hypothesis that "$(\exists x)(y) - xLy$" is a logical truth.

The infinitely long story generated by the tree method is not the only one that would do as a counterexample; it is by no means the only story in which every character is a lover, but it *is* the only story that the tree method will generate for the invalid "inference" that we are testing. The *simplest* counterexample is obtained by taking the universe of discourse to consist of a single person, a, who loves himself. This counterexample is described by the one-sentence story, "aLa."

Notice, finally, that the infinitely long, incomplete story generated by the tree method might be completed in such a way as to turn it into a version of the one-sentence story, "*aLa*," for one of the questions left unanswered in the infinite story concerns the number of characters. The fact that infinitely many names "*a*," "*b*," "*c*," ... are used does not mean that there are infinitely many distinct characters in the story: There might be only one character *a*, who has an infinity "*b*," "*c*," ... of aliases. If we complete the story in *this* way, stipulating that "*a*," "*b*," "*c*," ... are different names of one and the same person, then it becomes a very repetitious version of the one-sentence story "*aLa*."

EXERCISES

7.1   *Everyone has a father.*
          Anybody's father is his parent.
          ―――――――――――――――――――――
          Everyone has a parent.

7.2   *Horses are animals.*
          ―――――――――――――――――――――
          Horses' tails are animals' tails.

SOLUTIONS

7.1.

1	$(x)(\exists y)yFx$	[premise]
2	$(x)(y)(xFy \to xPy)$	[premise]
3	$\sqrt{}\ -(x)(\exists y)yPx$	[―conclusion]
4	$\sqrt{}\ (\exists x) - (\exists y)yPx$	[3 by $-$]
5	$\sqrt{}\ -(\exists y)yPa$	[4 by $(\exists x)$]
6	$(y) - yPa$	[5 by $-$]
7	$\sqrt{}\ (\exists y)yFa$	[1 by (x)]
8	bFa	[7 by $(\exists y)$]
9	$-bPa$	[6 by (y)]
10	$(y)(bFy \to bPy)$	[2 by (x)]
11	$\sqrt{}\ bFa \to bPa$	[10 by (y)]

$$12 \qquad -bFa \qquad bPa \qquad\qquad\qquad [11\ \text{by}\ \bigcirc \to \triangle]$$
$$\times \qquad\quad \times$$

7.2.

1	$(y)(Hy \to Ay)$	[premise]
2	$\sqrt{} \ -(x)[(\exists y)(Hy \ \& \ xTy) \to (\exists y)(Ay \ \& \ xTy)]$	[− conclusion]
3	$\sqrt{} \ (\exists x) - [(\exists y)(Hy \ \& \ xTy) \to (\exists y)(Ay \ \& \ xTy)]$	[2 by −]
4	$\sqrt{} \ -[(\exists y)(Hy \ \& \ aTy) \to (\exists y)(Ay \ \& \ aTy)]$	[3 by $(\exists x)$]
5	$\sqrt{} \ (\exists y)(Hy \ \& \ aTy)$	[4 by
6	$\sqrt{} \ -(\exists y)(Ay \ \& \ aTy)$	$-(O \to \triangle)]$
7	$\sqrt{} \ Hb \ \& \ aTb$	[5 by $(\exists y)$]
8	Hb	[7 by
9	aTb	$O \ \& \ \triangle]$
10	$(y) - (Ay \ \& \ aTy)$	[6 by −]
11	$\sqrt{} \ -(Ab \ \& \ aTb)$	[10 by (y)]

$$\diagup \quad \diagdown$$

12	$-Ab \qquad -aTb$	[11 by $-(O \ \& \ \triangle)]$
	$\times$	
13	$\sqrt{} \ Hb \to Ab$	[1 by (y)]

$$\diagup \quad \diagdown$$

14	$-Hb \qquad Ab$	[13 by $O \to \triangle]$
	$\times \qquad \times$	

Both inferences are valid.

FURTHER EXERCISES

7.3 *All the world loves a lover.*
  Andrew does not love Betty.
  Betty does not love herself.

Hint: The first premise can be construed in either of the following logically equivalent ways: $(x)(y)(x$ is a lover $\to y$ loves $x)$ or $(x)(x$ loves someone $\to$ everyone loves $x)$.

7.4 *Everyone loves every lover.*
  If even one person is loved, everyone loves everyone.

Hint: The conclusion says $(\exists x)(\exists y)xLy \to (x)(y)xLy$.

7.5   *Every lover loves everyone.*
_____
       Everyone loves every lover.

7.6   *Everyone loves every lover.*
_____
       Every lover loves everyone.

7.7   Are these logical truths?

    a $(x)(Px \to (x)Px)$ **b** $(\exists x)(Px \to (x)Px)$
    c $(x)(Px \to (\exists x)Px)$ **d** $(\exists x)xLx \to (\exists x)(\exists y)xLy$

7.8   The universe of discourse consists of the objects $a, b, c, \ldots$. Eliminate all quantifiers from each sentence in Exercise 7.7 by interpreting universal quantification as conjunction and existential quantification as disjunction.
7.9   According to DeMorgan's laws, the two sentences in **a** are logically equivalent, as are the two sentences in **b**.

    a $-(Pa \,\&\, Pb \,\&\, Pc \,\&\, \ldots),$ $-Pa \lor -Pb \lor -Pc \lor \ldots$
    b $-(Pa \lor Pb \lor Pc \lor \ldots),$ $-Pa \,\&\, -Pb \,\&\, -Pc \,\&\, \ldots$

Rewrite these four sentences with quantifiers, expressing conjunction as universal quantification and disjunction as existential quantification.
7.10   Is this consistent? "There is someone who shaves exactly those people who do not shave themselves," i.e., $(\exists x)(y)(xSy \leftrightarrow -ySy)$. Use the tree method.
7.11   Eliminate both quantifiers in Exercise 7.10 in favor of disjunction and conjunction. Is the resulting sentence truth-functionally consistent?

7.12   *There is a man in town who shaves all men in town who do not shave themselves.*
_____
       Some man in town shaves himself.

Hint: Use the class of all men in town as the universe of discourse.

7.13   *Alma has a brother who has no brother.* $(\exists x)(xBa \,\&\, (y) - yBx)$
_____
       Alma is no one's brother. $(x) - aBx$

7.14   *Anyone who can trap everyone Holmes can, can trap Holmes.*
_____
       Holmes can trap himself.

7.15 *Anyone who can trap Holmes can trap anyone Holmes can.*
 Unless Holmes can trap himself, no one he can trap can trap him.

7.16 Translate, using "*Rx*," "*Dx*," and "*Ex*" for "*x* is a Republican," "*x* is a Democrat," and "*x* is eligible."
  a *Only Republicans and Democrats are eligible.*
  b *All Republicans and Democrats are eligible.*
7.17 Translate, using "*xDy*," "*xGy*," and "*xBy*" for "*x* deserves *y*," "*x* gets *y*," and "*x* is better than *y*."
  a *Anyone who gets everything he deserves, deserves something he gets.*
  b *Everyone gets something that is better than anything he deserves.*
Pay attention to the distinction between people and things and to the choice of a universe of discourse.
7.18 Translate, using "*K*" for "knows":
  a *Everyone knows someone to whom he is unknown.*
  b *There is someone who knows everyone who knows him.*
7.19 Translate, using "*Mx*" for "*x* is male," "*P*" for "was a parent of," and "a_1," "a_2," "*c*," and "*e*" for "Adam," Abel," "Cain," and "Enos."
  a *Abel had no grandparents.*
  b *Cain and Abel were brothers.*
  c *Adam was Enos's paternal grandfather.*
  d *Abel was Enos's uncle.*
7.20 Translate, using "*Sx*" for "*x* is a stage," "*Px*" for "*x* is a path," and "*xOy*" for "(path) *x* is open at (stage) *y*."
  a *At each stage, one path or another is open.*
  b *There is a path which is open at all stages.*
  (The stages are stages in the construction of a tree.)
  c By the tree method, show that the inference from **b** to **a** is valid.
  d By the tree method, show that the inference from **a** to **b** is invalid.
7.21 A sentence in *prenex normal form* is one in which all quantifiers come at the left and govern the whole sentence. For every sentence, there is a logically equivalent sentence in prenex normal form. Examples: Prenex normal forms of the sentences "$(x)Px \to A$," "$(\exists x)Px \to A$," "$A \to (x)Px$," and "$A \to (\exists x)Px$" are "$(\exists x)(Px \to A)$," "$(x)(Px \to A)$," $(x)(A \to Px)$," and "$(\exists x)(A \to Px)$," respectively. Problem: Put the sentence "$(x)[Sx \to (\exists y)(Py$ & $yOx)] \to (\exists y)[Py$ & $(x)(Sx \to yOx)]$" in prenex normal form.

8

ADEQUACY OF THE TREE METHOD

In Chapter 5 we proved the adequacy of the tree method for testing the validity of inferences that involve only sentence letters, parentheses, and the signs "−," "&," "∨," "→," and "↔." We now extend that proof so as to apply to the inferences considered in Chapters 6 and 7. We continue to define validity of an inference as nonexistence of a counterexample to it, and we continue to define a counterexample as a valuation in which all premises are true and the conclusion is false. But we shall extend our definition of "valuation."

With our new definition of "valuation," it will remain true that the tree method is adequate in the following sense.

8.1   *There is an open path through a finished tree if and only if some valuation makes all initial sentences true.*

As in Chapter 5, we shall prove the "only if" clause of **8.1** by proving something a bit stronger:

8.2   *Each open path through a finished tree describes a valuation in which all full sentences in that path are true.*

And again, we shall prove the "if" clause of **8.1** by proving something a bit stronger (but superficially weaker than the corresponding statement **5.3**):

8.3   *If there is a valuation in which all initial sentences are true, then there is a valuation in which all full sentences in some path through the finished tree are true.*

As before, it will be the upward correctness of our rules of inference that ensures the truth of **8.2**, and it will be the downward correctness of our rules that ensures the truth of **8.3**, but we shall find that the rule for (x) is upward correct in only a rather special sense and that the rule for $(\exists x)$ is downward correct in only a rather special sense.

Then we shall have to broaden our concepts of valuation and correctness.

INFINITE TREES

We shall also have to broaden our notion of what constitutes a finished tree if **8.1**, **8.2**, and **8.3** are to make sense and be true even when the tree for the inference grows forever. In particular, we shall imagine that our trees are constructed by a superhuman creature—Zeus, say—who has an infinite amount of paper to write on and can write as fast as we please; no matter how long a finite string of symbols may be and no matter how short a time he has for the job (as long as he has *some* time, say, a billionth of a second), he can write the string of symbols out in a line within the alloted time. Now we imagine that in constructing a tree, Zeus spends half a second writing out the first full sentence that appears in the tree, a quarter of a second writing out the second full sentence, an eighth of a second writing out the third, and so on. In general, Zeus spends writing out each full sentence half the time he spent on its predecessor.

Example. The tree which shows that "$(x)(\exists y)xLy$" is consistent. At the right of each line we indicate the time Zeus spends writing out the initial portion of the tree, up to and including that line.

1     $(x)(\exists y)xLy$ [½ second]
2   √ $(\exists y)a_1Ly$ [¾ second]

3	a_1La_2	[⅞ second]
4	$\vee\ (\exists y)a_2Ly$	[¹⁵⁄₁₆ second]
5	a_2La_3	[³¹⁄₃₂ second]
6	$\vee\ (\exists y)a_3Ly$	[⁶³⁄₆₄ second]
7	a_3La_4	[¹²⁷⁄₁₂₈ second]

$$\vdots$$

Using "a_1," "a_2," and so on as names in this way, we can describe the tree as follows: Line 1 is "$(x)(\exists y)xLy$." If n is even ($n = 2, 4, 6, \ldots$), line n is "$(\exists y)a_mLy$," where m is half of n, and line $n + 1$ is "a_mLa_{m+1}," where again m is half of n. This defines the infinite tree since it defines each line in it; we have said quite explicitly how to fill in as much as we please of the material indicated by the three dots at the bottom of the displayed portion of the tree.

Writing faster and faster in this way, Zeus writes out as large a finite initial segment of the tree as we please in some length of time short of 1 second, and when the second has passed, he has written out the whole infinite tree! *At* the 1-second mark he is no longer writing, and the tree is finished. But no matter how short a time before the 1-second mark we choose to look, we shall find him busy writing—busier and busier, the closer he gets to the mark. Then putting matters vividly, we can define a finished tree as a tree that Zeus has constructed, keeping at it until all checkable sentences have been checked. Finishing a tree never takes Zeus more than 1 second. Or we can put matters more soberly, as at the end of the foregoing example, where we gave a definition which describes line number i of the tree for each value 1, 2, 3, ... of "i." There, we described the whole infinite tree by describing each part of it.

THE TREE THEOREM

As a prelude to proving the adequacy of the tree method, we shall prove the

TREE THEOREM

If at every stage in the construction of a tree, one or another path is open, then there is a path that is open at all stages.

As you saw if you did Exercise 7.20, the converse of this statement is a logical truth, but the statement itself is not. The tree theorem owes its truth to facts about the meanings of "path," "stage," and "tree" that are not explicit in the form of the theorem, which is

$$(x)_S (\exists y)_P yOx \to (\exists y)_P (x)_S yOx$$

in the restricted quantifier notation or

$$(x)[Sx \to (\exists y)(Py \ \& \ yOx)] \to (\exists y)[Py \ \& \ (x)(Sx \to yOx)]$$

in standard logical notation.

In terms of trees that Zeus has finished, the tree theorem amounts to the assertion that

Every infinite tree contains an infinite path,

which we shall also refer to as "the tree theorem." (An infinite path or tree is one that contains infinitely many sentences. An infinite path must be open at every stage in the construction of the infinite tree in which it occurs.) The tree theorem is true because each of our rules introduces at most a finite number of new paths. A nonbranching rule like the rule for O & △ simply extends the paths on which the conjunction occurs, while branching rules like those for O ∨ △, O ∨ △ ∨ □, and so on split paths into two or three or, in general, some *finite* number of paths.

Think of a tree as being formed of boxed lists in the manner of Figure 5.1. The list structure of that tree is shown in Figure 8.1. We need not look inside the boxes; for present purposes it is enough to know that each box contains some finite positive number of sentences. Think of trees such as these as family trees. The top list is the head of its family, and each list has some finite number 0, 1, 2, . . . of immediate descendants. Each list is the head of the family consisting of that list itself together with all its descendants (if any): its immediate descendants (if any), together with theirs (if any), and so on. Thus, the shaded boxes in Figure 8.1 compose the family headed by the highest shaded box. Call a box "fit" (as in the phrase "survival of the fit") if the family it heads is infinite, and call a box "unfit" if the family it heads is finite (and thus eventually dies out).

Figure 8.1

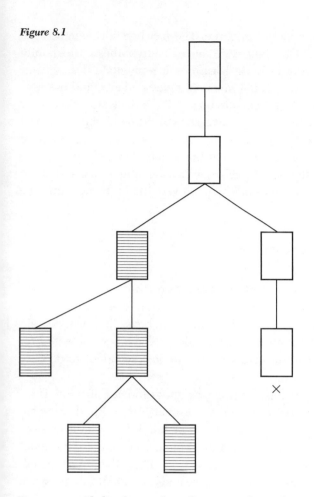

Because each list has only a finite number of immediate descendants, we have this situation:

If each immediate descendant of a box is unfit, so is that box.

The same matter can be put the other way round, as follows:

A fit list has at least one fit immediate descendant.

Now it is easy to prove the tree theorem "Every infinite tree contains an infinite path," for we can give a step-by-step procedure for finding an infinite path through any given infinite tree. The first box in the path is the box that heads the tree. This box is fit since by hypothesis the family it heads is infinite. Therefore it has at least one fit immediate descendant. Choose one, say the leftmost of its fit immediate descendants, and use it as the second box in the path. Since this box is fit, it will also have a fit immediate descendant which can serve as the third box in the path, and so on. At every stage in the construction of this path we can take one more step, for a fit box always has at least one fit immediate descendant.

This proves the tree theorem. In effect, we used mathematical induction in proving that the path never ends; we proved that for each positive integer n

the path contains at least n boxes.

The basis was our observation that since the tree is infinite, the top box must be fit so that the path contains at least one box. The induction step was our observation that if the path contains n boxes it must contain an $n + 1$st, for the nth box must be fit in order to have been selected for the path, and therefore it must have at least one fit descendant to do duty as the $n + 1$st box in the path.

The tree theorem assures us that if a tree grows forever (if the finished tree is infinite), then some path in it grows forever (the finished tree contains an infinite path). Any open path, finite or infinite, in a finished tree tells a consistent story describing a valuation which, according to statement **8.2,** makes every full sentence in that path true. Then the tree theorem assures us that when the construction of a tree ends at no finite stage (when it takes Zeus the full second to construct the tree), the corresponding inference is invalid.

RULES OF FORMATION

Before we can go on to the proofs of statements **8.2** and **8.3,** we must give our new definition of "valuation" and of the circumstances under which a sentence is *true in* a valuation. And in order to do this, we must get a clear idea of the shapes that sentences can assume. First, we itemize the ingredients of sentences.

Parentheses. "(," ")." These may also be written in somewhat different shapes, say "[," "]," as an aid to the eye in reading.

Names. An infinite assortment of symbols, say "a_1," "a_2," . . . .

Variables. An infinite assortment of symbols, say "x," "y," and "z," with or without subscripts "$_1$," "$_2$," "$_3$," . . . .

Quantifiers. Any result of writing a variable in the blank of "( )" or of "($\exists$)."

Predicate Symbols. An infinite assortment of symbols, say the roman capitals "A," "B," . . . , "Z," with or without subscripts.

With each predicate symbol there is associated a definite number 0, 1, 2, . . . called its *degree,* and with each predicate symbol of degree n there is associated a sequence of n *blanks.* Intuitively, the degree of a predicate symbol is the number of occurrences of names to which it must be applied in order to obtain a sentence. (To *apply* a predicate symbol of degree n to an n-termed sequence of names is to fill the predicate symbol's successive blanks with the successive terms of the sequence.)

Predicate symbols of degree 0 are also called "sentence letters"; they are sentences as they stand. Predicate symbols of degree 1 are also called "property symbols"; ordinarily, the blank associated with a property symbol is immediately to its right. Predicate symbols of degree 2, 3, . . . , n are called "binary" or "ternary" or . . . "n-ary" *relation symbols.* In the binary case, the associated blanks are ordinarily to the right and left of the symbol, and in other cases the blanks occur in a row to the right of the symbol.

Nothing momentous hangs on the choice of symbols as long as symbols in the various categories are distinguishable from each other in the contexts in which they appear. *Example:* If we used finite strings of small letters "a," "b," . . . , "z" as names, we would not be able to adhere to the convention that the blanks in ternary relation symbols occur in order at the right of the symbol, as when "$Bxyz$" is taken to mean that x is between y and z, for then the sentences which say that John is between Tom and Myron and that John is between Tommy and Ron would be indistinguishable: "Bjohntommyron." If this were our convention about names, we should have to use compound symbols like "$B($, , $)$" as property symbols with blanks separated by, say, commas.

Now an *atomic sentence* is the result of filling all blanks in a predicate symbol with names and variables. We may use just names or just variables or a mixture, and we may, but need not, write the same name or variable in two or more distinct blanks. An atomic sentence is called *open* or *closed* depending on whether it does or does not contain a variable. Then every sentence letter is a closed atomic sentence.

STORIES

Closed atomic sentences now play the role that sentence letters played in the trees of Part One. An open path in a finished tree contains at least one atomic sentence, or the denial of an atomic sentence, as a full line. The totality of atomic sentences and denied atomic sentences that appear as full lines in an open path through a finished tree compose the *story* told by that path. Usually, this story is incomplete.

Example. The consistency of the sentence "$(x)(\exists y)xLy$" is shown by the fact that the one-path tree that it begins is open. The closed atomic sentences in this path are

$$a_1La_2, \qquad a_2La_3, \qquad a_3La_4, \qquad \dots \; .$$

This story leaves various questions open. Thus, we do not know whether the universe of discourse is to be a set of people or numbers or stars or whatever, nor do we know how many things there are in the universe of discourse, for some or all of the distinct a's might denote one and the same object. Nor, finally, do we know the truth-values of any sentences except for those of form "a_nLa_{n+1}." But a full-fledged valuation of a set of sentences must answer all such questions.

A *valuation* of a set of sentences must specify a universe of discourse if the sentences contain any names or variables. It must specify the referent of each name that appears in a sentence of the set. It must specify the truth-value of each sentence letter that appears in a sentence of the set. For each property symbol that appears in a sentence of the set, it must specify exactly which objects in the universe that symbol is true of and which it is false of: it must specify the set of things in the universe that have the property in question. And for each relation symbol of degree n, it must specify exactly which n-tuples of objects in the universe of discourse that symbol is true of and which n-tuples it is false of: it must specify the set of all n-tuples of objects in the universe of discourse that stand to one another in the relation in question.

But the stories told by open paths in finished trees are as complete as they need to be for our purposes: They are consistent, and they can be enlarged in various ways to get complete stories. In particular, we shall always be able to suppose that distinct names denote distinct things in the universe of discourse, and in seeking counterexamples to invalid inferences we have great latitude in our choice of universes of discourse. For uniformity, we can and always shall choose a set of numbers as our universe: Our stories will be dull and arithmetical. Thus, the sentence "$(x)(\exists y)xLy$" might have been obtained as a translation of the English sentence "Everyone loves," in which it is clear that the universe of discourse is to be some class of people. But in inquiring into the mere *consistency* of the sentence "$(x)(\exists y)xLy$," we must make no use of information about the meaning of "L" that we have, knowing that "L" translates "loves," nor may we use the information that the universe of discourse is a class of people which we have, knowing that "(x)" translates "everyone" instead of "everything" or "everywhere." The sentence is *consistent* if and only if there is a valuation with *some* nonempty universe of discourse in which the sentence is true.

Then let us agree to choose as our universe, for the story told by an open path in a finished tree, the set of numbers given by the subscripts on names that appear in sentences in the path; if a name of form "a_n" appears in the path, that name denotes the number n, and the number n belongs to the universe of discourse of the story told by that path. If any sentence letters appear as full lines of the path, the story assigns them the value t while it assigns the value f to any sentence letters whose denials appear as full lines of the path. Predicate symbols of degree 1 may be true of certain members of the universe and false of others. In particular, "P" is true of 5 if "Pa_5" appears as a full line of the path, and "P" is false of 5 if "$-Pa_5$" appears as a full line. In general, a predicate symbol of degree n is true of a sequence of n numbers if the atomic sentence obtained by writing the corresponding sequence of names in the respective blanks of the predicate symbol appears as a full line of the path, and the predicate symbol is false of that sequence of numbers if the denial of the atomic sentence appears as a full line of the path.

Now the story told by an open path in a finished tree is more nearly complete than it was, but it may still fall short of specifying a complete valuation of the sentences in the path, as the following example shows.

Is the sentence "$(x)(y)xTy$" a logical truth? The answer is "no" because the tree which starts with the denial of that sentence is this:

1        $\sqrt{}\ -(x)(y)xTy$
2        $\sqrt{}\ (\exists x)-(y)xTy$
3        $\sqrt{}\ -(y)a_1Ty$
4        $\sqrt{}\ (\exists y)-a_1Ty$
5            $-a_1Ta_2$

According to our conventions, this open path tells a story for which the universe of discourse consists of the two numbers 1 and 2 and in which, according to line 5, the number 1 does not bear the relation T to the number 2; "T" is false of the pair 1,2 in that order. But the story leaves open the truth-values of the sentences

$a_1Ta_1,\qquad a_2Ta_2,\qquad a_2Ta_1$

and thus leaves it open whether "T" is true of the pair 1,1 or of the pair 2,2 or of the pair 2,1.

To ensure that the story told by an open path in a finished tree completely specifies a single valuation of the sentences that appear in the path, we now stipulate:

> In the story told by an open path through a finished tree, a predicate symbol of degree n that appears in the path is true of a sequence of n numbers in the universe of discourse if the path contains, as a full line, the sentence gotten by writing the names of these numbers in the respective blanks of the predicate symbol, and otherwise, the predicate symbol is false of that sequence.

Thus, we count a predicate symbol false of a sequence unless the story explicitly says that it is true of it. Similarly, we count a sentence letter that appears in a sentence of the path true only if it makes an appearance as a full line of that path; otherwise, we count it false, even if its denial does not make an appearance as a full line in the path. In our example about the sentence "$(x)(y)xTy$," the three sentences whose truth-values were left open by the story are now regarded as false, and the relation symbol "T" is to be understood as false of all four pairs of numbers in the universe of discourse, just as it would be if "T" meant *is three times as great as*.

RULES OF VALUATION

Now the *valuation described by an open path* through a finished tree will be identified with the valuation described by the story that the path tells, as we have specified it above. But not every valuation need be of this sort; a valuation need not have a set of positive whole numbers as its universe of discourse, nor need it be the *valuation described by* some open path through some finished tree. Thus, the valuation in statement **8.3** need not be of that sort. In general, a valuation of a set of sentences is determined by specifying a universe of discourse, truth-values for sentence letters, and sets of n-tuples of which predicate symbols of degree n are true. These specifications may but need not be made via the story told by an open path in a finished tree.

Preliminaries. A valuation directly determines the truth-values of closed atomic sentences and indirectly determines the truth-values of denials, conjunctions, disjunctions, conditionals, and biconditionals, in accordance with the rules of valuation given in Part One. Thus, a disjunction is true in a valuation if at least one of its components is true in that valuation and is false in a valuation if all components are. It only remains to consider quantified sentences. For this purpose, we must be a bit more explicit than we have yet been about the rules of formation for sentences involving variables.

We have already described the open and closed atomic sentences. Every occurrence of a variable in an atomic sentence is a *free* occurrence: an occurrence unlinked to any quantifier.

The free occurrences of variables in conjunctions, disjunctions, conditionals, biconditionals, and denials are precisely the free occurrences of variables in their components, and occurrences that are linked to quantifiers in the components are linked to the same quantifiers in the full sentences.

When a quantifier "(x)" or "$(\exists x)$" is written before a sentence, all occurrences of "x" that were free in the original sentence are linked to the quantifier in the resulting sentence, while all other occurrences of "x" remain linked to whatever quantifiers they were linked to in the original sentence, and all occurrences of other variables remain linked to whatever (if anything) they were linked to in the original sentence. Of course, it is inessential that "x" is the variable we have been speaking of: the same remarks hold good with any other variable written for "x" above.

The preceding paragraph simply codifies the material on linkage in Chapter 7.

Example. To find the pattern of linkage in the sentence

$$(x)[(x)Px \rightarrow (\exists y)xRy]$$

we retrace the steps by which this sentence was built out of its atomic constituents

$$Px, \qquad xRy$$

in which all occurrences of variables are free. The first step was to quantify these to obtain linkage patterns

$$(\widehat{x)Px}, \qquad (\widehat{\exists y)xRy}.$$

The second step was to form the conditional

$$[(\widehat{x)Px} \rightarrow (\widehat{\exists y)xRy}]$$

in which the linkages are the same as those in the components. The last step was to quantify again, with the result that the occurrence of "x" that was free in the conditional is now bound to the outer quantifier:

$$(x)[(\widehat{x)Px} \rightarrow (\widehat{\exists y)xRy}]$$

The resulting sentence is *closed:* it contains no free occurrences of variables.

Evaluating Quantified Sentences. Now we can explicitly state the conditions under which quantified sentences are true and false in a valuation. Again, we use "x" as the quantified variable, but the same remarks hold good for "y" or for any other variable.

If "x" has no free occurrences in the sentence . . . , then the sentences $(x) \ldots$ and $(\exists x) \ldots$ have the same truth-value that . . . has, in any valuation.

Now suppose that "x" does have one or more free occurrences in the sentence . . . x . . . , and ask what truth-values the sentences

$$(x) \ldots x \ldots, \qquad (\exists x) \ldots x \ldots$$

are to have in a valuation with a given universe of discourse. In answering this question, we choose a new name, perhaps "a," to which the given valuation assigns no referent; we form the sentence

. . . a . . .

by writing an "a" in place of each free occurrence of "x" in

. . . x . . . ;

and we consider a number of *new* valuations that are closely related to the given valuation. In particular, for each object o in the given universe of discourse, we consider the new valuation which is identical with the given valuation except that in the new valuation, the object o has the name "a" *in addition to* whatever names it had in the old. Now we can answer the question.

The sentence $(x) \ldots x \ldots$ *is true in the given valuation if the sentence* . . . a . . . *is true in each of the new valuations; the sentence* $(x) \ldots x \ldots$ *is false in the given valuation if the sentence* . . . a . . . *is false in one or more of the new valuations.*

This is the rule of valuation for (x). Similarly, the rule of valuation for $(\exists x)$ is this:

The sentence $(\exists x) \ldots x \ldots$ *is true in the given valuation if the sentence* . . . a . . . *is true in one or more of the new valuations; the sentence* $(\exists x) \ldots x \ldots$ *is false in the given valuation if the sentence* . . . a . . . *is false in each of the new valuations.*

Why Bother? We have labored greatly and brought forth a mouse—a familiar mouse. Our rules of valuation for quantified sentences are nothing but careful formulations of two familiar facts: that universal quantification works like conjunction and that existential quantification works like disjunction. Thus, suppose that the given valuation assigns referents to the names

$$a_1, \qquad a_2, \qquad a_3, \qquad \ldots$$

and that these referents exhaust the universe of discourse. The sentence

$$\ldots a \ldots$$

makes various statements in the various new valuations; these are identical with the statements made by the sentences

$$\ldots a_1 \ldots, \qquad \ldots a_2 \ldots, \qquad \ldots a_3 \ldots, \qquad \ldots$$

in the original valuation. Then to say, as in the rule of valuation for (x), that $\ldots a \ldots$ is true in every new valuation is to say simply that the conjunction

$$\ldots a_1 \ldots \quad \& \quad \ldots a_2 \ldots \quad \& \quad \ldots a_3 \ldots \quad \& \quad \ldots$$

is true in the original valuation. And to say, as in the rule of valuation for $(\exists x)$, that $\ldots a \ldots$ is true in one or more of the new valuations is to say simply that the disjunction

$$\ldots a_1 \ldots \quad \vee \quad \ldots a_2 \ldots \quad \vee \quad \ldots a_3 \ldots \quad \vee \quad \ldots$$

is true in the original valuation.

Why, then, did we bother to formulate our rules of valuation for the quantifiers? Simply because our interpretation of $(x) \ldots x \ldots$ as a conjunction and of $(\exists x) \ldots x \ldots$ as a disjunction is only a figure of speech when the universe of discourse is infinite. Conjunctions and disjunctions, like other sentences, can only be of finite length, so that when the universe of discourse is infinite, the conjunction which we offer as having the same truth-value as the sentence $(x) \ldots x \ldots$ does not really exist, nor does the disjunction which corresponds to the sentence $(\exists x) \ldots x \ldots$. We had to give perfectly literal rules of interpretation for the quantifiers in order to be sure that our figurative explanations make sense and in order to anticipate the sorts of confusion that might arise if we took the talk of conjunctions and disjunctions too literally.

Example. Interpret "H" as "is half of" and let the universe of discourse be the set of all positive real numbers: whole numbers, fractions, and irrational numbers like π and $\sqrt{2}$. This determines a valuation of the sentence

$(x)(\exists y)xHy.$

In this valuation, "H" is true of a pair of positive real numbers if and only if the second member of the pair is twice the first, and in this valuation the given sentence is true because, indeed, every positive real number can be doubled to get another positive real number. But it would be a mistake to suppose that the corresponding infinite "conjunction" could be written out (by Zeus) with the aid of some infinite sequence of names, say

$a_1,$ $a_2,$ $a_3,$ $\ldots,$

for as Georg Cantor proved in 1874, there are too many real numbers for that to be possible (even for Zeus). No sequence $a_1, a_2, a_3, \ldots$, finite or infinite, can exhaust the positive real numbers. Then the claim that the sentence

$\ldots a \ldots$

or, here,

$(\exists y)aHy$

is true *in each new valuation* is stronger than the claim that the infinite conjunction

$(\exists y)a_1Hy$ & $(\exists y)a_2Hy$ & $(\exists y)a_3Hy$ & $\ldots$

is true *in the original valuation,* no matter what positive real numbers are assigned to the names "a_1," "a_2," "a_3," $\ldots$ as their referents. Here, to make our figurative talk come out right, we would have to consider an infinite conjunction that has as many components as there are positive real numbers. This conjunction would have so *large* an infinity of components as to make it mathematically impossible for Zeus to write it out in his usual second or, indeed, in any length of time—so large an infinity as to vitiate our usual picture of infinite conjunctions.

But our fussy, literal rules of valuation for the quantifiers make sense for every universe of discourse, and they make the same sense no matter how large the universe of discourse may be. Using them, we can now study the correctness of our rules of inference for the quantifiers (x) and $(\exists x)$.

CORRECTNESS OF THE RULES

We first consider the rule for $(\exists x)$, which can be represented schematically in the form

$$\sqrt{\ \ (\exists x) \ldots x \ldots}$$
$$\ldots m \ldots$$

Here, upward correctness means that the premise $(\exists x) \ldots x \ldots$ is true in every valuation in which the conclusion $\ldots m \ldots$ is true, and downward correctness means that the conclusion is true in every valuation in which the premise is true. If the path under consideration already contains one or more sentences of form $\ldots n \ldots$ (where n is some name or other) as we are about to apply the rule, then we simply check the premise without adding a new sentence to the path. Here the rule for $(\exists x)$ is vacuous: there is no conclusion. Otherwise, we choose a name m that is new to the path and write the conclusion $\ldots m \ldots$ at the bottom.

The Rule for $(\exists x)$. The rule is upward correct. Intuitively, if $\ldots m \ldots$ is true in a valuation, then the universe of discourse for that valuation indeed contains an object x such that $\ldots x \ldots$ is true, namely, the object which m denotes. In terms of our rule of valuation for $(\exists x)$, the same matter can be put as follows. Suppose that $\ldots m \ldots$ is true in a valuation. Then in the universe of discourse for that valuation there is an object o which the name m denotes. Consequently $\ldots a \ldots$ will be true in the new valuation in which o is assigned to "a" as its referent. Since $\ldots a \ldots$ is true in at least one of the new valuations, $(\exists x) \ldots x \ldots$ is true in the original valuation.

But the rule for $(\exists x)$ is not downward correct; there may be valuations in which $(\exists x) \ldots x \ldots$ is true but $\ldots m \ldots$ is false.

EXAMPLE

The following tree shows that the sentence "$(\exists x)Px$" is consistent. (Here ... x ... is "Px" and m is "a_1.")

$$
\begin{array}{ll}
1 & \sqrt{}\ (\exists x)Px \\
2 & Pa_1
\end{array}
$$

In the valuation *described by this path,* premise and conclusion are both true, but there are other valuations in which the premise is true but the conclusion is false. One such valuation has a universe of discourse consisting of the numbers 1 and 2, assigns the number 1 to "a_1" as its referent, and stipulates that "P" is true of 2 but false of 1. In this valuation, line 2 is false but line 1 is true, for in the new valuation in which the referent of "a" is the number 2, "Pa" is true.

However, the rule for ($\exists x$) is close to being downward correct—close enough for our purpose, which is to prove statement 8.3:

> *If there is a valuation in which all initial sentences are true, then there is a valuation in which all full sentences in some path through the finished tree are true.*

(The assumption of downward correctness does not enter into the proof of 8.2.) For purposes of proving 8.3 it is sufficient that the rule for ($\exists x$) have the following sort of limited downward correctness.

LIMITED DOWNWARD CORRECTNESS

If there is a valuation in which the premise is true, then the conclusion (if any) is true either in that valuation or in a nominal variant of it.

A *nominal variant* of a valuation is a valuation that differs from it only in regard to the referents of one or more names. Valuations that are nominal variants of each other must have the same universe of discourse, must assign the same truth-values to all sentence letters, and must classify predicate symbols of degree n as true of exactly the same n-tuples; but a *name* that has a certain referent in one of the valuations may have a different referent in the other or may even be assigned no referent in the other. Thus, the "new" valuations that were mentioned in the rules of valuation for the quantifiers are nominal variants of the original valuation, which assigned no referent at all to a name, say "a," to which each "new" valuation assigns one or another referent in the universe of discourse. Similarly, the valuation that is described by the single path in our two-line tree for "$(\exists x)Px$" above is a nominal variant of the valuation that made line 1 true but made line 2 false.

It should be clear that the rule of inference for $(\exists x)$ *is* downward correct in this limited sense; the whole point of our insistence that the name m in the conclusion be new to the path was to guarantee this limited downward correctness of the rule. Since the name m is new to the path, its referent can be changed without disturbing the truth-values that the original valuation assigned to the sentences higher in the path, one of which is the premise $(\exists x) \ldots x \ldots$. If a valuation makes this premise true, there must be an object o in the universe of discourse which, assigned to m as its referent, makes $\ldots m \ldots$ true. If the original valuation does not assign o to m as its referent, some nominal variant of it does, a variant which need differ from the original only in regard to the referent of the new name m. Then the premise is true in the variant as it was in the original, and the conclusion is true in the variant as it need not have been in the original.

The Rule for (x). In discussing the correctness of the rule for (x), we must first make clear what sentences count as conclusions.

The list of conclusions of a premise of form $(x) \ldots x \ldots$ in a path through a finished tree consists of all sentences of form $\ldots n \ldots$ that occur as full lines in that path, where n is any name.

This list of conclusions may well be scattered through the path, for we do not check a sentence after applying the rule for (x) to it; only after the path is closed or the tree is finished can we be sure that no new names will appear in the path. And a sentence of form $\ldots n \ldots$ in a path is counted among the conclusions of a sentence of form $(x) \ldots x \ldots$ in the path whether or not the former was added to the path as a result of applying the rule for (x) to the latter.

EXAMPLE

The invalidity of the inference

$$\frac{(x)(\exists y)xRy}{-(\exists y)a_1Ry}$$

is shown by the fact that the following tree never closes.

1	$(x)(\exists y)xRy$	[premise]
2	$\checkmark$ $(\exists y)a_1Ry$	[$-$conclusion by $-$]
3	a_1Ra_2	[2 by $(\exists y)$]
4	$\checkmark$ $(\exists y)a_2Ry$	[1 by (x)]
5	a_2Ra_3	[4 by $(\exists y)$]
6	$(\exists y)a_3Ry$	[1 by (x)]

$$\vdots$$

Here the list of conclusions of line 1 includes line 2 as well as the other even-numbered lines, in spite of the fact that line 2 did not come from line 1 by an application of the rule for (x).

The rule for (x) comes within an ace of being downward correct:

If $(x)\ldots x \ldots$ is true in a valuation and n is any name, then $\ldots n \ldots$ is not false *in that valuation.*

In fact, if $(x)\ldots x \ldots$ is true in a valuation and the name n is assigned a referent by that valuation, the sentence $\ldots n \ldots$ is also true in the valuation. Then the rule for (x) is downward correct in at least the limited sense in which the rule for $(\exists x)$ is, and this limited downward correctness will be enough to see us through the proof of **8.3**.

It is in an even more limited sense that the rule for (x) is upward correct.

LIMITED UPWARD CORRECTNESS

If all conclusions of a premise which appear as full lines in an open path through a finished tree are true in the valuation *which that path describes,* so is the premise.

This strongly limited sort of upward correctness will see us through the proof of **8.2**:

Each open path through a finished tree describes a valuation in which all full sentences in that path are true.

It is clear that the rule for (x) does have this sort of upward correctness, for in the valuation described by an open path in which "a_1," "a_2," ... are all the names to appear, a sentence $(x) \ldots x \ldots$ which appears as a full line of the path must have the same truth-value (viz., *truth*) as the conjunction

$$\ldots a_1 \ldots \& \ldots a_2 \ldots \& \, \ldots$$

of all its conclusions in the path.

PROOF OF 8.2

At last we can proceed to the proof of **8.1** via **8.2** and **8.3**.

To prove **8.2**, we deduce a contradiction from its denial: from the assumption that

in some finished tree there is an open path which describes a valuation in which at least one full sentence in the path is *not* true.

From this assumption we deduce the conclusion that

among the full sentences in the path which are not true in the valuation that the path describes is an atomic sentence or the denial of one.

But this conclusion is impossible by definition of "the valuation described by an open path in a finished tree." Then when we have deduced the conclusion, we shall have refuted the assumption and thus proved **8.2**.

The deduction turns on the fact that all our rules of inference have at least limited upward correctness: If a list of conclusions is true in the valuation described by the path that contains it, so is the premise. A logically equivalent version of this statement is

If a premise is false in the valuation described by a path, so is at least one of its conclusions that appear as full lines in that path.

According to our assumption, some full sentence in the path is not true (and is therefore false) in the valuation which that path describes. Now either this given falsehood was used as the premise of some rule of inference in constructing the path, or it was not. If not, it must already be atomic or the denial of an atomic sentence, and we have our conclusion. Otherwise, this falsehood is the premise of a false conclusion in the path. Now reapply the same reasoning to this further falsehood. If it is atomic or the denial of an atomic sentence, there is nothing to prove. If not, it is in turn the premise of a further false conclusion in the path to which the same reasoning can again be applied. In this way we must eventually reach a falsehood that appears as a full line of the path and is either atomic or the denial of an atomic sentence. Why? Because a conclusion is always shorter than its premise: ... n ... is shorter than $(x) \ldots x \ldots$ and shorter than $(\exists x) \ldots x \ldots$; each of $-\bigcirc$, $\triangle$ is shorter than $\bigcirc \rightarrow \triangle$; each of $\bigcirc$, $-\triangle$ is shorter than $-(\bigcirc \rightarrow \triangle)$; and so on, through the other rules of inference. Since the falsehood which was assumed to occur in the path is of finite length, there must be some *finite* number of steps from false premises to false conclusions that will take us to a conclusion which is an atomic sentence or the denial of one.

This completes the proof of **8.2**.

PROOF OF 8.3

We now prove **8.3** by proving something a bit stronger:

If a valuation makes all initial sentences true, then either that valuation or one of its nominal variants makes all full sentences in some path through the finished tree true.

We proceed somewhat as in the proof of the tree theorem: We specify a step-by-step procedure that Zeus could follow in order to trace out a certain path through the finished tree and to construct a certain valuation, and we prove that the procedure is such that all full sentences in the path are true in the valuation. Zeus thinks of the tree as formed of boxed lists, each of which is either the list of initial sentences (in the box that heads the tree) or a list of conclusions of a premise that appears in a higher box; but when the premise is of form $(x) \ldots x \ldots$, we assign each conclusion ... n ... its own box.

At stage 1, Zeus traces the path down to the bottom of the list of initial sentences. All these sentences are true in the given valuation, which *may* assign referents to one or more names that do not appear in the initial sentences. If so, Zeus replaces the given valuation by the nominal variant in which the extraneous names are not assigned referents; if not, he keeps the given valuation.

At stage 2, Zeus surveys the immediate descendants (if any) of the top box. If there are none, his job is finished, for the initial sentences constitute a path (*the* path) through the finished tree in which all full sentences are true in the valuation he chose at stage 1. But if the top box has one or more boxed lists as immediate descendants, at least one of these lists must be true either in the valuation of stage 1 or in a nominal variant obtained by assigning a referent to a name that had no referent in the valuation of stage 1. Why? Because a list that is an immediate descendant of the top list must have been added to the tree when one of the rules of inference was applied to some sentence in the top list. If the rule in question was one of those for the connectives, downward correctness assures us that at least one of the lists which are immediate descendants of the top box is true in the valuation of stage 1. In that case, Zeus keeps the valuation of stage 1 and extends the path by adding to it one of the boxed descendants of the top list that are true in that valuation—say, the leftmost one. If the rule in question was one of those for the quantifiers and was not vacuous, the top list has only one immediate descendant: a box containing a single sentence of form . . . n . . . where n is some name. In this case, Zeus adds the sentence to the path and addresses himself to the question of whether he shall retain the valuation of stage 1 or replace it by a nominal variant. The answer depends on whether the name n is new to the path, as it *must* be if the rule in question was the one for $(\exists x)$, and as it *may* be if the rule was the one for (x). If the name is not new, he keeps the valuation of stage 1; if it *is* new, he replaces that valuation by a nominal variant in which the name n is assigned a referent that makes . . . n . . . true but which otherwise agrees with the valuation of stage 1. There is sure to be such a referent for n since the premise (x) . . . x . . . or $(\exists x)$ . . . x . . . is true in the valuation of stage 1.

Now the procedure that Zeus followed at stage 2 is typical of the general case. Having completed stage n (where n is 1 or 2 or 3 or . . .), Zeus has traced out a certain initial segment of a path and has in mind a valuation in which all full sentences in that segment are true. His next step is to see whether the boxed list he added at stage n has any immediate descendants. If not, his work is done: he has traced out a complete path and has in mind a valuation—the given valuation or a nominal variant of it—in which all full sentences in that path are true. But if the nth box has one or more immediate descendants, he knows he can take one more step in the procedure, for the immediate descendants of the nth box must have been added to the tree as a result of applying one of the rules of inference to a sentence in one of the first n boxes. The fact that all rules of inference are downward correct in at least the limited sense assures him that either in the valuation of stage n or in a nominal variant of it, one or more of the descendants of the nth box will be a true list. If any of the lists that descend immediately from the nth box are true in the valuation of stage n, he retains that valuation at stage $n + 1$ and adds the leftmost of the lists that are true in it to the path as the $n + 1$st list in it. Otherwise, he has no choice: The nth box must have exactly one immediate descendant, of form $\ldots n \ldots$, where n is a name that has no referent in the valuation of stage n. In this case he adds the sentence $\ldots n \ldots$ to the path as the $n + 1$st list in it and adopts at stage $n + 1$ a variant obtained by assigning to the name n a referent that makes $\ldots n \ldots$ true but which otherwise agrees with the valuation of stage n.

CONCLUSION

Having proved **8.2** and **8.3**, we have established statement **8.1** that

There is an open path through a finished tree if and only if some valuation makes all initial sentences true.

It follows from this and the tree theorem that the tree method is adequate for the purpose of testing inferences for validity in the sense that (referring to Figure 6.1):

8.4   *An inference is valid if and only if we answer "yes" at stage 2 of the flow graph after some finite number of steps.*

It also follows that the tree method is adequate for the purpose of testing individual sentences or sets of sentences for consistency and for the purpose of determining whether individual sentences are logical truths.

EXERCISES

8.1 Deduce statement **8.4** from statements **8.2** and **8.3** and the tree theorem.

8.2 When new names are required, choose them in order from the list "a_1," "a_2," .... What valuations are described by the open paths in the trees which show the consistency of each of the following sentences?

    a $(x)(y)xLy$ **b** $(\exists x)(\exists y)xLy$

    c $(x)(\exists y)xLy$ **d** $(\exists x)(y)xLy$

8.3 A sentence is said to be in *Skolem normal form* if and only if it is in prenex normal form (see Exercise 7.21) and all existential quantifiers (if any) are to the left of all universal quantifiers (if any). Explain why it is impossible to get an infinite tree in testing the consistency of a finite set of sentences, all of which are in Skolem normal form.

IDENTITY. FUNCTIONS

The sign "$=$" for *is identical with* is a relation symbol like the sign "L" for *loves* or the sign "T" for *can trap;* in all three cases, we form sentences by writing the sign between two names or between two occurrences of a single name. But although the relations T and L can hold only in rather special universes of discourse, the identity relation can hold in every universe, and although there are rather few interesting general truths about the relations T and L that we can formulate precisely, the identity relation has various important characteristics that are readily stated, such as the following three:

9.1	$(x)\ x = x$	*(Reflexivity)*
9.2	$(x)(y)(x = y \rightarrow y = x)$	*(Symmetry)*
9.3	$(x)(y)(z)[(x = y\ \&\ y = z) \rightarrow x = z]$	*(Transitivity)*

EXISTENCE

The relations "loves" and "can trap" have special subject matters: They make sense only as applied to such objects as men. But the identity relation has no special subject matter: We can write "$4 = 2 + 2$" to indicate that the expressions on the two sides of the sign of identity name the same number, and equally well, we can write "Venus = Aphrodite" to indicate that Venus and Aphrodite are one and the same goddess. In general, "$a = b$" means that a and b are one, not two: a and b are one and the same thing, no matter what kind of thing. The sentence formed by writing the sign "$=$" between two expressions is true (false) if those expressions do (do not) name the same thing, no matter whether that thing is a number, a man, or a god.

Warning: There is a difficulty about gods if there are none, just as there is a difficulty about the fictitious Holmes and his fictitious antagonist, Professor Moriarty, for the inference from **9.1** to "$(\exists x)\, x = a$" is a valid one, as the following tree testifies:

$$(x)\ x = x$$
$$-(\exists x)\ x = a$$
$$(x){-}x = a$$
$$a = a$$
$$-a = a$$

Then since the premise **9.1** is true, so is the conclusion "$(\exists x)\, x = a$." But if a is Holmes, the sentence "$(\exists x)\, x = a$" ("For some x, x is Holmes") falsely claims that Holmes exists. And the case is similar for Moriarty, Venus, and the rest of the fictional and mythical lot. In our system of logic, *to have a name for something is to commit ourselves to its existence.* Nor is this a peculiarity of our system of logic alone. In the English language, too, having a name for something seems tantamount to having a name for some *thing:* for some existent.

DEFINITE DESCRIPTIONS

In various examples we have spoken of Holmes, Crumm, and the rest—for the fun of it. Taken with obvious grains of salt, such talk serves well enough to illustrate the sober uses of logic where names have referents. But in literal talk, too, there may be doubt about the existence of one of the putative entities that are under discussion. Before 1930, someone might have speculated about the existence of a planet more remote than Neptune and provisionally assigned it the name "Pluto." The sentence "Pluto is less massive than the Earth" was not then known to be true or, indeed, to be a suitable vehicle for statement making. The sentence makes reference to the one and only planet (if such there be) that is more remote than Neptune. Assuming that there *is* exactly one such thing, we want to be understood as saying that it is less massive than the Earth, and if there is not, we are prepared to admit that the presupposition was false, on the basis of which we proposed to use the word "Pluto." Then the needs of communication can be met by saying

9.4   *There is exactly one planet more remote than Neptune, and that planet is less massive than the Earth*

instead of the shorter but trickier

9.5   *Pluto is less massive than the Earth.*

Sentence **9.5** is tricky in that it conceals a possibly false assumption, an assumption that is made quite explicit in **9.4**. Since it makes no use of the questionable name "Pluto," **9.4** must be more explicit than **9.5**; it must explicitly state the assumption which is masked in **9.5** by use of the name "Pluto." Then if "*a*" names Pluto, if "*Mx*" means that x is less massive than the Earth, and if "*Px*" means that x is a planet more remote than Neptune, **9.5** becomes

9.5'   *Ma*

and the more explicit sentence **9.4** has to be written more elaborately, say as

9.4' $(\exists x)[Px \ \& \ (y)(Py \rightarrow y = x) \ \& \ Mx]$

where "*a*" does not occur. It is the first two clauses in the brackets of **9.4'** that express the presupposition of **9.5**, that there is one and only one planet more remote than Neptune: "*Px*" says that there is at least one, x, and "$(y)(Py \rightarrow y = x)$" says that any other, say y, is in fact x itself (perhaps by another name). Finally, "*Mx*" says that this unique x is less massive than the Earth, and it says this only after the assumptions about x that are implicit in calling it "Pluto" have been made explicit.

NUMBER

One of the characteristic uses of the sign of identity is to say how many things there are that meet a certain description. Of course, we can say that there are no things at all that have the property P, without using the sign "=":

9.6   There are 0 P's: $-(\exists x)Px$

But to say that there is exactly one thing with the property P we must use the sign "=" somewhat as we did in **9.4'**:

9.7   There is exactly 1 P: $(\exists x)[Px \& (y)(Py \rightarrow y = x)]$

In **9.7**, we say that there is *exactly* 1 P by saying that there is *at least* 1—$(\exists x)[Px \ldots]$—and then adding that there is *at most* 1: $(\exists x)[\ldots \& (y)(Py \rightarrow y = x)]$. Similarly, we can say that there are at least 2 P's:

9.8 $(\exists x)(\exists y)(Px \& Py \& x \neq y).$

Here, "$x \neq y$" is shorthand for the denial of "$x = y$"; we write the dash of denial through the sign "=" instead of in its usual position "$-x = y$." It is essential that we specify that x and y are distinct, for distinct variables need not represent distinct objects. Thus, as we can easily verify by the tree method, "$(\exists x)(\exists y)(Px \& Py)$" is logically equivalent to (and is thus merely an elaborate way of saying) "$(\exists x)Px$." Similarly we can say that there are *at most* 2 P's:

9.9 $(x)(y)(z)[(Px \& Py \& Pz) \rightarrow (x = y \vee y = z \vee x = z)]$

This says that if x, y, and z are P's, they are not all distinct: Some pair of them and perhaps all three of them are identical. Then we know how to say that there are exactly two things with the property P:

9.10   There are exactly 2 P's:
$(\exists x)(\exists y)[Px \& Py \& x \neq y \& (z)(Pz \rightarrow (z = x \vee z = y))]$

Alternatively, we could have said that there are exactly 2 P's by asserting the conjunction of **9.8** and **9.9**, but statement **9.10** is logically equivalent to that conjunction and is neater.

INFERENCE RULES FOR IDENTITY

To prove the equivalence of **9.10** with the conjunction of **9.8** and **9.9** by the tree method, we need two more rules of inference. In effect, these rules will assert the general truths **9.1**, **9.2**, and **9.3**, as well as all other needful general truths about identity. Once these rules are adopted, **9.1**, **9.2**, **9.3**, and the rest will be provable by the tree method as logical truths; thus, the tree that starts with the denial of **9.1** will close when the first of the new rules is applied in conjunction with our old rule about the universal quantifier.

With only the old rules, we can get this far in the tree that starts with the denial of "$(x)\ x = x$":

$$\sqrt{}\ \ -(x)\ x = x$$
$$\sqrt{}\ \ (\exists x)\ x \neq x$$
$$a \neq a$$

But now we are stuck: None of the old rules apply to the single unchecked sentence, and the path is open since it fails to contain any sentence together with its denial. Obviously, the needed rule is as follows. (This rule is to be counted as one of the rules for denial mentioned at stage 2 of Figure 6.1.)

RULE FOR $\neq$

Close any path that contains a sentence of form $n \neq n$ where n is any name.

We are now entitled to write "$\times$" at the bottom of the path, thus closing the tree and indicating that the sentence "$(x)\ x = x$" is a logical truth.

To see what the other new rule must be, let us see how far we can get, using only the rules we have so far, in the tree which is to show that **9.2** is a logical truth:

1      $\sqrt{} \ -(x)(y)(x = y \rightarrow y = x)$
2      $\sqrt{} \ (\exists x) - (y)(x = y \rightarrow y = x)$
3      $\sqrt{} \ -(y)(a = y \rightarrow y = a)$
4      $\sqrt{} \ (\exists y) - (a = y \rightarrow y = a)$
5      $\sqrt{} \ -(a = b \rightarrow b = a)$
6                    $a = b$
7                    $b \neq a$

This tree is open, and none of our present rules can be applied to either of the unchecked sentences. Clearly, what we need is a rule that allows us to substitute equals for equals.

RULE FOR =

If an open path contains a sentence of form $m = n$ or $n = m$ and also a sentence of form $\ldots m \ldots$, write at the bottom of the path a sentence obtained from $\ldots m \ldots$ by replacing one of the m's by an n, unless that sentence already appears in the path.

Now we can close the tree: View line 7 as a sentence of form $\ldots a \ldots$ and, because of the presence of line 6, write a new line which is obtained by replacing the "a" in $\ldots a \ldots$ by "b":

8                    $b \neq b$

Now the rule for $\neq$ instructs us to close the tree, showing that **9.2** is a logical truth.

A further illustration of the use of the rule for $=$ is provided by the tree that shows **9.3** to be a logical truth. We condense some steps:

1      $-(x)(y)(z)[(x = y \ \& \ y = z) \rightarrow x = z]$ $[-9.3]$
2      $(\exists x)(\exists y)(\exists z) - [(x = y \ \& \ y = z) \rightarrow x = z)]$ [three steps, via $-]$
3      $-[(a = b \ \& \ b = c) \rightarrow a = c]$ [three steps, via $(\exists \ )$]
4                    $a = b$ [two steps:
5                    $b = c$ $-(\bigcirc \rightarrow \triangle)$
6                    $a \neq c$ and $\bigcirc \ \& \ \triangle]$
7                    $a = c$ [4: "a" for "b" in 5]
                       $\times$

To get line 7, we view line 5 as a sentence of form ... b ... and apply the rule for $=$, which, in virtue of line 4, allows us to replace "b" by "a" in ... b ... and write the result as a new line. Alternatively, we could have written "b" for "a" in 6 (because of 4) or "b" for "c" in 6 (because of 5) to get "$b \neq c$" or "$a \neq b$" as the seventh, closing line.

In practice, we are free to replace sentences by their logical equivalents, say "$a = b$" by "$b = a$." We are free to write at the bottom of any open path any logical consequence of sentences in that path; thus we may write "$a = c$" at the bottom of a path that contains both "$a = b$" and "$b = c$." And where a sentence of form $m = n$ appears in an open path along with any sentence containing m's or n's, we are free to write at the bottom any sentence obtainable from the latter by writing m's for n's and/or n's for m's. But it is of interest that the same results can be had, perhaps more laboriously, by routine applications of our rules for denial, identity, connectives, and quantifiers. When in doubt about the legitimacy of a shortcut, we can always return to the rules, taking a larger number of shorter, surer steps to the same destination.

For definiteness, we might enlarge Figure 6.1 by inserting the material shown in Figure 9.1 here in place of the arrow labeled "No" from stage 2 to stage 3. This amounts to a decision to apply the rule for $=$ as often as possible, immediately after applying the rules for denial and before applying the rules for the other connectives. The rule for $=$ could just as well have been inserted at various other points in the flow graph, and in practice, there is no need to apply the rules in the same order for all problems. If a tree closes, the corresponding inference has been shown to be valid, regardless of the order in which the rules were applied. It is only when a tree *fails* to close that we must be wary of the order of application of the rules of inference. In such a case we must ask whether the order of application is such that if the tree *can* close, it *will*.

Figure 9.1

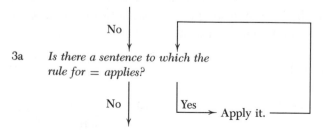

Examples. a   The validity of the inference

$$\frac{(x)(\exists y)xLy}{(\exists y)aLy}$$

is shown by the fact that the following tree closes:

1    $(x)(\exists y)xLy$ [premise]
2    $(y)-aLy$ [— conclusion by —]
3    $\sqrt{}\ (\exists y)aLy$ [1 by (x)]
4   aLb [3 by $(\exists y)$]
5        $-aLb$ [2 by (y)]
        $\times$

If we had taken our order of application from Figure 6.1, we would have obtained a larger closed tree, as shown at the left below. But if we had simply alternated applications of the rules for (x) and for $(\exists y)$ we would have generated the infinite tree at the right below.

1    $(x)(\exists y)xLy$ [premise] $(x)(\exists y)xLy$ [premise]
2    $(y)-aLy$ [— conclusion by —] $(y)-aLy$ [— conclusion by —]
3    $\sqrt{}\ (\exists y)aLy$ [1 by (x)] $\sqrt{}\ (\exists y)aLy$ [1 by (x)]
4        $-aLa$ [2 by (y)] aLb [3 by $(\exists y)$]
5   aLb [3 by $(\exists y)$] $\sqrt{}\ (\exists y)bLy$ [1 by (x)]
6        $(\exists y)bLy$ [1 by (x)] cLb [5 by $(\exists y)$]
7        $-aLb$ [2 by (y)] $(\exists y)cLy$ [1 by (x)]
        $\times$ $\vdots$

The trouble with the tree at the right above is that in it, we never get around to applying the rule for (y) to line 1 and thus closing the tree.

   Further examples, in which order of application of the rules is of no great moment, may be obtained by testing the following five inferences for validity. In **e** and **f** on the next page, **9.11** is the sentence

9.11 $(\exists x)(y)(Py \leftrightarrow y = x)$

Since inferences **e** and **f** are both valid, **9.11** is formally equivalent to statement **9.7** and is thus another way of saying that there is exactly one P.

b $\dfrac{a = b}{Pa \leftrightarrow Pb}$ **c** $\dfrac{Pa \leftrightarrow Pb}{a = b}$ **d** $\dfrac{(\exists x)Px \quad\quad\quad\quad\quad\quad\quad}{\begin{array}{c}(x)(y)[(Px \,\&\, Py) \to x = y]\\ (\exists x)[Px \,\&\, (y)(Py \to x = y)]\end{array}}$

e $\dfrac{9.7}{9.11}$ **f** $\dfrac{9.11}{9.7}$

Solutions. Inferences **b** and **d** are valid; **c** is not.

b
$$a = b$$
$$-(Pa \leftrightarrow Pb)$$
$$\sqrt{} \;\; -(Pa \leftrightarrow Pa)$$

```
        -(Pa ↔ Pa)
         /      \
      -Pa        Pa
      Pa        -Pa
       ×         ×
```

c
$$\sqrt{} \;\; Pa \leftrightarrow Pb$$
$$a \neq b$$

```
       /    \
     Pa     -Pa
     Pb     -Pb
```

d
$$\sqrt{} \;\; (\exists x)Px$$
$$(x)(y)[(Px \,\&\, Py) \to x = y]$$
$$\sqrt{} \;\; -(\exists x)[Px \,\&\, (y)(Py \to x = y)]$$
$$(x)-[Px \,\&\, (y)(Py \to x = y)]$$
$$Pa$$
$$\sqrt{} \;\; -[Pa \,\&\, (y)(Py \to a = y)]$$

```
        /                \
     -Pa        √ (∃y)-(Py → a = y)
      ×         √ -(Pb → a = b)
                      Pb
                     a ≠ b
                √ (Pa & Pb) → a = b
                   /        \
         -(Pa & Pb)        a = b
           /    \            ×
        -Pa     -Pb
         ×       ×
```

e $\quad\sqrt{\ }(\exists x)[Px \mathbin{\&} (y)(Py \to y = x)]$
$\quad\quad\sqrt{\ }\sqrt{\ }-(\exists x)(y)(Py \leftrightarrow y = x)$
$\quad\quad(x)(\exists y)-(Py \leftrightarrow y = x)$
$\quad\quad\quad\quad Pa \mathbin{\&}$
$\quad\quad\quad(y)(Py \to y = a)$
$\quad\quad\sqrt{\ }(\exists y)-(Py \leftrightarrow y = a)$
$\quad\quad\quad\sqrt{\ }-(Pb \leftrightarrow b = a)$

$\quad\quad Pb \qquad\qquad\qquad -Pb$
$\quad\quad b \neq a \qquad\qquad\quad b = a$
$\quad\sqrt{\ }Pb \to b = a \quad -Pa \text{ [by rule for } =]$
$\qquad\qquad\qquad\qquad\quad \times$
$-Pb \qquad b = a$
$\times \qquad\quad \times$

f $\quad\sqrt{\ }(\exists x)(y)(Py \leftrightarrow y = x)$
$\quad\sqrt{\ }-(\exists x)[Px \mathbin{\&} (y)(Py \to y = x)]$
$\quad(x)-[Px \mathbin{\&} (y)(Py \to y = x)]$
$\quad\quad(y)(Py \leftrightarrow y = a)$
$\quad\sqrt{\ }-[Pa \mathbin{\&} (y)(Py \to y = a)]$

$\quad\quad -Pa \qquad \sqrt{\ }(\exists y)-(Py \to y = a)$
$\quad\sqrt{\ }Pa \leftrightarrow a = a \quad \sqrt{\ }-(Pb \to b = a)$

$\quad Pa \qquad -Pa \qquad\qquad Pb$
$\quad a = a \quad\ a \neq a \qquad\quad b \neq a$
$\qquad \times \qquad \times$

$\qquad\qquad\qquad \sqrt{\ }Pb \leftrightarrow b = a$

$\qquad\qquad\qquad Pb \qquad -Pb$
$\qquad\qquad\quad b = a \qquad b \neq a$
$\qquad\qquad\quad \times \qquad\quad \times$

FUNCTIONS

Adam begat Seth; Seth begat Enos; Enos begat Cainan. Writing "F" for "was the father of" and "a," "b," "c," and "d" for "Adam," "Seth," "Enos," and "Cainan," we can convey the foregoing information as follows:

$$aFb, \qquad bFc, \qquad cFd$$

On the other hand, we might construe "was" as "$=$" and introduce the *function symbol* "f" for "the father of," so as to write the same information as follows:

9.12 $a = f(b), \qquad b = f(c), \qquad c = f(d)$

These three sentences say that

$a =$ the father of b, $b =$ the father of c, $c =$ the father of d

When a function symbol is applied to a name, the result may be treated as a name. And the process of forming names in this way can be reiterated; thus, substituting equals for equals in **9.12**, we get

$a = f(f(c)), \qquad\qquad\qquad\qquad a = f(f(f(d))).$

These sentences say that

$a =$ the father of the father of c, $a =$ the father of the father of
the father of d

or, equivalently, that

$a =$ the paternal grandfather of c, $a =$ the paternal great grandfather of d

If the function symbol "f" is to produce a name whenever it is applied to a name, the function must be defined in such a way that there is always exactly one object $f(x)$ corresponding to each object x. Then according to Genesis, *the (biological) father of* will not do as an interpretation of the function symbol "f," for if x is Adam (or Eve), there is no such object as $f(x)$. We might remedy this defect by arbitrarily assigning values to the function f corresponding to these two arguments. Thus, we might define f as follows:

9.13 $f(x) = \begin{cases} \text{the father of } x, \text{ if } x \text{ has a father} \\ x, \text{ if } x \text{ has no father} \end{cases}$

Then since Adam had no father, we have

$$a = f(a), \qquad a = f(f(a)), \qquad \ldots$$

(These sentences do *not* mean that Adam was his own father, his own paternal grandfather, etc., for according to **9.13**, "*f*" does not simply mean *the father of*.) Similarly, *the teacher of* is not an allowable interpretation of the function symbol "*f*," for some have no teacher, and some have more than one.

Our general requirement about the interpretation of any function symbol, say "*f*," can be put as follows:

9.14 $(x)(\exists y)(z)(f(x) = z \leftrightarrow z = y)$

This says that for each x there is one and only one object y such that $f(x) = y$. We might think of using **9.14** as an additional premise in any inference in which the function symbol "*f*" occurs in a premise or in the conclusion. But this is not necessary, for if we take the line that a name always results when a function symbol is applied to a name, *the tree method classifies **9.14** as a logical truth:*

1	$\sqrt{}\sqrt{}\sqrt{}\ -(x)(\exists y)(z)(fx = z \leftrightarrow z = y)$	[$-$**9.14**, abbreviating "$f(x)$" by "fx"]
2	$\sqrt{}\ (\exists x)(y)(\exists z)-(fx = z \leftrightarrow z = y)$	[1 by three uses of rule for $-$]
3	$(y)(\exists z)-(fa = z \leftrightarrow z = y)$	[2 by rule for $(\exists x)$]
4	$\sqrt{}\ (\exists z)-(fa = z \leftrightarrow z = fa)$	[3 by rule for (y) with "fa" as name]
5	$\sqrt{}\ -(fa = b \leftrightarrow b = fa)$	[4 by rule for $(\exists z)$; "b" as *new* name]
6	$fa \neq b \qquad\qquad fa = b$	[by rule
7	$b = fa \qquad\qquad b \neq fa$	for $-(\bigcirc \leftrightarrow \triangle)$]
8	$fa \neq fa \qquad\qquad b \neq b$	[6 and 7 by rule for $=$,
	$\times \qquad\qquad\quad \times$	viewing "fa" as a name]

As the proof of **9.14** shows, only a very minor adjustment is needed in our rules to allow us to reason in terms of functions:

Construe function symbols as always yielding names when applied to names, but where a *new* name is called for in the rule for ($\exists$), use a new *single letter*.

Examples. The following inferences yield further examples of this final extension of the tree method. (The "inferences" **j** and **k** are, of course, assertions that the sentences under the bars are logical truths.)

g	$fa = b$	**h**	$a = b$	**i**	$fa = fb$		
	$fb = c$		$\overline{fa = fb}$		$\overline{a = b}$		
	$\overline{ffa = c}$						

i (under) *invalid*

j $\overline{(\exists x)fa = x}$ **k** $\overline{(x)(y)[(fa = x \,\&\, fa = y) \to x = y]}$

Solutions

g	1	$fa = b$	[premise]	**h**	$a = b$
	2	$fb = c$	[premise]		$fa \neq fb$
	3	$ffa \neq c$	[−conclusion]		$fa \neq fa$
	4	$ffa \neq fb$	[2 and 3 by =]		×
	5	$ffa \neq ffa$	[1 and 4 by =]		
		×			

i $fa = fb$ **j** $\sqrt{} -(\exists x)fa = x$
    $a \neq b$ $(x)fa \neq x$
    open; no rules apply $fa \neq fa$ [2 by rule for (x); "fa" as name]
                                              ×

k   1 $\sqrt{}\sqrt{} -(x)(y)[(fa = x \,\&\, fa = y) \to x = y]$
      2      $\sqrt{}\sqrt{} (\exists x)(\exists y) -[(fa = x \,\&\, fa = y) \to x = y]$
      3            $\sqrt{}\sqrt{} -[(fa = b \,\&\, fa = c) \to b = c]$ [2 by $(\exists x)$ and $(\exists y)$;
                                                                      "b" and "c" *new*
                                                                      names]

      4                  $fa = b \,\&$ [3 by $-(\bigcirc \to \triangle)$
      5                  $fa = c$ and
      6                  $b \neq c$ $\bigcirc \,\&\, \triangle$]
      7                  $b = c$ [4 and 5 by =]
                            ×

MATHEMATICAL REASONING; GROUPS

Functions of two or more arguments are treated similarly. Thus, we might define a function g such that $g(x,y)$ is the first offspring of x and y if x and y have offspring. To ensure that $g(x,y)$ exists for *all* persons x, y, we stipulate that if x and y have no offspring, $g(x,y)$ is to be x:

9.15 $g(x,y) = \begin{cases} \text{the first offspring of } x \text{ and } y \text{, if any} \\ x \text{, if } x \text{ and } y \text{ have no offspring} \end{cases}$

Then if a, b, and c are Adam, Eve, and Cain, we have

$$g(a,b) = c, \qquad g(b,a) = c$$

but

$$g(a,c) = a, \qquad g(c,a) = c, \qquad g(a,a) = a$$

where the last statement is true if "offspring" is interpreted in the usual biological sense, and does *not* mean that Adam was his own offspring. (In general, according to **9.15**, "$g(x,y) = x$" means that x and y have no offspring.)

Functions are much used in mathematical reasoning, although in the case of functions of two arguments, it is common to write the function symbol *between* the arguments: "$(x + y)$" instead of "$+(x,y)$" and "$(x + (y + z))$" instead of "$+(x, +(y,z))$." Sometimes, too, the function symbol is suppressed, as when multiplication is indicated by juxtaposition: "(xy)" for the product of x and y. And still other notations are used, as when the square of 3 is written "3^2." Here, the result of applying the two-place function of exponentiation to two arguments is indicated by writing the second argument as a superscript on the first: "(x^y)" for the yth power of x.

To see how the tree method applies to mathematical reasoning, consider the theory of which the axioms are the following three sentences:

G1 $(x)(y)(z)\ x + (y + z) = (x + y) + z$
G2 $(x)\ x + 0 = x$
G3 $(x)\ x + \bar{x} = 0$

This theory (*group theory*) can be interpreted in various ways. The interpretation suggested by our notation is that in which the universe of discourse is, say, the set of real numbers—positive, negative, and zero—and "$+$," "0," and "$-$" have their usual arithmetical interpretations. We write the dash of negation *above* its argument to avoid confusion with the dash of denial.

The sentence

G4 $(x)(y)(z)(x + z = y + z \rightarrow x = y)$

is a logical consequence of the three axioms; it is thus a *theorem* of group theory. The tree method yields a proof of **G4** as follows.

1	$(x)(y)(z)\, x + (y + z) = (x + y) + z$	[premise: **G1**]
2	$(x)\, x + 0 = x$	[premise: **G2**]
3	$(x)\, x + \bar{x} = 0$	[premise: **G3**]
4	$\sqrt{}\sqrt{}\sqrt{}\; -(x)(y)(z)\, (x + z = y + z \rightarrow x = y)$	[$-$conclusion: $-$**G4**]
5	$\sqrt{}\sqrt{}\sqrt{}\; (\exists x)(\exists y)(\exists z) -(x + z = y + z \rightarrow x = y)$	[4, by three uses of $-$]
6	$\sqrt{}\; -(a + c = b + c \rightarrow a = b)$	[5, by $(\exists x)$, $(\exists y)$, and $(\exists z)$]
7	$a + c = b + c$	[6, by
8	$a \neq b$	$-(\bigcirc \rightarrow \triangle)$]
9	$a + (c + \bar{c}) = (a + c) + \bar{c}$	[1, by (x), (y), and (z), with "a," "c," and "$\bar{c}$" as names]
10	$a + (c + \bar{c}) = (b + c) + \bar{c}$	[7 and 9, by $=$]
11	$b + (c + \bar{c}) = (b + c) + \bar{c}$	[1, by (x), (y) and (z)]
12	$c + \bar{c} = 0$	[3, by (x)]
13	$a + (c + \bar{c}) = b + (c + \bar{c})$	[10 and 11, by $=$]
14	$a + 0 = b + 0$	[12 and 13, by $=$ (twice)]
15	$a + 0 = a$	[2 by (x)]
16	$b + 0 = b$	[2 by (x)]
17	$a = b + 0$	[15 and 14 by $=$]
18	$a = b$	[16 and 17 by $=$]

$$\times$$

In this eighteen-line proof we combined steps at several points, but took no serious shortcuts. To show that **G4** is a theorem of group theory is to show that the inference from **G1**, **G2**, and **G3** to the conclusion **G4** is a valid one, so we dutifully began the tree with the three axioms:

1   **G1**
2   **G2**
3   **G3**
4    $-$**G4**

But since the three axioms would be used as premises in the proof of any theorem, there is no point in writing them at the top of every tree; instead, we shall *imagine* that they are present and shall feel free to write instances of them, obtained via the rules for (x), (y), and (z), at any point in any proof of a theorem of group theory. Then lines 1, 2, and 3 would not appear in the tree: this corresponds to normal mathematical practice.

Similarly, in normal mathematical practice, elementary logical operations such as the three uses of the rule for " $-$ " (transforming " $-($ $)$ " into " $(\exists)-$ ") in going from line 4 to 5 would not be mentioned explicitly; rather, the denial of the conclusion $-$ **G4** would be written immediately in the form it takes in line 5, which would thus be the first line of the tree. Indeed, the transition from line 5 to line 6 would normally be left tacit, too; typically, we would start the tree with line 6 together with a parenthetical remark to the effect that the line is an immediate consequence of $-$ **G4**.

In practice we should also feel free to combine several applications of the rule for $=$, with a parenthetical note identifying the line from which the given line follows, as at 9 below. Then in practice, our eighteen-line proof would be written somewhat as follows:

1    $\sqrt{\ } -(a + c = b + c \rightarrow a = b)$ [from $-$**G4**]
2    $a + c = b + c$ [from 1 by
3    $a \neq b$ $-(\bigcirc \rightarrow \triangle)]$
4    $a + (c + \bar{c}) = (a + c) + \bar{c}$ [from **G1**]
5    $b + (c + \bar{c}) = (b + c) + \bar{c}$ [from **G1**]
6    $c + \bar{c} = 0$ [from **G3**]
7    $a + 0 = a$ [from **G2**]
8    $b + 0 = b$ [from **G2**]
9    $a = b$ [from 4, 5, 6, 7, 8, and 2 by $=$]
$\times$

Combining simple steps in this way serves to illuminate the overall structure
of the proof.

With $+$ and $-$ interpreted as summation and negation, group theory
tells the truth, but not the whole truth; thus, the truth

9.16 $(x)(y)\ x + y = y + x$

is not implied by axioms **G1** to **G3.** We shall now show that the following
special case of **9.16** *is* a theorem of group theory.

G5 $(x)\ x + 0 = 0 + x$

In proving **G5** we shall make use of theorem **G4,** which we have already
proved; line 7 in the following proof is obtained from **G4** via the rules for
(x) and (y). The legitimacy of this move follows from a fact that we have
already noted: No harm can be done by writing at the bottom of an open
path a logical consequence of sentences that appear in that path.

1	$a + 0 \neq 0 + a$	$[-\mathbf{G5}$ by $-$ and $(\exists x)]$
2	$0 + (a + \bar{a}) = (0 + a) + \bar{a}$	$[\mathbf{G1}]$
3	$a + \bar{a} = 0$	$[\mathbf{G3}]$
4	$0 + 0 = 0$	$[\mathbf{G2}]$
5	$0 = (0 + a) + \bar{a}$	$[3, 4,$ and 2 by $=]$
6	$a + \bar{a} = (0 + a) + \bar{a}$	$[3$ and 5 by $=]$
7	$\vee\ a + \bar{a} = (0 + a) + \bar{a} \rightarrow a = 0 + a$	$[\mathbf{G4}:$ "a" for "x" and "$(0 + a)$" for "y"$]$

```
8    a + ā ≠ (0 + a) + a        a = 0 + u
9         ×                      a + 0 = a     [G2]
10                              a + 0 = 0 + a   [8 and 9 by =]
                                    ×
```

At line 5 of the proof of the next theorem we again use the shortcut,
using previously proved theorems as we do axioms.

G6 $(y)[(x)\ x + y = x \rightarrow y = 0]$

This says that 0 is the only object which has the property described in axiom **G2**.

1	$\sqrt{\ } -[(x)\ x + a = x \rightarrow a = 0]$	$[-\mathbf{G6}$ by $-$ and $(\exists y)]$
2	$(x)\ x + a = x$	$[1$ by
3	$a \neq 0$	$-(\bigcirc \rightarrow \triangle)]$
4	$0 + a = 0$	$[2$ by $(x)]$
5	$a + 0 = 0 + a$	$[\mathbf{G5}$ by $(x)]$
6	$a + 0 = 0$	$[4$ and 5 by $=]$
7	$a + 0 = a$	$[\mathbf{G2}]$
8	$a = 0$	$[6$ and 7 by $=]$
	$\times$	

INFINITE TREES AGAIN

Is the sentence "$(x)(\exists y)xLy$" consistent? Yes, because the tree which begins with that sentence never closes:

$(x)(\exists y)xLy$
$\sqrt{\ } (\exists y)aLy$
    aLb
$\sqrt{\ } (\exists y)bLy$
    bLc
  $(\exists y)cLy$

$\vdots$

This tree is infinite: The presence of a universal quantifier before an existential quantifier at the beginning results in the generation of infinitely many new names.

Function symbols are another source of infinitely many new names, as illustrated by the tree we construct to see whether the sentence "$(x)\ a \neq fx$" is consistent:

1	$(x)\ a \neq fx$	
2	$a \neq fa$	$[1$ by (x) with "a" as name$]$
3	$a \neq ffa$	$[1$ by (x) with "fa" as name$]$
4	$a \neq fffa$	$[1$ by (x) with "ffa" as name$]$

$\vdots$

The sentence in line 1 is indeed consistent, for this tree tells an infinitely long story in which that line is true. One interpretation of this story identifies a with the number 1, identifies fx as $x + 1$, and takes the positive whole numbers as the universe of discourse. But other interpretations are possible, one of which is the extremely simple interpretation in which the universe of discourse consists of the two numbers 0 and 1, in which a is the number 1, and in which fx is $x - x$. For every x in this interpretation, fx is 0, and therefore it is true that $(x)\, a \neq fx$. Here, the infinity

$$a, \quad fa, \quad ffa, \quad fffa, \quad \ldots$$

of distinct names refers to only two distinct things: "a" names 1 while all the rest name 0.

Clearly, distinct names need not name distinct things either in logic or in English, where "Mark Twain" and "Samuel Clemens" name one and the same man. Where, as in the last example, the tree method tells a story that uses an infinity of different names, it may be possible to give an interpretation in which these names refer to only a finite number of distinct objects. An extreme case of this sort arose at the end of Chapter 7 when we worked out the tree for the "inference"

$$\overline{(\exists x)(y) - xLy}$$

The tree told an infinitely long story

$$aLb, \quad bLc, \quad cLd, \quad dLe, \quad \ldots$$

in which infinitely many distinct names appeared. In this story a was said to love b, who in turn was said to love c, who in turn was said to love d, and so on without end. But the story did not specify that a, b, c, and the rest were all distinct; the sentences

$$a \neq b, \quad b \neq c, \quad c \neq d, \quad d \neq e, \quad \ldots$$

did not appear in the story, and as we saw, the story would still have been consistent if we had assumed that the universe of discourse was composed of a single person named "a" and *also* named "b," "c," "d," and so on without end.

ADEQUACY

The tree method is adequate for testing validity of inferences in which function symbols and the sign of identity may occur, but the adequacy proof in Chapter 8 must be rather carefully modified in order to show that this is the case. Thus, we must establish that the rules for $=$ and $\neq$ have the appropriate sorts of upward and downward correctness, we must carefully examine the consequences of treating expressions like "$g(a,b)$" as names, and we must redefine the notion of *the valuation described by an open path through a finished tree*, for where the sign of identity occurs in a path, we may not be free to suppose that distinct names in the path denote distinct objects. The necessary adjustments are not very difficult, but they require a careful revision of the definitions and proofs of Chapter 8 which fits more comfortably at the beginning of a second course in logic than at the end of the first.

EXERCISES

9.1   Show that statement **9.4′** implies and is implied by

9.17 $(\exists x)(Mx \,\&\, (y)(Py \leftrightarrow y = x))$,

which is thus shown to be another way of saying that the one and only P is an M.

9.2   Use statement **9.17** to express the following statements, with "Hx" for "x was a husband of Xantippe" and "Px" for "x taught Plato."

    a   *Xantippe's (one and only) husband taught Plato.*

    b   *Plato's (one and only) teacher was a husband of Xantippe.*

    c   *Plato's (one and only) teacher = Xantippe's (one and only) husband.*

9.3   Translate and test for validity. Use "xTy" for "x taught y" or (what comes to the same thing) "y was x's student." (An autodidact is someone who taught himself.)

    a   *Socrates taught Plato.*
       Socrates had at most one student.
       <u>*Aristotle was a student of someone whom Socrates taught.*</u>
       Plato taught Aristotle.

    b *No one has more than one student.*
        Plato was taught by an autodidact.
        Plato was an autodidact.

9.4   Symbolize the following valid inferences, but do not bother to test them for validity.

    a *Everyone has exactly one father.*
        Everyone has exactly one paternal grandfather.

    b *Everyone has exactly two parents.*
        No one has more than four grandparents.

If the premises seem ambiguous to you, choose the interpretations that make them true.

9.5   Which of the following are logical truths? (Use the tree method.)

a $(x)(y)\ x = y$
b $(\exists x)(\exists y)\ x = y$
c $(\exists x)(y)(Py \leftrightarrow y = x) \rightarrow (\exists x)Px$

9.6   Which, if any, of the three sentences in Exercise 9.5 are logical truths when the sign "$=$" of identity is replaced by the sign "$\neq$" of diversity throughout? (Do not use the tree method: just think.)

9.7   Where "R" and "S" are relation symbols, the expressions

      $aRbRc,$ $aRbSc$

are often used as shorthand for

      $aRb\ \&\ bRc,$ $aRb\ \&\ bSc$

respectively. Thus, we write

      $a = b = c,$ $a \neq b \neq c,$ $a = b \neq c$

as shorthand for

      $a = b\ \&\ b = c,$ $a \neq b\ \&\ b \neq c,$ $a = b\ \&\ b \neq c.$

Write the following inferences in unabbreviated form and test their validity by the tree method.

a $\dfrac{aRbRc}{aRc}$ b $\dfrac{a = b \neq c}{a \neq c}$ c $\dfrac{a \neq b \neq c}{a \neq c}$

d $\dfrac{-(a = b = c)}{a \neq b \neq c}$ e $\dfrac{a \neq b \neq c}{-(a = b = c)}$

9.8 Symbolize each of the following, using "f" as a function symbol for *the father of* and "m" as a function symbol for *the mother of*.

   a   *a* is *b*'s paternal grandmother.   b   *a* is *b*'s grandmother.
   c   *a* is a father.   d   *a* is a grandfather.
   e   *a* is *b*'s full sibling.   f   *a* is *b*'s first cousin.

9.9 Interpret "f" and "m" as in Exercise 9.8, read "P" as "is a parent of," and read "Mx" as "x is male." Describe the relationship between *a* and *b* as concisely as you can in English on each of the following assumptions.

a $fa = fb \lor ma = mb$ d $Mb \& (\exists x)(xPa \& fb = fx \& mb = mx)$
b $aPfb$ e $-Ma \& (\exists x)(xPa \& fbPx \& mbPx)$
c $faPb \& maPb \& Ma$ f $fa = fb \leftrightarrow ma \neq mb$

9.10 Test for validity by the tree method:

a $\dfrac{(x)(y)x = y}{(x)fx = x}$ d $\dfrac{(x)fgx = x}{(x)(y)(fx = y \rightarrow gy = x)}$

b $\dfrac{(x)fa = x}{(x)fx = a}$ e $\dfrac{(x)ffx = x}{(x)(y)(fx = fy \rightarrow x = y)}$

c $\dfrac{(x)fx = a}{(x)fa = x}$

9.11 Test "$fa = a$" for consistency. (You should get an infinite tree.)

9.12 Prove that the following are theorems of group theory.

G7 $(x)\ x + \bar{x} = \bar{x} + x$
G8 $(x)(y)(z)(z + x = z + y \rightarrow x = y)$
G9 $(x)(y)(x + y = 0 \rightarrow y = \bar{x})$
G10 $(x)\ \bar{\bar{x}} = x$

10

UNDECIDABILITY. INCOMPLETENESS

We have now completed our formalization of logic: We could program a computing machine to test inferences for validity by the tree method. Presented with a valid inference, the machine would eventually inform us of its validity, and presented with an invalid inference, the machine would never erroneously classify it as valid. In this sense, the tree method adequately formalizes logic.

But in another sense, the method is inadequate. The process of building a tree to test an invalid inference may go on forever, so that there need be no finite number of steps after which the machine classifies a given invalid inference as invalid. Thus, presented with the invalid inference

$$\frac{(x)(\exists y)xLy}{aLa}$$

the machine will never finish the tree and will therefore never give a "yes" or "no" answer to the question "Is this inference valid?" If at some point the machine could predict that it will never finish the tree, it could tell us at that point that the correct answer is "no"; but as matters stand, we have an adequate "yes" machine which is inadequate as a "no" machine.

In this sense, the tree method is inadequate, but in this sense, *every mechanical routine is inadequate:* there can be no adequate "no" machine for quantificational validity. It follows that there can be no adequate mechanical routine for determining whether inferences have finite or infinite trees. Confronted with any particular inference whose tree is infinite, we may be able to recognize, after some finite number of steps, that the tree will never stop growing. But there is no uniform mechanical procedure for doing this; a procedure that works for some inferences must always fail for others, so that there is always place for human ingenuity in the matter of recognizing invalidity.

We shall put the matter in this way:

10.1   *There is no mechanical decision procedure for quantificational validity.*

This means that there is no clerical routine which, applied by a man or a machine to arbitrary inferences in the notation of quantification theory, eventually classifies them (correctly) as valid or invalid. This fact was first proved in 1936 by Alonzo Church. After proving Church's theorem we shall be able to prove a version of Kurt Gödel's remarkable *incompleteness theorem* (1931) on the limits of the axiomatic method. The theorems of Gödel and Church are of the first importance, both mathematically and philosophically. In particular, on the philosophical side, Gödel's theorem dealt the deathblow to the theory which identified mathematical truth with provability, and Church's theorem established that logic can never be fully mechanized.

THE FRAGMENT A OF ARITHMETIC

Church's theorem **10.1** is a claim about *all* mechanical procedures: The claim is that they all are inadequate as decision procedures for quantificational validity. Then to prove the theorem, we must somehow obtain a bird's-eye view of the capabilities of all mechanical procedures. Toward this end we now describe an axiom system due to Raphael Robinson (1950).

The system A of Robinson arithmetic uses just one predicate symbol: the sign " $=$ " of identity. It uses just one name, the symbol "0," which is interpreted as denoting the number zero. And it uses just three function symbols corresponding to the operations of adding 1 to a number, of finding the sum of two numbers, and of finding the product of two numbers: the symbols

$$', \qquad +, \qquad \cdot$$

will represent the *successor* function, the *sum* function, and the *product* function. In particular, the expressions

$$x', \qquad x + y, \qquad x \cdot y$$

will represent the successor of x (the next whole number after x), the sum of x and y, and the product of x and y. The universe of discourse is the set $0, 1, 2, \ldots$ of all *natural numbers*.

The axioms of A are the following seven sentences:

A1 $(x)(y)(x' = y' \to x = y)$
A2 $(x)(x \neq 0 \to (\exists y)\, x = y')$
A3 $(x)\, 0 \neq x'$
A4 $(x)\, x + 0 = x$
A5 $(x)(y)\, x + y' = (x + y)'$
A6 $(x)\, x \cdot 0 = 0$
A7 $(x)(y)\, x \cdot y' = (x \cdot y) + x$

All the axioms are true in the valuation we have indicated. **A1** says, in effect, that distinct natural numbers have distinct successors. **A2** says that every natural number other than zero is the successor of some natural number, and **A3** denies that zero is the successor of any natural number. **A4** and **A5** are rules for computing sums, and **A6** and **A7** are rules for computing products. In particular, **A5** says that

$$x + (y + 1) = (x + y) + 1,$$

and **A7** says that

$$x \cdot (y + 1) = (x \cdot y) + x.$$

Here we have used a name, "1," which is not part of the vocabulary of the system A. In A itself, we write the numerals

0, 1, 2, 3, . . .

as

$0, 0', 0'', 0''', \ldots$

In general, the *numeral* for the number n, in the system A, is obtained by writing n accents after the symbol for zero. Thus, in A, we write

$$0''' \cdot 0'' = 0''''''$$

to indicate that

$$3 \cdot 2 = 6.$$

REPRESENTABILITY

Consider a sentence, say

10.2 $\ldots x \ldots,$

in the notation of A which has free occurrences of one and only one variable (here, "x"). Let n be any natural number, and let "$\bar{n}$" be an abbreviation for the numeral which denotes the number n. Then "$\bar{n}$" is short for "0" followed by n accents; thus, "$\bar{3}$" is short for "$0'''$." Now consider the sentence

10.3 $\ldots \bar{n} \ldots$

which is obtained by substituting "n" for all free occurrences of variables in **10.2**. It may be that for each natural number n, the sentence **10.3** is either *provable* or *refutable* in A. In other words, it may be that for each n, either sentence **10.3** or its denial is implied by the axioms of A. If this is the case, sentence **10.2** is said to *represent* a certain set of natural numbers in A. In particular, the number n is in the set represented by **10.2** if **10.3** is provable in A, and n is outside that set if the denial of **10.3** is provable in A.

   Example: The set

10.4 $0, 2, 4, \ldots$

of even natural numbers is represented in A by the sentence

10.5 $(\exists y)\, x = y + y.$

This means that each of the sentences

10.6 $(\exists y)\, 0 = y + y, \quad (\exists y)\, 0'' = y + y, \quad (\exists y)\, 0'''' = y + y, \quad \ldots$

is provable in A, as is each of the sentences

10.7 $-(\exists y)\, 0' = y + y, \qquad -(\exists y)\, 0''' = y + y,$
   $-(\exists y)\, 0''''' = y + y, \qquad \ldots.$

In effect, the sentences **10.6** say that the various even natural numbers belong to the set **10.4** and the sentences **10.7** say that the various odd natural numbers do not.
   The case is similar for open sentences having free occurrences of two or more distinct variables. Thus, a sentence

10.8 $\ldots x \ldots y \ldots$

in which the variables "x" and "y," but no others, have free occurrences, represents a set of *pairs* of natural numbers if and only if for each pair m,n the sentence

10.9 $\ldots \bar{m} \ldots \bar{n} \ldots$

is either provable or refutable in A. In such a case, the pair m,n of natural numbers does (does not) belong to the set which **10.8** represents if **10.9** is implied (refuted) by the seven axioms of A.

Example: The set

10.10 (0,0),   (1,2),   (2,4),   . . .

of all pairs of natural numbers in which the second member is twice the first is represented in A by the sentence

10.11 $y = x + x.$

This means that when numerals are written in place of "x" and "y" in **10.11**, the resulting sentence is provable (refutable) in A if the numeral written for "y" does (does not) have exactly twice the number of accents that the numeral written for "x" has. Then it means that each of the sentences

10.12 $0 = 0 + 0,$ $0'' = 0' + 0',$ $0'''' = 0'' + 0'',$ . . .

is provable in A, and that when n is *not* twice m, the unabbreviated form of the sentence "$\bar{n} = \bar{m} + \bar{m}$" is refutable in A.

CHURCH'S THESIS

If a set of natural numbers is representable in A, the tree test provides a mechanical procedure for obtaining "yes" or "no" answers to questions of the form "Is the number n in the set?" If the set is represented by a sentence **10.2**

   . . . x . . . ,

we simply apply the tree test to the two inferences

Axioms of A	Axioms of A
. . . $\bar{n}$ . . .	$-$ . . . $\bar{n}$ . . .

simultaneously. Since the sentence **10.2** represents the set and since the tree test is adequate for validity, one of the two trees must eventually close, and since the axioms of A are clearly consistent, *only* one of the two trees will close. Then the correct answer is "yes" ("no") if the first (second) tree is the one that closes.

Let us speak of a set of natural numbers as *decidable* if and only if there is a mechanical decision procedure for it: a mechanical procedure which, applied to any numeral, eventually yields a "yes" or "no" answer to the question "Does the number denoted by this numeral belong to the set?" We have just seen that

10.13 *Every representable set is decidable.*

If the converse of this statement is also true, then

10.14 *Decidability = representability,*

and we have achieved our bird's-eye view of the capabilities of all mechanical decision procedures, as far as sets of natural numbers are concerned.

There is excellent reason to suppose that **10.14** is true, despite the seeming weakness of the system A. Thus, it is far from obvious that the operation of exponentiation is definable in A, and therefore it might seem that the set

10.15 1, 10, 100, 1000,   . . .

of all powers of 10 is not representable in A. If the set **10.15** is not representable in A, then statement **10.14** is false, for the set **10.15** is surely decidable. But in fact the operation of exponentiation is definable in A (in a roundabout manner), and the set **10.15** is representable in A.

More generally, it might seem that some decidable sets might be representable in systems obtained by adding extra axioms and notation to A but might not be representable in A itself. Thus, we might have thought of adding the function symbol "exp" to the notation of A and adding the following two axioms:

A8 $(x)\ x \exp 0 = 0'$
A9 $(x)(y)\ x \exp y' = (x \exp y) \cdot x$

Here, "exp" symbolizes the exponentiation function: $x \exp y$ is the number

x^y

obtained by multiplying together a string of y x's. Similarly, we might think of adding other function symbols, together with axioms that govern computations involving those symbols, in order to represent new sets in the enlarged system. As long as the whole set of axioms is finite and consistent, the argument which established **10.13** will apply to the enlarged system, so that we might expect to find decidable sets which are representable in the enlarged system but not in A, as when we represent the set **10.15** of powers of 10 by the sentence

10.16 $(\exists y)\ x = 0''''''''''\ \text{exp}\ y$

in the enlarged system. But as we have already remarked, there is in A itself a much more complicated sentence which, like **10.16**, represents the set **10.15**. And in general, it can be shown that any set which is representable in a finite, consistent extension of A is actually representable in A itself.

But although there is excellent reason to think **10.14** true, we can never strictly prove it. **10.14** is not the sort of statement that admits of mathematical proof; it is a *thesis* ("Church's thesis"), not a theorem, because the notion of decidability that appears in it is to be understood in terms of our intuitive idea of *mechanical procedure* or *clerical routine*. Such procedures can take a limitless variety of forms, and it is always at least barely conceivable that one day, a new and essentially more powerful procedure will be invented which will conform to our intuitive idea of a mechanical procedure but which will provide a decision procedure for some unrepresentable set. If that day should ever come, Church's thesis will have been refuted, to the amazement of almost all logicians.

Then Church's thesis **10.14** is the sort of statement that admits of refutation, but not of proof. The longer such a thesis survives, unrefuted, the more confident of its truth can we reasonably be—unless we have been wearing dogmatic blinders and neglecting opportunities to refute it.

ARITHMETIZATION

If Church's *thesis* is true, we now have our bird's-eye view of all decidable sets of natural numbers, but Church's *theorem* **10.1** is an assertion about decidable sets of another sort. To say that an inference is quantificationally valid is to make a claim about sentences, not numbers.

To be more precise, the claim is that the members of a certain finite sequence of sentences (the premises) stand in a certain relationship (implication) to a certain sentence (the conclusion). Church's theorem then says that a certain set of pairs is not decidable, where the first members of the pairs are finite sequences of sentences and the second members are individual sentences. The theorem might be put in this way:

10.17 *Let I be the set of all those pairs in which the first member is a finite sequence of sentences and the second member is a sentence which that sequence implies. Then I is not decidable.*

To make sense of **10.17**, we must extend our notion of decidability to nonnumerical sets like I. We do this by a variant of Gödel's original method (1931).

We need a way of assigning code numbers to sentences and to sequences of sentences in the notation of quantification theory. Once this has been done, we can discuss the decidability of sets like I indirectly, by way of the code. Church's theorem **10.17** can then be stated as follows, by way of Church's thesis and the code:

10.18 *Let I* be the set of pairs (x,y) of natural numbers in which x is the code number of a finite sequence of sentences and y is the code number of a sentence which sequence number x implies. Then I* is not representable in A.*

The details of how the coding is accomplished are unimportant; all that matters is that the processes of coding and decoding be of the sort for which we can specify clerical routines. There must be a mechanical procedure which, applied to any natural number, eventually tells us whether or not it is the code number of a sentence (and if so, *which* sentence) or of a finite sequence of sentences (and if so, *which* sequence). And there must be a mechanical procedure which, applied to any sentence or finite sequence of sentences in the notation of quantificational logic, eventually yields the correct code number. It goes without saying that the coding must be unambiguous: No two distinct sentences or sequences may have the same code number.

To show that the thing can be done, we now describe a particular code. To begin, we assign numbers to all the single symbols in the notation of quantificational logic.

First come the propositional connectives, to which we assign code numbers as follows:

−	12
&	122
∨	1222
→	12222
↔	122222

These numbers get very large very soon. No matter; we shall not actually have to write out any code numbers, except for purposes of illustration.

Next come an assortment of symbols. For good measure, we include the special notation of the theory A.

(	13
)	133
,	1333
⊒	13333
=	133333
+	1333333
·	13333333
′	133333333
0	1333333333

Now the variables must be assigned numbers. There are infinitely many variables, say

$$x, \quad y, \quad z, \quad x_1, \quad y_1, \quad z_1, \quad x_2, \ldots$$

The corresponding code numbers are as follows:

14, 144, 1444, 14444, 144444, 1444444, 14444444, . . .

In decimal notation, the code number for the nth variable in our list is expressed by a "1" followed by n occurrences of the symbol "4."

The other infinite arrays of symbols are treated similarly. In addition to "0," which has already been assigned its number, there are infinitely many distinct names, say

$$a_1, \ a_2, \ \ a_3, \ldots,$$

to which we assign code numbers

$$15, \ 155, \ 1555, \ldots.$$

For each positive integer n, there are infinitely many distinct function symbols of degree n. For uniformity of notation, suppose that "f" is the basic function symbol with the degree indicated by a superscript and with subscripts distinguishing the various symbols of each degree. Thus, the distinct function symbols of degree 2 would be these:

$$f_1{}^2, \ f_2{}^2, \ \ f_3{}^2, \ldots$$

The corresponding code numbers in decimal notation will be these:

$$116, \ 1166, \ 11666, \ldots$$

Here the number of symbols "1" identifies the superscript, and the number of symbols "6" identifies the subscript. In general, the mth function symbol of degree n will have, as the decimal representation of its code number, a string of n "1"'s followed by a string of m "6"'s. The only exceptions are the three special function symbols for the theory A, to which we have already assigned code numbers.

Sentence letters and predicate letters of various degrees can be treated similarly. Perhaps the sentence letters are "A_1," "A_2," "A_3," ... with code numbers $17, \ 177, \ 1777, \ldots$, and perhaps the mth predicate letter of degree n is of form "$P_m{}^n$," with a code number which is written in decimal notation as a string of n "1"'s followed by a string of m "8"'s. The exception, of course, is the predicate symbol "$=$" of degree 2, which has the code number 133333.

Now that we have a code number for each individual symbol, we can make short work of sentences and sequences of sentences. Sentences are finite sequences of individual symbols. To get the decimal expression for the code number of a finite sequence of individual symbols, we just replace each symbol by the decimal expression for its code number.

Example: The sentence

$$(x)(\exists y)\ x = y$$

has the code number

13141331313333144133141333333144.

For examples of the process of decoding, consider the numbers

1967,   1413333311,   141333331161314133313333333333133.

The first two of these are not code for anything, and the third is code for
the sentence "$x = f_1{}^2(x,0)$." In general, given the decimal expression for a
number, we decode it as follows. Starting at the extreme left, find the
longest consecutive string of digits which represents the code number of
some single symbol, and replace this string of digits by the symbol; but if
no initial string of digits represents the code number of any symbol, the
whole number is code for nothing whatever. Now repeat this process,
applying it again and again to whatever digits remain, until the whole
decimal expression has been either decoded or classified as code for nothing
whatever.

Finally, to code a sequence of sentences or, more generally, to code a
finite sequence of finite sequences of symbols, write a "9" between each
two adjacent sequences of symbols and then replace those sequences by
the decimal expressions for their code numbers. Thus, the sequence consisting of the three sentences

$$A_1,\qquad (A_1 \to A_2),\qquad A_2$$

has

1791317122221771339177

as its code number.

DECIDABLE SETS OF EXPRESSIONS. SUBSTITUTION

By means of the code, we can now discuss the decidability of sets of expressions in terms of the decidability of corresponding sets of natural numbers. Roughly speaking, we extend Church's thesis to sets of expressions as follows:

10.19 *A set of expressions in the notation of quantificational logic is decidable if and only if the set of code numbers of those expressions is representable in A.*

If Church's thesis **10.14** is correct for sets of natural numbers, then thesis **10.19** is correct for sets of expressions, and similar formulations will correctly apply to sets of pairs of expressions, to sets of triples of expressions, and to sets of finite sequences of expressions generally.

Example: The set S of triples of expressions.

A triple (e_1,e_2,e_3) belongs to the set S if and only if e_1 and e_3 are sentences in the notation of quantificational logic, e_2 is a numeral in the notation of A, and sentence e_1 is the result of substituting the numeral e_2 for all free occurrences of variables in e_3.

We define the corresponding set S* of triples of natural numbers as follows:

A triple (n_1,n_2,n_3) belongs to the set S* if and only if n_1 and n_3 are code numbers of sentences in the notation of quantificational logic, n_2 is a natural number, and sentence number n_1 is the result of substituting $\bar{n}_2$ for all free occurrences of variables in sentence number n_3.

Here, n_2 is the numeral in the notation of A that denotes the number n_2: a "0" followed by a string of n_2 accents. This represents a slight departure from the pattern indicated in **10.19**. If we had strictly followed that pattern, the number n_2 would have been *the code number of* the numeral e_2, but in our definition of S*, n_2 is *the number denoted by* the numeral n_2. Thus, if e_2 is the numeral "0''," our n_2 is the number 2, which that numeral denotes in the intended interpretation of A; but according to **10.19**, we should have $n_2 = 133333333313333333313333333$, which is the code number of the expression e_2, namely, a "0" followed by two accents. It is because of this departure that **10.19** is introduced above by saying "*Roughly speaking,* we extend Church's thesis to sets of expressions as follows."

Clearly, S is a decidable set. It is a trivial and mechanical procedure to examine a triple of expressions and determine whether the first is a sentence, the second is a numeral, and the third is a sentence from which the first is obtainable by substituting the second for all free occurrences of variables in the third. Since the decoding procedure is mechanical, it follows that the set S* must be decidable. Given a triple of numerals in the notation of A, we can mechanically determine what (if any) sentences of A are encoded by the first and third of them. If the numerals pass this first test, we apply the decision procedure for S to the triple of which the first member is the sentence encoded by the first numeral, the second member is the second numeral itself, and the third member is the sentence encoded by the third numeral. This argument serves to *illustrate* the claim that Church's thesis **10.19** is true for sets of expressions if the corresponding thesis **10.14** is true for sets of numbers.

Further, the argument *establishes* the claim that if Church's thesis is true for sets of natural numbers, then there must be a sentence in the notation of A, say

10.20 $—x—y—z—,$

containing free occurrences of the variables "x," "y," and "z," but of no other variables, which represents the set S* in the sense that for any three natural numbers m, n, and p, the sentence

10.21 $—\bar{m}—\bar{n}—\bar{p}—$

is provable (refutable) in A if the triple (m,n,p) does (does not) belong to the set S*.

THE SET N^*

We are almost ready to prove Church's theorem **10.18**:

Let I be the set of pairs (x,y) of natural numbers in which x is the code number of a finite sequence of sentences and y is the code number of a sentence which sequence number x implies. Then I* is not representable in A.*

To prove **10.18** we first observe that the sequence

A1   A2   A3   A4   A5   A6   A7

has a code number whose decimal representation is obtained by writing the decimal representations of the code numbers of the seven axioms of A in a row separated by "9"'s. Let us call this number "a" and let "$\bar{a}$" stand for the corresponding numeral in the notation of A: a "0" followed by the immense number a of accents. If the set I^* is represented in A by the sentence

$$\ldots x \ldots y \ldots,$$

then the sentence

10.22 $\ldots \bar{a} \ldots y \ldots$

will represent in A the set of code numbers of sentences that are implied by the axioms of A. This sentence has free occurrences of one and only one variable, "y."

There is nothing special about the variable "y"; we can easily rewrite **10.22** in a logically equivalent form

10.23 $\ldots \bar{a} \ldots x \ldots$

where there are free occurrences of "x" in exactly the places where "y" occurs free in **10.22**. Now **10.23** represents the property of being the code number of a sentence that is provable in A—the property of being the code number of a theorem of A. If n is any natural number, then

10.24 $\ldots \bar{a} \ldots \bar{n} \ldots$

is provable (refutable) in A if n is (is not) the code number of a theorem of A. Furthermore, the sentence

10.25 $-\ldots \bar{a} \ldots \bar{x} \ldots$

must represent the set N^* of numbers that are *not* code numbers of theorems of A. If n is any natural number, the sentence

10.26 $-\ldots\bar{a}\ldots\bar{n}\ldots$

is refutable in A if n is the code number of a theorem of A, but **10.26** is provable in A if n is the code number of nothing at all or if n is the code number of an entity that, for any reason, fails to be a theorem of A. Thus, the sentence

$-\ldots\bar{a}\ldots\bar{a}\ldots$

is provable in A because a is the code number of a *sequence*, not a sentence, and the sentence

$-\ldots\bar{a}\ldots 0''\ldots$

is provable in A because 2 is not the code number of anything.

Church's theorem says that the set I^* is not representable in A, and we have just seen that if I^* is representable in A, so is the set N^* of numbers which are not code numbers of theorems. We shall prove Church's theorem by deducing contradictory conclusions from the assumption that N^* is representable in A.

SELF-REFERENCE. CHURCH'S THEOREM

The proof that N^* is not representable in A will turn on the fact that if it *is* representable, there is a sentence in the notation of A which says of itself, via the code, that it is not a theorem of A. It is as if **10.27** were a sentence in the notation of A:

10.27   *Sentence* **10.27** *is not a theorem of* A.

If **10.27** were a theorem of A, the statement it makes about itself would be false, and the axioms of A would have been shown to imply a falsehood. But it is clear that the axioms of A are all true, and we know that no false conclusion can be inferred from true premises. Then sentence **10.27** cannot be a theorem of A. This argument shows that

10.28   *If* N^* *is representable in* A *then* **10.27** *is not a theorem of* A.

Now suppose we were also able to demonstrate the following:

10.29 *If N^* is representable in A then* **10.27** *is a theorem of A.*

From **10.28** and **10.29** it would follow that N^* is not representable in A.

Our proof that N^* is not representable in A will have the form outlined above, with the following sentence playing the role of **10.27**:

10.30 $(\exists x)(-x-\bar{b}-\bar{b}-\ \&\ -\ldots\bar{a}\ldots x\ldots)$

Here, b is the code number of the sentence

10.31 $(\exists x)(-x-y-z-\ \&\ -\ldots\bar{a}\ldots x\ldots)$

in which "$-x-y-z-$" is the sentence **10.20** which represents the set S^* and "$-\ldots\bar{a}\ldots x\ldots$" is the sentence **10.25** which represents the set N^* if I^* is representable in A. We have seen that if Church's thesis is true, there really is a sentence **10.20** which represents S^* in A. But the existence of a sentence **10.25** which represents N^* in A is an *assumption,* which we make only in order to deduce contradictory conclusions from it and thus refute it.

To see that sentence **10.30** says of itself, via the code, that it is not a theorem of A, we translate it into English:

> There is a number x that is the code number of a sentence obtained by substituting the numeral $\bar{b}$ for all free occurrences of variables in sentence number b; and sentence number x is not a theorem of A.

Now **10.31** is sentence number b, and when we substitute the numeral $\bar{b}$ for all free occurrences of variables in that sentence, we obtain sentence **10.30**. Then sentence number x, which **10.30** says is not a theorem of A, is **10.30** itself.

We now prove the analogue of **10.28**: we prove that

10.32 *If N^* is representable in A and Church's thesis is true, then sentence* **10.30** *is not a theorem of A.*

The hypothesis that Church's thesis is true assures us of the existence of a sentence "$-x-y-z-$" which represents the decidable set S^* in A, and the hypothesis that N^* is representable in A implies the existence of a sentence, say "—...$\bar{a}$...x...," which represents the set N^* in A. Then the two hypotheses together imply the existence of sentence **10.30** in the notation of A. We have seen that each of **A1** to **A7** is *true in the intended interpretation of A*—true in the valuation in which the universe of discourse is the set 0, 1, 2, ... of natural numbers, in which the sign "0" denotes the number zero and in which the signs "$'$," "$+$," and "$\cdot$" represent the successor, sum, and product functions, respectively. Then if **10.30** were a theorem of A, there would have to be a natural number, say c, for which the sentences

10.33 $-\bar{c}-\bar{b}-\bar{b}-$, $-...\bar{a}...\bar{c}...$

both assume the value t in the intended interpretation of A. Intuitively, the first of these sentences says that c is the code number of sentence **10.30**, and the second says that sentence number c is not a theorem of A, so that we may conclude that **10.30** is not a theorem of A after all; or we may establish the same conclusion rigorously, as follows.

By hypothesis, the sentences

10.34 $-x-y-z-$, $-...\bar{a}...x...$

represent the sets S^* and N^* in A. Consequently, each of sentences **10.33** is either provable or refutable in A. If both are true in the intended interpretation, neither is refutable. Then on our hypotheses, both of sentences **10.33** are provable in A, and since sentences **10.34** represent S^* and N^* in A, the triple (c,b,b) belongs to S^* and the number c belongs to N^*: c is the code number of the result **10.30** of substituting "$\bar{b}$" for all free occurrences of variables in sentence number b, and sentence number c is not a theorem of A. Then **10.30** is not a theorem of A, and **10.32** is proved.

The point of taking the long way round here is to meet the objection that in the intended interpretation of A, sentences **10.33** make arithmetical statements which do not, on the face of them, say anything about sentences, substitution, free occurrences of variables, or theoremhood. It is only by way of the coding that sentences **10.34** represent the sets S^* and N^* so that sentences **10.33** *say* that c is the code number of **10.30** and that sentence number c is not a theorem of A. Thus, the claim that

10.35   "...$\bar{a}$...$\bar{c}$..." *says that sentence* **10.30** *is a theorem of A*

really amounts to this:

10.36 "...$\bar{a}$...$\bar{c}$..." *is provable (refutable) in* A *if* **10.30** *is* (*is not*) *a theorem of* A.

Still, **10.36** is not an outrageously distorted way of saying **10.35**, for if "...$\bar{a}$...x..." represents a set of natural numbers, then for any n

10.37 "...$\bar{a}$...$\bar{n}$..." *is provable (refutable) in* A *if it is true* (*false*) *in the intended interpretation of* A.

Combining **10.36** and **10.37**, we have this:

10.38 "...$\bar{a}$...$\bar{c}$..." *is true* (*false*) *in the intended interpretation of* A *if sentence* **10.30** *is* (*is not*) *a theorem of* A.

Then **10.35** may be construed as a brief but somewhat foggy way of saying **10.38**; and in a similar way we construe other claims about what sentences of A say by way of the code. In particular, notice that **10.38** does not say that "...$\bar{a}$...$\bar{c}$..." is *about* sentence **10.30** or *about* theoremhood. On the contrary, **10.38** is perfectly compatible with the view that "...$\bar{a}$...$\bar{c}$..." is about natural numbers or about sums, products, and successors—a plausible view since, in addition to the basic notation of quantificational logic, the sentence we abbreviate by "...$\bar{a}$...$\bar{c}$..." contains only pluses, dots, accents, and occurrences of the symbol "0."

It only remains to prove the analogue of **10.29**:

10.39 *If* N^* *is representable in* A *and Church's thesis is true, then sentence* **10.30** *is a theorem of* A.

Here, too, the proof is by contradiction; we assume that **10.30** is not a theorem of A and deduce from the hypotheses of **10.39** that **10.30** *is* a theorem of A. Conclusion: It is.

Assume, then, that **10.30** is not a theorem of A. Then its code number, say c, belongs to N^*, and since "$-$...$\bar{a}$...x..." represents N^*, "$-$...$\bar{a}$...$\bar{c}$..." is a theorem of A. Furthermore, since **10.30** is the result of substituting "$\bar{b}$" for all free occurrences of variables in sentence number b and "$-x-y-z-$" represents S^*, "$-\bar{c}-\bar{b}-\bar{b}-$" is a theorem of A. Finally, since the inference

$$\frac{\begin{array}{l} -\ldots\bar{a}\ldots\bar{c}\ldots \\ -\bar{c}-\bar{b}-\bar{b}- \end{array}}{(\exists x)(-x-\bar{b}-\bar{b}-\ \&\ -\ldots\bar{a}\ldots x\ldots)}$$

is a valid one, the conclusion, which is **10.30**, is also a theorem of A. This proves **10.39**.

Now from **10.32** and **10.39** we conclude that

If Church's thesis is true, N* is not representable in A.

Since N* is representable in A if I* is, we have now shown that

*If Church's thesis **10.14** is true, so is Church's theorem.*

Translating back into the terms in which the problem was originally posed, we have shown this:

10.40   *If every decidable set is representable in A, then there is no mechanical decision procedure for quantificational validity.*

Therefore, there can be no adequate "no" machine for quantificational validity; the tree method cannot be radically improved upon.

ANOTHER FORM OF CHURCH'S THEOREM

This rounds out our treatment of quantificational logic. In proving the adequacy of the tree method we established the scope of one formalization of logic, and in proving Church's theorem we established that the limits of formal quantificational logic are essentially the same as the limits of the tree method.

But our proof of adequacy in Chapter 8 applied only to inferences in which the sign " = " of identity does not appear and in which function symbols do not appear. Therefore, we have not strictly proved the adequacy of the tree method as applied to inferences in the notation of theories like A. The adequacy proof could be extended, but we shall not trouble to do so. Instead, we shall observe that we could have worked with an alternative formulation of the system A in which no use is made of the sign of identity or of function symbols. Call this system "B." We could have formulated

Church's thesis as a claim about the system B and then carried through the argument as before to prove the following version of **10.40**:

10.41 *If every decidable set is representable in B, then there is no mechanical decision procedure for quantificational validity, even when inferences are restricted to those that do not involve function symbols or the sign of identity.*

We formulated Church's thesis as a claim about A rather than B because of the relative familiarity of the notation of A. But we can easily eliminate the signs "$=$," "$'$," "$+$," and "$\cdot$" so as to reduce A to a system B in which the sign of identity and function symbols do not appear. To eliminate the sign "$=$," with its dependence on the special rules of inference for $=$ and $\neq$, we must choose some ordinary predicate symbol of second degree, say "E," and provide axioms which effectively give the sign "E" the force which the rules for $=$ and $\neq$ give to the sign "$=$":

B1 $(x)\ xEx$
B2 $(x)(y)(xEy \to yEx)$
B3 $(x)(y)(z)[(xEy\ \&\ yEz) \to xEz]$

Furthermore, we must use three other predicate symbols in order to make statements to the same effect as

10.42 $x' = y, \qquad x + y = z, \qquad x \cdot y = z$

For this purpose we use a second-degree predicate symbol, say "A" (for "accent"), and two third-degree predicates, say "S" and "P" (for "sum" and "product"), in such a way that the sentences

10.43 $Axy, \qquad Sxyz, \qquad Pxyz$

will have the same effect as the corresponding sentences **10.42**. To assure that the sentences **10.43** are effectively equivalent to the corresponding sentences **10.42**, we must provide axioms which explicitly formulate the assumptions that are packed into the functional notation: that for each number x there is one and only one number y such that $y = x'$ and that for each pair x,y of numbers there is one and only one number z such that $x + y = z$ and one and only one number z such that $x \cdot y = z$:

B4 $(x)[(\exists y)(z)(Axz \leftrightarrow zEy)$ & $(x_1)(x_1 Ex \rightarrow Ax_1 y)]$
B5 $(x)(y)[(\exists z)(z_1)(Sxyz_1 \leftrightarrow z_1 Ez)$ & $(x_1)(y_1)((x_1 Ex$ & $y_1 Ey) \rightarrow Sx_1 y_1 z)]$
B6 $(x)(y)[(\exists z)(z_1)(Pxyz_1 \leftrightarrow z_1 Ez)$ & $(x_1)(y_1)((x_1 Ex$ & $y_1 Ey) \rightarrow Px_1 y_1 z)]$

Now we can transcribe the seven axioms of A into the notation of B as follows.

B7 $(x)(y)(z)[(Axz$ & $Ayz) \rightarrow xEy]$

This corresponds to **A1**, "$(x)(y)(x' = y' \rightarrow x = y)$." In place of **A2**, "$(x)(x \neq 0 \rightarrow (\exists y)x = y')$," we have

B8 $(x)(-E0x \rightarrow (\exists y)Ayx)$

In place of **A3**, "$(x)\ 0 \neq x'$," and **A4**, "$(x)\ x + 0 = x$," we have

B9 $(x) - Ax0$
B10 $(x)\ Sx0x$

So far, the transcriptions of the axioms of A have been no more complex than the axioms themselves. But to transcribe **A5** we must introduce three new variables, "z," "w," and "u," as follows:

$$x + \underbrace{\underbrace{y'}_{z} = \underbrace{(x + y)'}_{u}}_{}$$

$$w \qquad\qquad w$$

Then we write **A5**, "$(x)(y)\ x + y' = (x + y)'$," as follows:

B11 $(x)(y)(z)(w)(u)[(Ayz$ & $Sxzw$ & $Sxyu) \rightarrow Auw]$

A6, "$(x)\ x \cdot 0 = 0$," is simple enough:

B12 $(x)\ Px00$

But for **A7**, "$(x)(y)\ x \cdot y' = (x \cdot y) + x$," we must introduce new variables as we did for **A5**:

B13 $(x)(y)(z)(w)(u)[(Ayz \,\&\, Pxzw \,\&\, Pxyu) \rightarrow Suxw]$

It only remains to fill a gap left by the disappearance of the accent in the transition from A to B: in B we have the numeral "0" for the number zero, but we no longer have numerals for the other natural numbers. Consequently we can no longer view sentence **10.3**

$$\ldots \bar{n} \ldots$$

as obtained from **10.2**

$$\ldots x \ldots$$

by substituting occurrences of the numeral $\bar{n}$ for all free occurrences of the variable "x," unless n happens to be zero. Thus, if n is zero, $\ldots \bar{n} \ldots$ is still $\ldots 0 \ldots$; but if n is 1, $\ldots \bar{n} \ldots$ will now be

10.44 $(x)(A0x \rightarrow \ldots x \ldots)$

and if n is greater than 1, $\ldots \bar{n} \ldots$ will be

10.45 $(x_1)(x_2) \ldots (x_{n-1})[(A0x_1 \,\&\, Ax_1x_2 \,\&\, \ldots \,\&\, Ax_{n-1}x) \rightarrow \ldots x \ldots]$

If the definitions of the sets S, S^*, and N^* are modified according to this pattern, the proof of form **10.41** of Church's theorem is essentially the same as our earlier proof of statement **10.40**.

THE UNAXIOMATIZABILITY OF ARITHMETIC

The system A of Robinson arithmetic is very weak. Small wonder that although all its theorems are true, there are truths in A which are not theorems of A. We might hope to repair this defect by adding more axioms. Thus, we might adopt, as axioms, all sentences in the notation of A that have the following form:

10.46 $[\ldots 0 \ldots \,\&\, (x)(\ldots x \ldots \rightarrow \ldots x' \ldots)] \rightarrow (x) \ldots x \ldots$

The axioms of form **10.46** allow us to prove theorems by mathematical induction.

Example: If "... x ..." is "$(y) \, x + y = y + x$," then **10.46** is

10.47 $[(y) \, 0 + y = y + 0 \,\&\, (x)((y) \, x + y = y + x \rightarrow$
$$(y) \, x' + y = y + x')] \rightarrow (x)(y) \, x + y = y + x$$

In the extension of capital A in which every sentence of form **10.46** is an axiom we can prove both components of the conjunction which is the antecedent of **10.47.** Then in that extension of capital A we can also prove the consequence of **10.47,** namely, the commutative law of addition, which is not provable in A itself.

By adding to A the infinity of new axioms of form **10.46,** we greatly increase the range of truths that are provable in our system, but there still remain unprovable truths, for we can show that

10.48 *If Church's thesis is true, no decidable set of axioms in the notation of quantificational logic implies all the true sentences of A and none of the false ones.*

This is the version of Gödel's incompleteness theorem which is most directly relevant to the theory which identifies truth with provability, in mathematics.

Gödel's theorem **10.48** concerns axiomatizations of arithmetic in which, although the axioms may be infinite in number, there is a mechanical decision procedure for determining whether any given sentence is an axiom. Any finite set of axioms is clearly decidable in this sense. So is any set in which the axioms, although infinitely numerous, have only a finite number of different forms.

Example: The set consisting of the seven axioms of A together with all sentences of form **10.46** is decidable, for the procedure is straightforwardly mechanical whereby we compare a given sentence with each of **A1** to **A7** to see whether it is identical with one of them and, if not, examine the sentence to see whether it is of form **10.46.**

In philosophical talk of an axiomatic system in which all the truths and none of the falsehoods of arithmetic are provable, it is tacitly assumed that the set of axioms is, if not finite, at least decidable in the intuitive sense. Theorem **10.48** shows that there is no such system if Church's thesis is correct, for in particular, the theorems of such a system would have to include all the truths and none of the falsehoods that are expressible in the fragment A of arithmetic, in contradiction to **10.48.**

We prove **10.48** by deducing a contradiction from Church's thesis together with the assumption that

10.49 *There is a system C of arithmetic which has a decidable set D of axioms and in which all the true sentences of A are theorems and none of the false ones are theorems.*

The system C may also have theorems that are not expressible in the notation of A; we neither assume nor exclude this.

As a first step in the proof of **10.49** we observe that the property of being a closed tree for an inference from a certain decidable set of premises to a certain conclusion is a decidable one: It is a mechanical matter to determine whether a finite array of symbols is a finished tree, whether each path is closed, and whether each initial sentence is either the denial of the conclusion or a member of the decidable set of premises. Notice further that we can represent a tree as a sequence of sequences of sentences, simply by writing each path through the tree as a sequence of sentences and representing the tree itself as the sequence of its paths. For a closed tree, each path is finite, and there are finitely many paths, so that we are dealing with finite sequences of finite sequences of sentences. We can readily extend our coding scheme so as to assign code numbers to such entities. One way of doing this is to code sequences of sentences as before and then to use *pairs* of symbols "9" to separate the decimal representations of adjacent sequences of sentences.

Now by Church's thesis, the following set T^* of pairs of natural numbers is representable in A:

The pair (x,y) belongs to T^* if and only if x is the code number of a sentence in the notation of A and y is the code number of a closed tree for an inference from the decidable set D of axioms to sentence number x.

In particular, suppose that T^* is represented in A by the sentence

10.50 $-x-y-$

and consider the sentence

10.51 $(\exists y) -x-y-$.

Sentence **10.51** has the characteristic that for any natural number n,

10.52 $(\exists y) -\bar{n}-y-$

is true (false) in the intended interpretation of A if n is (is not) the code number of a sentence in the notation of A which is a theorem of the system C. Then by assumption **10.49**,

10.53 *Sentence **10.52** is true (false) in the intended interpretation of A if n is (is not) the code number of a sentence in the notation of A that is true in the intended interpretation.*

Now consider the sentence

10.54 $(x)(-x-y-z- \rightarrow -(\exists y) -x-y-)$

in which "$-x-y-z-$" is the sentence **10.20** which represents the set S^* in A and "$-x-y-$" is the sentence **10.50** which represents the set T^* in A. Clearly, **10.54** is a sentence in the notation of A and has a code number, say d. Form the sentence

10.55 $(x)(-x-\bar{d}-\bar{d}- \rightarrow -(\exists y) -x-y-)$

by substituting "$\bar{d}$" for both free occurrences of variables in **10.54**. Sentence **10.55** says something about all natural numbers, x: that

If x and d are code numbers of sentences and sentence number x is the result of substituting "$\bar{d}$" for all free occurrences of variables in sentence number d, then sentence number x is not a theorem of C.

Since sentence number d is **10.54**, there is one and only one sentence, **10.55**, which has a code number x of the sort described here. Thus, sentence **10.55** says of itself that it is not a theorem of C.

To put matters more precisely:

10.56 *Sentence* **10.55** *is true in the intended interpretation of A if and only if* **10.55** *is not a theorem of C.*

Since **10.55** is a sentence in the notation of A, assumption **10.49** assures us that

10.57 *Sentence* **10.55** *is a theorem of C if and only if it is true in the intended interpretation of A.*

Together, **10.56** and **10.57** yield a contradiction:

10.58 *Sentence* **10.55** *is true in the intended interpretation of A if and only if sentence* **10.55** *is false in the intended interpretation of A.*

Since Church's thesis and assumption **10.49** were the premises from which we deduced **10.56** and **10.57**, and hence the contradiction **10.58**, we may conclude that

10.59 *If Church's thesis is true, assumption* **10.49** *is false.*

This completes the proof of form **10.48** of Gödel's incompleteness theorem.

EXERCISES

10.1 Construct trees for the inferences

a $A4$ b $A1$
    $A5$ $A3$
    $\overline{0'' + 0'' = 0''''}$ $A4$
                     $A5$
                     $\overline{0'' + 0'' \neq 0'''}$

and thus prove in Robinson arithmetic that 2 and 2 are 4, not 3.
10.2 Prove in Robinson arithmetic that 2 times 2 is 4, not 3.
10.3 To illustrate the fact that the sentence **10.5** represents the set **10.4**

of even natural numbers in A, construct trees which prove **a** and **c** below and refute **b** in Robinson arithmetic:

a $(\exists y)\, 0 = y + y$
b $(\exists y)\, 0' = y + y$
c $(\exists y)\, 0'' = y + y$

10.4   The sentence

$$(\exists z)\, z + x = y$$

represents in A the set of all pairs (x,y) of natural numbers in which x is less than or equal to y. To illustrate this fact, prove **a** and **b** below in A and refute **c** in A:

a $(\exists z)\, z + 0 = 0$
b $(\exists z)\, z + 0 = 0'$
c $(\exists z)\, z + 0' = 0$

10.5   Robinson arithmetic is strong on particulars but weak on generalities. Thus, although all sentences

$$0 \neq 0', \qquad 0' \neq 0'', \qquad 0'' \neq 0''', \qquad \ldots$$

of form $\overline{m} \neq \overline{m}'$ are provable in A, the corresponding generalization

10.60 $(x)\, x \neq x'$

is not, and similarly, neither of the generalizations

10.61 $(x)\, 0 + x = x, \qquad (x)\, 0 \cdot x = 0$

are provable in A, although all their instances are: for each numeral $\overline{m}$, both of the sentences

$$0 + \overline{m} = \overline{m}, \qquad 0 \cdot \overline{m} = 0$$

are provable in A. Demonstrate that the three sentences in **10.60** and **10.61** are indeed unprovable in A by verifying that all seven axioms of A are true in the following valuation but that none of the sentences in **10.60** and **10.61** are true in that valuation. Universe of discourse: the natural numbers together with two additional distinct objects a and b. The functions $'$, $+$, and $\cdot$ are defined as follows, where n and m are any natural numbers and p is any positive natural number.

$n' = n \text{ plus } 1$
$a' = a$
$b' = b$

$+$	m	a	b
n	$n \text{ plus } m$	b	a
a	a	b	a
b	b	b	a

$\cdot$	0	p	a	b
n	0	$n \text{ times } p$	a	b
a	0	b	b	b
b	0	a	a	a

Note that "0" has its usual meaning in A and that the new objects a and b have no names *in A*.

10.6   Prove the commutative law of addition in the extension of Robinson arithmetic in which every sentence of form **10.46** is an axiom.

10.7   If e_1, e_2, and e_3 are the respective expressions

$$0 = 0, \qquad 0, \qquad x = x$$

then (e_1, e_2, e_3) belongs to the set S of triples of expressions. What is the corresponding member of the set S^* of triples of natural numbers? Answer in the decimal notation.

10.8   Describe the numeral of A that denotes the code number of the name "0." Answer in English.

GUIDE TO FURTHER STUDY

The reader who has come this far without skipping very much has at least a fair grounding in the fundamentals of logic and is in a position to pursue the subject either in further courses or in independent reading. The following remarks provide a preliminary sketch of some of the main divisions of the subject. Bracketed numbers refer to entries in the Bibliography at the end of the book, which represents a necessarily small selection from a vast and growing literature.

NOTATIONS

Our notation is only one among many that are in current use. Corresponding to our symbols

$$- \quad \& \quad \vee \quad \rightarrow \quad \leftrightarrow \quad (x) \quad (\exists x) \quad A \quad Bx \quad xCy \quad Dxyz \quad \ldots$$

the reader may encounter these

$$\sim \quad \cdot \quad \vee \quad \supset \quad \equiv \quad (x) \quad (\exists x) \quad p \quad Px \quad Qxy \quad Rxyz \quad \ldots$$

or these

$$- \quad \wedge \quad \vee \quad \rightarrow \quad \leftrightarrow \quad \bigwedge x \quad \bigvee x \quad \ldots$$

or these

$$- \quad \cdot \quad + \quad \supset \quad \equiv \quad \Pi x \quad \Sigma x \quad \ldots$$

or still others. The case is similar for jargon: Disjunctions are often called "alternations" or "logical sums"; denials are often called "negations"; biconditionals, "equivalences";

conditionals, "material implications." In practice, this variety of notations and termi-
nologies presents little more difficulty than the variety of typefaces in printed books.

Perhaps the greatest expense of ingenuity on the invention of notations has
occurred in the matter of grouping. For simplicity we have followed W. V. Quine in
compounding sentences by filling the blanks of

$$(\quad \vee \quad \vee \quad), \qquad\qquad (\quad \rightarrow \quad)$$

and the like with sentences. The more common practice is to write sentences in the
blanks of

$$(\quad)\vee(\quad)\vee(\quad), \qquad (\quad)\rightarrow(\quad)$$

and the like. To save parentheses, some writers use conventions according to which
the connectives

$$\&, \qquad \vee, \qquad \rightarrow, \qquad \leftrightarrow$$

are successively weaker in binding strength. Thus, the inscription

$$A \vee B \,\&\, C \rightarrow D$$

becomes an unambiguous abbreviation of the sentence

$$[A \vee (B \,\&\, C)] \rightarrow D.$$

Further, dots are often used in place of parentheses, so that even without the
convention about binding strengths of connectives, the foregoing sentence can be
written without parentheses as

$$A \vee\cdot B \,\&\, C : \rightarrow D$$

where the break marked by a dot or dots on one side of a connective extends in the
indicated direction until a larger number of dots is encountered or, failing that, to the
end of the sentence.

Of special interest is the so-called "Polish notation," in which no separate signs
are needed to indicate grouping.

Denial (Negation) of "p":	Np
Conjunction (Konjunction) of "p" with "q":	Kpq
Disjunction (Alternation) of "p" with "q":	Apq
Conditional with antecedent "p" and consequent "q":	Cpq
Biconditional (Equivalence) of "p" with "q":	Epq

In the Polish notation, conjunctions and disjunctions always have exactly two terms: Instead of *"Apqr,"* corresponding to our *"p ∨ q ∨ r,"* we write either *"ApAqr"* or *"AApqr,"* corresponding to *"p ∨ (q ∨ r)"* and *"(p ∨ q) ∨ r"* respectively. Since the connective *"N"* applies only to single sentences and all other connectives apply only to pairs of sentences, there can be no ambiguity in decoding such sentences as

$CpCCqrp,$

which is Polish for our

$$p \rightarrow [(q \rightarrow r) \rightarrow p].$$

ALTERNATIVES TO THE TREE METHOD

Methods of demonstrating validity of inferences are as numerous as notations. The tree method derives from Beth's method of *semantic tableaux* [3 and 4] and equally from Hintikka's method of *model sets* [16 and 17].

A very different approach, more commonly encountered than the tree or tableau method, proceeds by providing axioms and rules of inference with the aid of which inferences can be shown valid in the manner of Exercise 5.6 (but with additional axioms and rules of inference for use with quantified sentences). Often, methods of this sort are designed only to demonstrate logical truth of single sentences. Validity of an inference is then demonstrated indirectly by forming a conditional whose antecedent is the conjunction of the premises and whose consequent is the conclusion of the inference; the inference is valid if and only if this conditional is a logical truth. Here, the *locus classicus* is Hilbert and Ackermann [15]. Chapter 2 of Mendelson [22] is concise and thorough. For more extensive treatments of the same matter, see Church [7] and Novikov [23].

Equally common are methods of *natural deduction,* in which rules of inference allow construction of direct proofs of conclusions from premises in patterns meant to correspond to intuitive modes of reasoning. (In effect, the coupled tree method described at the end of Chapter 5 is a method of natural deduction for inferences which do not involve quantifiers.) Here, the standard textbook is Quine [26], the appendix to which contains a concise statement of a technique much like our tree method. Mates's more recent textbook [21] is differently but equally valuable; it incidentally contains an exposition (chapter 10) of the axiomatic approach mentioned above. Our treatment of group theory at the end of Chapter 9 follows Mates's very closely and may be compared with pages 184 to 185 of reference [21] to see the close effective resemblance between the tree method and the method of natural deduction. Finally, the reader may wish to consult Lyndon's very concise book [19] for a treatment of the axiomatic approach (pages 43ff.) and of three variants of the method of natural deduction (pages 64ff.).

HIGHER-ORDER LOGIC; TYPE THEORY

The expressive power of our notation is greatly increased if we introduce new variables "X," "Y," ... which bear the same relation to the predicate letters "A," "B," ... that the familiar variables "x," "y," ... bear to the names "a," "b," .... In the resulting system of *second-order logic* we can formulate such statements as these:

$$(x)(y)(\exists X)xXy, \qquad x = y \leftrightarrow (Y)(Yx \leftrightarrow Yy)$$

The first of these statements says that any two things bear some relation to each other. The second statement can serve as a definition of the identity relation, for it gives a necessary and sufficient condition for two things x and y to be one and the same: Each must have every property that the other has. In the first statement, the variable "X" ranges over two-place relations of individuals; in the second statement, the variable "Y" ranges over properties of individuals. We shall say that "Y" and "X" range over *first-level* properties and relations.

First-level properties and relations—properties and relations of individuals—will in turn have properties and bear relations to each other and to individuals; such properties and relations of first-level properties and relations are said to be of *second level*. Thus, if the individuals are people, the property P of being an eighteenth-century President of the United States is of first level and has two instances: Washington and Adams. Then the first-level property P has the second-level property 2 of having two instances, which can be defined as follows:

$$2Y \leftrightarrow (\exists x)(\exists y)(x \neq y \,\&\, (z)[Yz \leftrightarrow (z = x \vee z = y)])$$

(As Bertrand Russell points out in his valuable if rather outdated book [28], the natural numbers 0, 1, 2, ... can plausibly be construed as properties of properties, viz., as the properties of having 0, 1, 2, ... instances.) In general, a property or relation of nth level properties or relations is said to be of level $n + 1$. Thus, the relation $>$ (*is greater than*), which the second-level property 2 bears to the second-level property 1, is itself of third level.

In Part Two we studied *first-order* quantificational logic, where no use is made of variables for properties and relations. In general, nth order quantificational logic makes use of variables for properties and relations of all levels up to n, but makes no use of variables of level n or more. General *type theory* is the system of logic in which we have variables of all levels. Part IV of Hilbert and Ackermann [15] is a lucid introduction to higher-order logic; a detailed treatment of second-order logic is contained in Church [7], chapter IV.

The same considerations which show that there can be no effective decision procedure for first-order logical truth show that in second-order logic, too, there can be no adequate "no" machine for questions of the form "Is this sentence a logical truth?" For first-order logic the tree method described the program of an adequate "yes" machine for such questions; but no such method and no such machine can exist for second-order logic, since any such machine could be used as follows to provide an adequate "no" machine for first-order logical truth. Given a first-order sentence O which is to be tested for logical truth, replace all names and predicate letters in O by suitable variables, and then universally quantify these variables and prefix a dash to the whole to get a sentence Δ of second-order logic. Thus, if O is the sentence "$(\exists x)xRa$" of first-order logic, Δ will be the sentence "$-(y)(X)(\exists x)xXy$" of second-order logic. Now if O is to be a logical truth, it must remain true no matter what objects are denoted by the names that occur in O and no matter what properties or relations are represented by the predicate letters that occur in O. Then O fails to be a first-order logical truth if and only if Δ manages to be a second-order logical truth, and therefore an adequate "yes" machine for second-order logic would at the same time be an adequate "no" machine for first-order logic. Conclusion: For higher-order logic there can be no analogue of the tree method. There can be no effective procedure for identifying valid inferences as such in higher-order logic. For details, see Hermes [14], section 26.

SET THEORY

Many of the purposes of higher-order logic are served by formulating a deductive theory of the ordinary sort—a first-order theory—about sets. Here there are no predicate variables, and the individual variables "x," "y," and the like range over sets as well (perhaps) as over such nonsets as Socrates and Alma, and over sets of sets, and sets of sets of sets. We can get along with only one predicate symbol, say the Greek letter epsilon "ϵ," interpreted as the two-place relation *is a member of*. Other notions can be defined in terms of membership. Thus, since two things are in fact one and the same if and only if they belong to all the same sets, we can define identity as follows:

$$x = y \leftrightarrow (z)(x \epsilon z \leftrightarrow y \epsilon z)$$

One might suppose that corresponding to any condition on x there is a set of things that meet the condition—even if, as in the case of the condition "$x \neq x$," the corresponding set is empty. But there are difficulties when we consider the condition "$x \notin x$" of non-self-membership. The things in the universe of discourse that satisfy this condition cannot themselves compose a set y in the universe of discourse, for the assumption that they do is self-contradictory, as the following tree shows:

$$\sqrt{} \; (\exists y)(x)(x \epsilon y \leftrightarrow x \notin x)$$
$$(x)(x \epsilon a \leftrightarrow x \notin x)$$
$$\sqrt{} \; a \epsilon a \leftrightarrow a \notin a$$

```
        /     \
    a ε a     a ∉ a
    a ∉ a     a ε a
      ×         ×
```

Then we cannot consistently suppose that corresponding to each condition on x there must exist a set in the universe of discourse consisting of the things in that universe which satisfy the condition. Instead, we must place restrictions on the conditions which are assumed to determine sets; and since there is no one completely natural way of doing this, there are many variants of axiomatic set theory. Some of these are surveyed briefly in section 42 of Quine [26]; for further particulars, see part three of Quine [27], part one of Bernays [2], or chapter 3 of Fraenkel and Bar-Hillel [12].

In a sense, set theory comprises all of mathematics. Thus, the arithmetic of natural numbers can be represented within set theory as described in section 39 of Quine [26], and then statements about rational numbers, real numbers, functions, limits, derivatives, and integrals can be reduced to statements about sets, or sets of sets, or sets of sets of sets . . . of natural numbers. Russell's somewhat outdated book [28] remains an informative and enjoyable nontechnical survey of the situation, with type theory in the role of set theory. For modern axiomatic treatments within set theory, see chapters 4 through 6 of Quine [27] or the first six chapters of Suppes [32] or chapter 6 of Quine [25].

The deepest questions in set theory arise in Georg Cantor's theory of transfinite numbers [5], which David Hilbert called "the finest product of mathematical genius and one of the supreme achievements of purely intellectual human activity" (David Hilbert, "On the Infinite," in Benacerraf and Putnam [1]). Chapters 8 and 9 of Russell [28] provide a brief introductory sketch of the theory with a minimum of technicality, and Fraenkel [11] gives an ample introductory exposition. For axiomatic treatments, see part two of Quine [27], chapter 4 of Mendelson [22], the last two chapters of Suppes [32], or Bernays [2]. Finally, the reader who becomes seriously interested in the subject will want to read Cohen [8] for an illuminating review of logic and set theory (chapters 1 and 2) and an account of recent developments at the frontier (chapters 3 and 4).

METAMATHEMATICS

It is only incidentally that logicians are concerned with the elaboration of particular deductive systems such as group theory and Robinson arithmetic; the primary focus is rather on general facts about particular systems or classes of systems. Thus, Alfred Tarski's proof [34] that the first-order theory of groups is undecidable gives us a theorem *about* group theory, not a theorem *of* group theory. The theorem is not deduced from the axioms of group theory; nor, indeed, is it expressed in the notation of group theory. Rather, Tarski's theorem belongs to *metamathematics*, the theory of mathematical theories. If we view quantificational logic as a mathematical theory, then the adequacy theorem of Chapter 8 and the undecidability theorem of Chapter 10 are also seen as *metatheorems:* theorems of metamathematics. But the line between mathematics and metamathematics is not a clear one, for metamathematics itself can be viewed as a branch of mathematics, and one can inquire into such problems as the axiomatizability and decidability of various portions of metamathematics. Basic texts in the subject are Kleene [18] and Tarski, Mostowski, and Robinson [34]. For a careful treatment of the incompleteness of arithmetic, see chapter 3 of Mendelson [22]. For less strenuous surveys of metamathematics, see chapter 9 of Stoll [31] and chapter 5 of Fraenkel and Bar-Hillel [12].

One of the most important metamathematical concepts is that of a *mechanical* or *effective* procedure. Logic and mathematics abound in examples of such procedures; some, like Euclid's algorithm for finding the greatest common divisor of two positive integers, are known from antiquity, but it was only in the 1930s that the whole class of effective procedures was characterized in mathematically precise terms. It was then that Kurt Gödel, Alonzo Church, Alan Turing, and Emil Post independently gave four superficially different definitions, which proved to determine one and the same class of procedures. The original papers are reprinted in Davis [10], where pages 305 to 316 present Post's brilliantly clear exposition of the concept of effectiveness and the generalized Gödel theorem based upon it. Less readily accessible but equally valuable is Turing [36], and another very clear introduction is Trakhtenbrot [35]. Chapter 5 of Mendelson [22] presents three different definitions of effectiveness and proves their equivalence. For a detailed exposition of the subject based on Post's ideas, see Smullyan [29]; Kleene develops Gödel's approach in part three of [18] and compares it with Turing's; and Turing's approach is worked out in detail in Davis [9] and Hermes [14]. Finally, a leisurely exposition of a fifth concept of effectiveness is given by Markov in [20].

SEMANTICS; MODAL LOGIC

The early successes of modern logic were mainly connected with the process of formalization which came to its full flowering in the work of Gödel and the development of the concept of effectiveness. It was these successes that lent plausibility to the view that mathematics is a game played according to formal rules with meaningless marks on paper—a view in which the semantical concepts of meaning and truth have no place. But at the same time that Gödel's incompleteness theorem undermined the plausibility of the strict formalist view, Alfred Tarski created a framework [33] within which the concept of truth can fruitfully be brought to bear on mathematical theories. In particular, Tarski showed how to define the set T of true sentences of first-order arithmetic; the definition is, of course, noneffective and is formulated in a metatheory, not in arithmetic itself. But one might wonder whether there is an open sentence . . . x . . . of arithmetic which is true when x is taken to be the Gödel number of a truth, and is otherwise false. The answer is "no," for if there were such a sentence we could readily find another open sentence, with Gödel number n, which is true if its free variable denotes the Gödel number of a *falsehood*, and is otherwise false. But then the sentence obtained by substituting the numeral for n for the free variable in sentence number n would be true if and only if false—an impossibility which establishes that no such sentence as . . . x . . . can exist. This proves to be another road to Gödel's incompleteness theorem, for as Gödel showed, there *is* an open sentence . . . x . . . of arithmetic which is true (false) if x is (is not) the Gödel number of a theorem; but if the class of theorems were identical with the class T of truths, Tarski's foregoing argument would show that no such sentence could exist.

Tarski's theory put the concept of truth on a sure metamathematical footing, but the status of the concept of meaning is less clear. Gottlob Frege, the creator of the first complete formalization of quantificational logic, was much concerned with meaning ("Sense and Reference," [13]). More recently, Tarski's success with the theory of truth has inspired others to seek an adequate theory of meaning; here, the most ambitious attempt has been that of Rudolf Carnap [6], whose approach is a modification of Frege's. But there are some who, on logical or philosophical grounds, dispute the feasibility or intelligibility of the project—notably, Quine [24]. Where the notion of meaning is available, a concept of necessity can be defined: A sentence is necessarily true if and only if its truth can be ascertained by an examination of the meanings of the constituent terms, including the quantifiers and connectives. Conversely, given the concept of necessary truth, we can define likeness of meaning: Two sentences have the same meaning if and only if their biconditional is a necessary truth. Then an adequate theory of meaning would be tantamount to an adequate theory of truth for languages in which we have a non-truth-functional operator $\Box$, which may be read "It is necessarily the case that." But as Quine points out in chapter 8 of [24], the modal operator $\Box$ does not mix well with identity and quantification. Thus, we would be inclined to say that such identities as "$a = a$" are necessary truths, but that identities like "$a = b$," in which different names appear, may be true without being necessary. Yet the following tree is surely closed, for "$\Box a = a$" is true if any modal statement is:

1           $a = b$ [premise]
2     $-\Box a = b$ $[-$conclusion$]$
3     $-\Box a = a$ $[1, 2$ by $=]$

Then the invalid inference

$$\frac{a = b}{\Box a = b}$$

passes the tree test! Clearly, some of our familiar rules of inference prove unsound when the language to which they are applied contains the modal operator. Modal logic is at present in a lively state of development. For an introduction to current work, see the articles by Saul Kripke and Jaakko Hintikka in [30].

BIBLIOGRAPHY

[1] Benacerraf, Paul, and Hilary Putnam: *Philosophy of Mathematics*, Prentice-Hall, Inc., Englewood Cliffs, N.J., 1964.

[2] Bernays, Paul: *Axiomatic Set Theory*, North-Holland Publishing Company, Amsterdam, 1958.

[3] Beth, Evert W.: *Formal Methods*, D. Reidel Publishing Co., Dordrecht, Holland, and Gordon and Breach, Science Publishers, Inc., New York, 1962.

[4] ————: *The Foundations of Mathematics*, North-Holland Publishing Company, Amsterdam, 1959 (rev. 1964), and Harper Torchbooks, Harper & Row, Publishers, Incorporated, New York, 1966.

[5] Cantor, Georg: *Contributions to the Founding of the Theory of Transfinite Numbers*, The Open Court Publishing Company, La Salle, Ill., 1915.

[6] Carnap, Rudolf: *Meaning and Necessity*, The University of Chicago Press, Chicago, 1947, and Phoenix Books, The University of Chicago Press, Chicago, 1956.

[7] Church, Alonzo: *Introduction to Mathematical Logic*, Princeton University Press, Princeton, N.J., 1956.

[8] Cohen, Paul J.: *Set Theory and the Continuum Hypothesis*, W. A. Benjamin, Inc., New York, 1966.

[9] Davis, Martin: *Computability and Unsolvability*, McGraw-Hill Book Company, New York, 1958.

[10] ————: *The Undecidable*, The Raven Press, Hewlett, N.Y., 1965.

[11] Fraenkel, Abraham A.: *Abstract Set Theory*, 2d ed., rev., North-Holland Publishing Company, Amsterdam, 1961.

[12] ————, and Yehoshua Bar-Hillel: *Foundations of Set Theory*, North-Holland Publishing Company, Amsterdam, 1958.

[13] Frege, Gottlob: *Translations from the Philosophical Writings of Gottlob Frege*, Basil Blackwell & Mott, Ltd., Oxford, 1952.

[14] Hermes, Hans: *Enumerability, Decidability, Computability*, Springer-Verlag OHG, Berlin, and Academic Press, Inc., New York, 1965.

[15] Hilbert, David, and W. Ackermann: *Principles of Mathematical Logic*, Chelsea Publishing Company, New York, 1950.

[16] Hintikka, K. Jaakko J.: "Form and Content in Quantification Theory," *Acta Philosophica Fennica*, no. 8, pp. 7–55, Helsinki, 1955.

[17] ———: "Notes on Quantification Theory," *Societas Scientiarum Fennica, Commentationes Physico-Mathematicae*, vol. 17, no. 12, Helsinki, 1955.

[18] Kleene, Stephen Cole: *Introduction to Metamathematics*, D. Van Nostrand Company, Inc., Princeton, N.J., 1952.

[19] Lyndon, Roger C.: *Notes on Logic*, D. Van Nostrand Company, Inc., Princeton, N.J., 1966.

[20] Markov, A. A.: *Theory of Algorithms*, trans. for the National Science Foundation, Washington, D.C., and the U.S. Department of Commerce by the Israel Program for Scientific Translations, Jerusalem, 1961.

[21] Mates, Benson: *Elementary Logic*, Oxford University Press, Fair Lawn, N.J., 1965.

[22] Mendelson, Elliott: *Introduction to Mathematical Logic*, D. Van Nostrand Company, Inc., Princeton, N.J., 1964.

[23] Novikov, Peter Sergeevich: *Elements of Mathematical Logic*, Oliver & Boyd Ltd., Edinburgh and London, 1964.

[24] Quine, Willard Van Orman: *From a Logical Point of View*, Harper Torchbooks, Harper & Row, Publishers, Incorporated, New York, 1961.

[25] ———: *Mathematical Logic*, rev. ed., Harvard University Press, Cambridge, Mass., 1951.

[26] ———: *Methods of Logic*, rev. ed., Holt, Rinehart and Winston, Inc., New York, 1959.

[27] ———: *Set Theory and Its Logic*, Harvard University Press, Cambridge, Mass., 1963.

[28] Russell, Bertrand: *Introduction to Mathematical Philosophy*, George Allen & Unwin, Ltd., London, 1919.

[29] Smullyan, Raymond M.: *Theory of Formal Systems*, rev. ed., Princeton University Press, Princeton, N.J., 1961.

[30] Societas Philosophica Fennica: "Proceedings of a Colloquium on Modal and Many-valued Logics," *Acta Philosophica Fennica*, vol. 16, Helsinki, 1963.

[31] Stoll, Robert R.: *Set Theory and Logic*, W. H. Freeman and Company, San Francisco, 1963.

[32] Suppes, Patrick: *Axiomatic Set Theory*, D. Van Nostrand Company, Inc., Princeton, N.J., 1960.

[33] Tarski, Alfred: "The Concept of Truth in Formalized Languages," *Logic, Semantics, Metamathematics*, Clarendon Press, Oxford, 1956.

[34] ———, Andrezej Mostowski, and Raphael M. Robinson: *Undecidable Theories*, North-Holland Publishing Company, Amsterdam, 1953.

[35] Trakhtenbrot, B. A.: *Algorithms and Automatic Computing Machines*, D. C. Heath and Company, Boston, 1963.

[36] Turing, Alan M.: "Solvable and Unsolvable Problems," *Science News* 31, Penguin Books, Inc., Baltimore, 1954, pp. 7–23.

INDEX